Dedication

To my children, BJ, Rob, and Lyn

You are my anchors. You have given my life meaning. I hope that through reading my memoir you will gain a broader and deeper picture of your mother's journey.

"Cecelia Hurwich is her own best example in her research on how people successfully navigate the aging process. She brings the wisdom of joy to her life every day."

Joel Selvin
Author; Columnist, San Francisco Chronicle

"In her groundbreaking memoir, Cecelia shares her pioneering insights into aging, how and why women should use this time to go for it, to toss out expectations about who they should be in their fifties, sixties, seventies, and beyond into elderhood. I am blessed, as you will be, to have her autobiography to midwife us into our later years."

Karen Sands
Author of **Visionaries Have Wrinkles**
Founder of Broad Minded Publishing

"Cecelia will dance right into your heart and soul, endlessly inspiring you with her positive energy, her commitment to all that is good and just in our world, and her loving, caring spirit—constantly working to make everything better. She listens—hears—and dances to "the music of life.""

The Honorable MeraLee Goldman
Cultural Ambassador, City of Beverly Hills, CA

"Cecelia's memoirs remind us that life doesn't end at hardship, disappointment, or, as many people think, middle age. Through Cecelia's memoirs, the concept of aging may still have some wrinkles and sags, but it can be full of enthusiasm, excitement, and vitality."

Judith Adamson
Author, Editor

March 2013

To Deborah
Here is my memoir the fruition
of your encouraging me many years ago to
get on with my research on vital
older women. *With warm*
regards
Cecelia

92 and dancing

Cecelia Hurwich, Ph.D.

Vitality in Aging Press
Berkeley, California USA

Vitality in Aging Press
P.O. Box 5017
Berkeley, CA 94705 USA

ISBN 978-0-615-73676-1

All photographs in this book are the property of the Hurwich family.

Cover and text design by Carol Salvin

Orders, inquiries, and correspondence should be addressed to:
Vitality in Aging Press
P.O. Box 5017
Berkeley, CA 94705 USA

Contents

Foreword

The note on the bulletin board at the aging conference read: "Sorry I missed your presentation on positive psychology. Would love to chat with you. Please post your reply on the board. " That was my introduction to Cecelia Hurwich, at the Western Gerontological Society of America meeting in Albuquerque, New Mexico, in 1983. When we met, I figured her to be about my age (mid-forties), and could not believe it when she announced that she was actually 63 years old. Wow. She may have been petite in stature, but she exuded a tremendous amount of energy and zest for life. That was the beginning of numerous personal communications via email and occasional visits at her home in Berkeley, California. On one of my later visits, Cecelia showed me a file that she had kept on my work and announced that my research had had a profound influence on her life journey, as well as on her own research on successful aging.

For years I have researched the positive side of the aging process and have written about the important role of mental and physical health, social and emotional support, personal optimism, meaning and purpose in life, resilience, and spirituality as factors in successful aging. Every one of these themes is clearly and eloquently illustrated throughout this book, *92 and Dancing*, which is the life story of this remarkable, vital woman. Cecelia's life is itself a testament to positive aging, a path she has consciously and adamantly chosen to follow. Her memoirs reveal an individual with a great deal of inner strength and flexibility, and remarkable resilience in the face of numerous difficult life circumstances.

Born into a life of comfort, Cecelia was devastated by her parents' divorce. She gained inner strength and optimism for the future from her mother, grandmother, and other supportive family members. During the Great Depression, when she and her mother struggled to make ends meet, she learned to truly appreciate the love of her family, which gave her the confidence that would get them through hard times; she also learned to work diligently and take on responsibilities, which contributed greatly to her inner strength. In her late teens, while working in Yosemite National Park, Cecelia developed a strong spiritual connection with the natural environment, together with a love for hiking and mountain climbing—meaningful activities that have helped sustain her ever since. Again and again we see how her positive attitude allowed her to prevail, as she recalls serving in the Navy as a WAVE officer during World War II, the discrimination she experienced in the Navy, and later her own failed marriage.

In her sixties, Cecelia turned her attention to studying the qualities that help women maintain vitality as they age. Returning to college, she conducted an in-depth study of vital older women, finding that her subjects were passionately and actively engaged with life, and pursued activities outside of themselves that gave their lives meaning. This work, which earned her a Ph.D. at the age of seventy, inspired and informed the way she has lived her own life as she has aged. She has continued to be active in the field of aging, and her research on aging and activism in the environmental movement have made a positive difference in the world. Her activism and her passion for travel and the outdoors have continued to provide Cecelia with a deep sense of meaning and purpose in her later years. In the final two chapters of the memoir, Cecelia documents how physical aging brings with it unique challenges, and how a positive mental attitude of acceptance and optimism, along with a renewed sense of personal meaning, contributed to her recovery from serious health issues and the emotional responses that accompany such events.

92 and Dancing recounts a lifetime of achievements, personal sacrifices, good times, and bad times. Most of all, this book stands as a testimony to the remarkable resilience of the human spirit.

Gary T. Reker, Ph.D.
Professor Emeritus of Psychology
Trent University, Peterborough, ON

Acknowledgments

I am indebted to the many people who have helped make this memoir possible. In particular, I want to thank the women who came to hear me speak on vitality in aging, and whose enthusiasm for my presentations first inspired me to write. Initially I intended to share the findings of my research on vital older women, yet I found that what I wrote read too much like a guide to "how to grow old," when my intention was to show women how to reap the rewards of aging. My friends, family, and colleagues kept urging me to write about my life, for they knew I had an important message to pass on not only from my research, but from the wisdom acquired during my many years.

Brainstorming with Annie Stine about the direction to pursue, I realized that what I really wanted was to write a book about my life. I am forever grateful for the valuable suggestions of Justine Fixel, my dear friend from Navy years, in the beginning stages of my interviews. Judith Adamson was most instrumental in organizing my voluminous stories into chapters. She was always patient, encouraging, and wonderful to work with. Janet Leese came to me as a bright graduate student at the University of California, Berkeley, interested in gerontology. Remaining through her two pregnancies, she provided invaluable assistance and encouragement with my memoir, from its formative stages through near-completion. Chris Hebdon, another bright graduate student at UC Berkeley, in anthropology, contributed much as my assistant in the book's final phases. His skills with the computer and with words were both greatly valued. Without the support of editor Eileen Ecklund, I could not have finished the book. In a few months' time she not only pulled together the last chapters but made astute suggestions for changes throughout the book.

I am grateful to Marilyn Kriegel, my inspiring instructor, and Dr. Will Schutz, the director of our master's program and a founder of the human potential movement, both of whom had faith in me and my ability to undertake my research. Others who encouraged me during this master's period were Dolores Bermak, Mary Balkowitsch, and John Radcliff. I thank Ginger Alafi, Sylvia Sussman, Lillian Cartwright, and Emily Hancock, colleagues and friends who supported me during my doctoral research.

Thank you Aline Mayer, Susan Ives, Christina Fisher, and Alicia Roldan for your time and caring energy. Bob Colwell, a friend from Outward Bound, was of utmost help in designing the visually appealing "Vitality in Aging" brochure. A special acknowledgment to my friend Marian Penn, who carefully read each chapter and helped refine it. Malcolm Margolin, whose memoir class I recently had the distinct pleasure of attending, advised and urged me to go ahead and get the manuscript out there as a memoir! I am deeply grateful to the members of my memoir-writing group, who have given me many helpful critiques and much positive support over this last year.

My heartfelt thanks to Edith Gladstone for reading and rereading the manuscript with such a joyful spirit. Her first-class editing skills, grammatical expertise and keen insights provided invaluable assistance. My deepest appreciation to Carol Salvin for her design talents, layout design and help with including the photographs for this book. I could not have published this book without her patience, support, and dedication in guiding me through the self publishing process.

Above all I am fortunate to be with my partner, Don Ross, who has given up vacations and outings while patiently waiting for me to finish yet another chapter. His love and support have kept me vital and dancing.

Father, Mother, and me

My Early Years

My parents met and fell passionately in love when my mother was only seventeen. Their marriage took them back and forth across the Pacific four times, spanned two continents and three cultures, and produced a beloved child. After a decade it ended with an admission that their relationship could not endure, but also with a poignant vow that neither would have another child with anyone else.

My mother, Lillian Lowenstein, had been raised in Oakland, the youngest of four girls and six boys. Adored by her older sisters and brothers, she was also a favorite of her father, who early on taught her the workings of his corner grocery store business. My mother played the piano exquisitely, taught from the time she was six by her older brother Harry, a concert pianist. She was exceptionally intelligent and excelled in mathematics, doing the bookkeeping for her father's store while still in high school. Lillian was determined to go to college even though none of her brothers and sisters had had the chance—the minute they finished high school, they had gone to work to help support the large family. Even though not many young women attended college at the time, my mother's parents were excited about the possibility of their youngest daughter doing so and were willing to make sacrifices to send her there, but she chose love and marriage instead.

As a young woman, my mother was a beauty. She had dark, thick braids that were long enough for her to sit on, and with her large brown eyes and petite hourglass figure, she looked as if she had stepped out of a Renaissance painting. But Lillian didn't know she was beautiful because her mother didn't allow anyone to tell her. My grandmother, Eva Lowenstein, was terrified that what had happened to my mother's sister Agnes—a married man had gotten her pregnant, resulting in a hushed abortion—would happen to her youngest daughter. Consequently she raised Lillian strictly, forbidding her to go out with young men.

My father, Jack Steinberg, was born in Harbin, China, to an affluent family. As a child he was surrounded by Chinese servants, taught several languages at an early age, and doted on by his parents, Gregory and Cecelia Steinberg, who thought him intelligent and clever. He was a good-looking boy who grew into a handsome and charming young man. When he reached college age, his parents sent him to study business at the University of California, Berkeley, so he could eventually manage the family import/export business with his younger brother, Henry.

The Steinbergs had been in business for years in Khabarovsk, a Russian city thirty miles from the Chinese border, manufacturing uniforms for the Russian army and navy. As Jews, they had to practice extreme care and tact in their business dealings with czarist officials in order to avoid reprisals. In the mid-1890s, when Russian pogroms were particularly horrific, the Steinbergs and other Jews fled on the Trans-Siberian Railroad to Vladivostok. From there they moved to Harbin, China, where they were able to reestablish their business.

By the time my mother met him, Jack had matured into a slender, dark, handsome, and—in Lillian's inexperienced eyes—an exciting young college student. Jack moved fast and talked even faster. Gifted in languages, he could speak at least five and often jumped from one language to another at whim, using whichever expressed his meaning best without particular concern for his listeners. He was outgoing, flamboyant, and gregarious. People found him captivating, and he became a favorite in the lively group of Russian Jews who lived in Oakland.

He was a regular visitor at my mother's home, invited by my mother's cousin Sadie for the family's weekly Shabbat dinners. After dinner the young people gathered around the piano for songs and dancing. Eventually Jack, absolutely smitten by my mother, admitted that he was coming to Shabbat dinners only to see her. Lillian was swept off her feet.

When the Russian Revolution broke out in 1917, Jack returned to China to help his father and brother run their business. Before he left, he presented my mother with a ring, and they considered themselves secretly engaged. "I was very much in love with him," my mother told me years later. "He was making such love to me in his letters." Eva suspected something was going on with her daughter but didn't know what, or with whom. When Jack returned to California in 1918, he announced to the Lowensteins that he wanted to marry Lillian. Eva had never allowed her daughter to set foot outside the door with any man, and now here was this young suitor suddenly declaring his intention to marry her!

Lillian graduated from Technical High School in Oakland on May 31, 1918. She had abandoned her plans for college and instead began preparing her trousseau. She was an excellent seamstress and made all her negligees, slips, and dresses by hand in preparation for her wedding and the trip to China. Later that same year, Lillian Lowenstein married Jack Steinberg at Temple Sinai in Oakland. The entire Lowenstein family, by now totally enchanted with Jack, shared wholeheartedly in the joyous celebration.

Life in China

Soon after their wedding, my father and mother boarded an ocean steamer from San Francisco for the two-week crossing to China. My father was eager to introduce his beautiful young bride to his family, and also to rejoin his father and brother in the family business. Jack's mother, Cecelia, had tragically died while he was studying at Berkeley, and his father had soon married a younger woman named Olga. Upon arriving in China, my parents stayed with Grandpa Gregory and Olga in Tientsin. The young couple traveled throughout China, meeting the many Steinbergs not only in Tientsin, Tsingtau, and Harbin, but also across the border in Vladivostok. They were met everywhere with open arms and lavish parties. Lillian was quickly embraced as a sister by Jack's brother, Henry, and his sister, Annie.

Jack's father adored my mother, always introducing her as "my beautiful American daughter-in-law." Mother was fond of him but put off by his ostentatious behavior, spending a fortune on showy dinner parties and doing things way beyond his means. She found it offensive, especially as she came from thrifty, hard-working roots. She couldn't help noticing how easily Jack's father seemed to make and lose fortunes.

Yet, it was an exciting time for my mother, who had never been out of California. My parents moved to Harbin, where G. P. Steinberg & Sons was thriving making military supplies for General Kolchak, a Russian admiral and White Russian leader fighting the Bolsheviks. Grandpa Gregory owned four flats in Harbin, with a hotel on top. My parents settled comfortably into one of the flats.

Harbin was known as the "Little Paris of the East," not only for its western architecture but also for its cosmopolitan cultural and intellectual leanings. Over the years it had become a city of sophistication and culture, attracting diverse groups—White Russians seeking asylum from the Bolsheviks, Russian Jews seeking refuge from anti-Semitism, Chinese businessmen, and railroad workers. Here Russian Jews enjoyed political, economic, and cultural liberties unavailable in Russia.

By the time my parents settled in Harbin, the Russian Jewish community was deeply entrenched, nurtured by the wealth of its new entrepreneurs. The Jewish community welcomed immigrants, who often arrived with their entire lives packed in a single suitcase, and gave them food and a place to live until they could get on their feet. My grandfather and other businesspeople went out of their way to find jobs for the newcomers, teaching them the ropes of doing business in China.

My parents were overjoyed when I was conceived later that year. Mother, concerned about the unsanitary conditions in Chinese hospitals, wanted me to be born in the United States. She also longed to be close to her family. In the sixth month of her pregnancy, she and my father boarded a steamer for the return voyage to California. In Oakland they lived with Mother's sister Sadie Strom, her husband, Abe, and their sons, Sid and Harold, who were about nine and seven.

I was born at Saint Mary's Hospital in Oakland on December 21, 1919, and named for my father's mother, Cecelia. We stayed on at Aunt Sadie's for almost another year, a particularly happy time for my parents, surrounded as they were by the warm and hospitable Lowenstein clan. Sid and Harold were absolutely crazy about me and thrilled to have a baby girl around. They rocked me to sleep, pushed my buggy, and played endlessly with me, thoroughly spoiling me and creating a lifelong bond that kept us closely connected throughout our lives.

The entire family fell in love with my charming father, who never arrived at a relative's home without flowers, candy, and a lot of style. He generously brought bicycles and other extravagant toys to my young cousins, whom he treasured. Although the family wondered how Father could spend money so freely since he didn't seem to be working, they didn't dwell on it. Even when it became clear that he was a compulsive gambler and liked women, they were so captivated by him that they were more than willing to forgive his erring ways.

When I was almost a year old, my parents returned to Harbin so Father could once again take his place in the family business. One day my grandfather took Mother aside to ask what they had been doing that prompted my father to spend close to fifty thousand dollars during the year we were in the United States. Mother was shocked when she connected the dots and realized that my father had supported a mistress, not only in China during the early months of her pregnancy, but also in Oakland, while waiting for me to be born. That explained much of the extravagant sum. In the early days of their marriage, when my mother, so happy and in love with Jack, was told that he had mistresses, she wouldn't believe it. She thought others were just jealous and, in her desire to trust her husband, brushed aside any talk of his philandering. It was deeply disturbing for Mother to learn that it was common practice for men in their social circle to take a mistress; even Grandpa Gregory was said to keep a woman.

My father's betrayals notwithstanding, Harbin presented my mother with a glamorous new world, replete with servants and the luxuries that well-connected Russian Jewish society could offer. My parents set up their own flat with a cook and Mandarin-speaking amah to help care for me. Mother threw herself into studying Mandarin and Russian, overseeing the servants, entertaining guests, and raising me.

My father showered her with jewels and beautiful clothes. Their life was a whirlwind of parties, dances, picnics, and sumptuous dinners in friends' homes. I vividly remember my handsome father and beautiful mother, dressed up in tuxedo and ball gown, stopping to give me a hug and kiss before leaving for the evening. I recall seeing Russian couples dressed in the latest Parisian fashions—the women either in the long-sleeved, tight-bodiced, floor-length dresses or in shorter, looser gowns in sleek satins or rayon with pleats or slits, designed to allow greater ease of movement. It was a privileged and opulent life for Mother, whose parents had labored so hard just to feed their ten children and countless refugees.

I learned to speak Mandarin from my Chinese amah. By the time I was two I spoke it fluently, as well as Russian, which my parents spoke at home. I had a remarkable memory. By the age of three I could recite by heart a Russian poem that lasted twenty minutes. I was often brought downstairs before bedtime in my pink raw silk pajamas so Father could show off my linguistic prowess to his guests.

On one such evening I was summoned to appear before a group that included two fashionably dressed Russian couples; a Chinese business associate of my father's and his lovely wife, who wore a tight, sleek Mandarin gown of blue silk with diagonally embroidered flowers; and a French couple wearing Coco Chanel designs, who were in Harbin obtaining rare Chinese silks to transport along with furs from Siberia to

France. I had just learned a new poem in Russian and Father asked me to recite it. Then he had me speak in Mandarin. He beamed with pride as I captivated the guests. I loved that Father was proud of me and reveled in his attention. Mother nodded approvingly, and when I was finished led me to my room to be put to bed by my devoted amah.

Hunger in Harbin

One of my first memories in Harbin was eating in the warm kitchen with my amah as numerous servants came in and out. Harbin, situated in the northernmost part of China, was bitterly cold in the winter, with temperatures often well below thirty degrees. Servants entering the kitchen hurried to the stove for warmth, rubbing their hands against the chill. Even to my young eyes these grown-ups looked small and thin, different from my parents' families and friends, who were plump, a trait considered attractive in those days. Knowing the servants were hungry, I often held out my plate to them, but they averted their eyes nervously, shaking their heads "no." Later I discovered it was inappropriate for servants to accept food from the child of their master. Concerned and curious, I asked my father where our servants lived and ate, and he dismissively waved, "Out there."

One day when I was playing in the garden I noticed a pile of bedding in a wooden storeroom, and realized this was "out there." I felt sad for the servants. It was a window into a life very different from mine, and my first experience of poverty.

The imperious side of my father's nature was a part of him that I was not comfortable with as a child. "Slippers, boy," he'd call to a servant who might have been older than he. It made me wince. Father had grown up with workers and servants, and although he gave them generous tips and gifts, he dismissed them with a flip of his wrist, for he considered them of a lower class.

Our big, two-story flat had large picture windows facing a busy street and a garden where I played by myself. My grandfather and Olga had a son, Nathan, who was my age, and occasionally we played together, but most of the time I played alone. I liked watching the bustle on the street below through the huge windows.

One bitterly cold day when I was three, I was looking out the window as a horse-drawn wagon loaded with cabbages drove by. Two peasants pulling small carts ran in front of the wagon; to avoid hitting them, the driver swerved sharply to the left. The wagon overturned, hurling hundreds of cabbages onto the street. Within seconds a mob of ravenous men, women, and children descended on the cabbages and began eating them as the driver frantically tried to stop them. Minutes later, every last cabbage had disappeared—eaten or tucked away in carts, aprons, and dresses. This vivid image of raw hunger will be with me forever.

During these years in China, my father's extramarital affairs and gambling caused a great deal of strife in my parents' marriage, although Mother later told me that Father claimed the affairs meant nothing to him, that she was his only love. I remember lying in my crib, hearing the hushed, angry tones of my parents arguing in the middle of the night, the quick footsteps, and the sudden quiet after the front door slammed. I was terrified my father wouldn't return, and spent the rest of the night hardly able to rest, anxiously listening for the door to open. When I awoke the next morning, Mother and Father were sitting together at breakfast as if nothing had happened. I didn't know how to talk to them about their quarrels in the dead of night, which caused a nagging ache in my young life.

Father's unethical business ventures landed G. P. Steinberg & Sons deep in debt. Naively believing that a change of environment and steady work would help stabilize their marriage and finances, Mother persuaded Father to return to the United States. Shortly after returning to California, Mother and I moved into my grandmother's house in Oakland because Father was unable to support us. Father found a room with a Russian family in San Francisco, and it was arranged for me to see him every Saturday.

Grandmother lived in a cozy chocolate-colored bungalow on Forty-third Street near San Pablo Avenue, conveniently located right across from Annie Yates Grammar School. I spoke no English when I entered first grade but Miss Nelson was patient and encouraging. My friendly classmates, fascinated by this little girl from China who spoke Mandarin but couldn't speak any English, eagerly helped me—for example, by gesturing and pointing to a pencil or book and saying its name. The big calendar on the wall taught me numbers, months, days of the week, and the playground became a rich language classroom. Within a few months I'd become fluent in English.

The other children kindheartedly included me in their play, a novel experience since other than playing with Nathan in China, I hadn't had any real friends my age. My new friends and I shared secrets, swung on the rings in the school playground, visited each other's houses, and walked to the library for books. *Treasure Island* made the rounds, inspiring our imaginations to figure out what we'd do if shipwrecked on a remote island.

Mother worked as a corsetiere in my Aunt Agnes's lingerie store in San Francisco. Every day except Sunday she took a train to the Oakland ferry, which brought her across the bay to San Francisco. From the ferry she boarded a streetcar to the store in the Mission District. She left early in the morning, worked for ten hours, and then commuted back for another two hours, usually not returning home for dinner until eight in the evening or later, totally exhausted.

I lived for Saturday—my day with Father. I woke up way too early, put on my best dress, little white socks and patent leather pumps, and waited for Mother to comb my curly hair and gather it into a big bow. Then on went the coat, gloves, and little purse. I'd sit on the front steps watching for Father to appear around the corner, his familiar cape fluttering around his knees.

"Ah, my beautiful little daughter," he'd say, picking me up. "What will it be today? The merry-go-round or the zoo?"

Sometimes he had an elaborate plan already laid out. If the circus was in town, he was sure to have tickets. Often we'd have lunch of piroshkis or soup on Geary Boulevard in Outer Richmond where the Russian community lived, then catch a matinee at the nearby Alexandria Theater. If it was sunny we might take the streetcar all the way out to Ocean Avenue to frolic on the beach, picking up shells and chattering about anything and everything. My absolute favorite was going to Golden Gate Park and riding the horses on the carousel. At each go-around, I'd wave at Father, who was seated on a nearby bench. I could see him talking to whoever was sitting near him, pointing proudly at me, bragging to them that I was his daughter.

He let me do whatever I pleased. I remember one Saturday it poured rain and after lunch I wanted to walk in puddles. Father, game for anything, splashed right along with me, laughing like a child. That evening after Father brought me home, Mother was predictably upset. "Cecelia, you've got mud splattered all over your best dress and your feet are so wet you'll certainly catch a cold. What on earth was your father thinking, Cecelia? That man has no common sense."

I adapted to going back and forth between my parents' completely opposite ways of childrearing. Father, spontaneous and fun, and Mother, strict yet caring and dependable. There was never any doubt in my mind that Mother loved and lived for me and that my father loved me when we were together— but I wondered if he loved me and thought about me when he was far away. Being flexible and resilient, I learned to tailor my feelings and behavior to whichever parent I was with.

My father soon found a job selling life insurance in San

Francisco. He was so charismatic and persuasive that he became the top salesman in his company. Unfortunately, he pocketed his clients' payments, and within a year he landed in jail. My mother's family posted bail, but with his release he was ordered to leave the United States because he wasn't an American citizen. Obliged to move, the three of us headed for Vancouver, Canada.

A Tragic Episode

We began every day at school in Canada singing "God Save the King." King George was not my king, but I mouthed the words anyway, eager to fit in. I continued in second grade without difficulty, working diligently on the load of homework given to children in Canada. When I came home from school my parents were still at work, so I let myself into the empty apartment and busied myself with homework, washing the breakfast dishes and straightening the apartment. I wrote letters to my schoolmates back in Oakland describing a happy life, not admitting my loneliness. I wasn't allowed to have friends over or leave the apartment until Mother or Father returned home, but we didn't even remain long enough in Vancouver for me to have a chance to make friends.

After a few months on his job, Father's old habits landed him right back in jail. Mother visited him, returning home with eyes swollen and red from crying. Years later, she told me that the jail sentence, plus finding out about his latest girlfriend in Canada, was the final straw. She had hoped he'd be a faithful husband and find work to help support us, but she finally concluded he'd never change. Heartbroken and angry, she decided to proceed with a divorce. Though she still loved my father, she could not continue in the marriage.

Moving to Canada was a tragic episode for us all. It was the end of our life together. Mother's family once again paid for Father's release from jail. Without either U.S. or Canadian citizenship, he was forced to return to China. When we said goodbye I had no idea I wouldn't see my beloved father again until I was an adult.

Mother and I returned home to Oakland and Father returned to China, making and losing fortunes as he had done in the past. I missed him terribly but his letters came regularly and I'd rush to open them. He always said the same things: that all was going well for him in China; that he missed me and loved me very much; that he was making lots of money and would soon be sending some for a new dress or whatever I wanted.

I watched Mother read her letters. She read them hastily, often ripping them up and storming out of the room. She didn't hide her anger that Father did not contribute to my upkeep or help us with any of our living expenses. Gradually I began to resent his lack of support and how sad he made my mother. I wondered if he really did love me. His letters claiming he loved me felt phony; I would let them lie on my dresser for days before reading them.

Life with Grandma

When we moved back to Grandma's house on Forty-third Street in Oakland I was almost nine. Though still missing my father, I loved living with Grandma and with Mother's youngest brother, Robert, who was in his early twenties and still living at home. Mother returned to the long workdays at Aunt Agnes's shop, but Grandma was always there when I came home from school.

Robert was about ten years older than I was and felt more like a brother than an uncle. He was kind and taught me to do male things such as toss and catch a ball. He rode a motorcycle—unusual in those days—and flew airplanes for the sheer exhilaration it brought him. He taught himself to play the saxophone and played regularly in a jazz band. A part time magician, he performed in full regalia of a black, crimson-lined cape and top hat. When I saw one of his performances, I gasped as he pulled rabbits out of his hat and made women disappear from boxes. When he reached his mid-twenties, his brothers and sisters, who viewed having a profession as necessary for the son of immigrants, decided he must enroll in pharmacy school, for they were worried about his future.

Saturday visits with Father were replaced by piano lessons with Mr. Windemeir in the Richmond district of San Francisco. Mother, and my uncles and aunts who contributed money for my lessons, believed it was worth sacrificing and scrimping so that I could play the piano and thus gain the cultural exposure our immigrant family valued.

The long trip to Mr. Windemeir's studio started by train in

Oakland to the docks, where I took a ferry to the San Francisco Ferry Building, and boarded a streetcar. The ride was made even longer because I became nauseous and had to get on and off the streetcar to throw up. It took me all Saturday to get to my lesson and return home. Then I was obliged to practice each day after school. At first it was a chore, as I'd glance longingly out the window to where my friends were outdoors playing. As I improved, I enjoyed practicing more until playing the piano became deeply satisfying. It made me happy that Grandma loved to hear me play. She'd stop whatever she was doing, come into the living room, and sit with her hands folded in her lap, eyes closed, with a totally peaceful look on her face. My piano lessons laid the groundwork for my lifetime love of music.

When I came home from school, there was Grandma, gray hair swept into a bun, offering me fresh-baked cookies and her loving attention. If she wasn't cooking, we went into her garden in our backyard. It was small, with several fruit trees (perfect for climbing!) and lush with colorful patches of roses, lilacs, and snapdragons. She was a passionate gardener, and she taught me how to dig, plant, and prune while we laughed and talked. There was a big, canopied swing on the porch, which Grandma occasionally let me sleep on overnight in warm weather, but mostly we sat swinging on it after we did our gardening. It was then that she often told me stories about her life in the old country, Russia.

Grandma was a spiritual woman with a strong belief in God. She had to have faith to withstand the oppressive conditions of czarist Russia, the devastating anti-Semitism and the pogroms against Jews. She came from a village in Siberia called Nerchinsk, where she married Samuel Lowenstein when she was only fifteen. Samuel was conscripted into the army, and, as a Jew, was required to spend eight long years, whereas non-Jews served only four. When her younger brother Morris was about to be called into the army, Samuel and Eva fled with Morris and their four small children, not wanting him to experience the same hardship as Samuel. They arrived in San Francisco by steerage, with one suitcase and a samovar, and moved into a house south of Market with cousins and friends from Russia. Six more children followed, my mother being the youngest daughter, doted upon by her older siblings.

One of my favorite stories of Grandma's was about the 1906 San Francisco earthquake. "Early one morning in April," she would recount, "the house shook like a train was going through it. Your grandfather knew to shut off the gas, and then we went running through the house to be sure everyone was out. Your mother's door had slammed shut and couldn't be opened so Schmul pulled off a piece of the banister and broke through one of the door panels to pull your terrified mother, who was then ten, out. He found your two uncles trapped under a bed that had turned over on them when the floor fell through and dragged them out. Just before the house next door began to fall onto ours, and as we started to see flames, your Aunt Agnes bravely ran back into the burning house and grabbed the samovar. Later we used that samovar to make hot tea for the hundreds of other homeless people camping in tents in Golden Gate Park." The samovar now graces my home and is cherished as part of my Russian-Jewish heritage.

Eventually my grandpa found a horse and wagon to drive Grandma and ten children on the long trip around the bay from San Francisco to Oakland (in those days no bridge existed from San Francisco to Oakland). It was in Oakland that Grandpa found a good corner location to open a grocery store—a practical business venture that could also feed his large family. When other young Jewish men, usually between ages eighteen and twenty-one, had to flee Nerchinsk, Grandma waited for them at the docks in San Francisco, as they came off the boats with one small suitcase and no English skills, to welcome them and bring them into my grandfather's and her home to live. I can remember Grandma saying, "We weren't well off, but there was always plenty of food and we made room until these immigrant guests of ours could find a place of their own and a job."

My other favorite story that Grandma told was how my grandfather teased her with displays of affection in front of their children. "You don't remember your grandfather because you were living in China when he died. He would have loved you, Cecelia. That Schmul, he was always sneaking up behind me and throwing his arms around me when I was stirring the soup or grabbing me around the waist when I had my head poking into the oven. He'd kiss me in front of the children! I tried to stop him. 'Schmul, the children!' I'd say. But, between you and me, really I loved it. Don't you ever be afraid of showing someone you love them, no matter how old you are, Cecelia." With that, Grandma hugged me, and happily I felt myself enveloped by her large bosom.

Grandma adored me but I knew it drove her crazy that I was so mischievous and played baseball with boys in the neighborhood. She hadn't allowed Mother to play with boys as a child, not even her own brothers, for fear she'd become a tomboy, and here I was the leader of the whole bunch! Sometimes my grandma had no idea where I might be and told my mother she worried about me, but luckily the neighborhood was safe. It was mostly working-class Italian, Swedish and Portuguese people who all looked out for everyone else's children.

As a girl I was athletic and could climb anything. Mother once told me she'd have me all dressed up ready to go visiting on a Sunday morning and suddenly she couldn't find me. She'd look up on the roof and there I was smiling impishly down at her in my best dress!

When Mother came home at night I sat with her while she ate the dinner Grandma had kept warm for her. We talked about what I had done at school but I could see she was tired, her short curly hair collapsed around her face and sadness around her eyes. It was during the depth of the Depression and I knew Mother was worried about making ends meet. I couldn't help sensing that she felt the huge empty space left by my father.

There were many wonderful times, however. Every Friday Grandma cooked Shabbat dinner for the whole family of thirty or forty aunts, uncles, cousins, and any stray friends who needed a meal. Thursday afternoons when I came home from school, Aunt Sadie took Grandma and me in her car on a huge shopping expedition for the groceries. Grandma sent me up and down the aisles in search of matzo meal or butter while she stopped at the kosher fish and poultry counters. Friday morning when I left for school the stove was filled with huge pots already bubbling and by the time I got home, the smells were so tantalizing that I planted myself in the kitchen, peeking into huge pots while Grandma gave me little tastes. When I offered to help, Grandma showed me how to chop, roll, or stir. I was blissfully happy whenever I was in the kitchen with Grandma.

By six o'clock, the family began to arrive, hugging and talking as if they hadn't seen each other just a week ago. I loved feeling myself pulled into a hug against my aunt's fur coat, a big kiss planted on my cheek, or being scooped up onto my uncle's shoulder. While the men took a brandy in the living room, the women packed into the kitchen to help, and soon plates heaped with gefilte fish, mounds of chopped herring, matzo balls, chickens, brisket, and stacks of latkes poured out of the kitchen. There was a silent moment of deep thanks for the food and lighting of the Shabbat candles and prayers and then everyone began eating and talking over, under and through each other as they passed the food up and down the large table—extended by leaves—that ran from one end of the dining room to the far end of the living room, with a card table at either end for us young cousins.

It was impossible not to notice how Grandma's delicious food sparked great conversation and high spirits. Piano music and dancing added gaiety and warmth after dinner. I knew I wanted this feeling for the rest of my life. It's no wonder that I love cooking for friends and gatherings as I've recreated this celebration many times over throughout my life. To me there's hardly anything more satisfying than a full refrigerator—the prelude to tables laden with tasty food, nourishing beloved people.

While I was in high school, Mother became reacquainted with one of the Russian immigrants my grandmother had taken into her home when Mother was ten and he was a young man of eighteen. They reestablished their earlier connection and began dating. This young Russian, Walter Ashe, had come to San Francisco to escape conscription into the Russian army and had worked his way through UC Berkeley, majoring in chemistry. He was a socialist, who was interested in literature, current events, concerts, lectures, but mostly my mother.

I adored Walter, a kind and generous man, and was thrilled for Mother. She had been only twenty-eight—a young woman —when she divorced my father. Though she never complained, I knew she came home tired and felt lonely for male company. Walter idolized Mother, constantly telling her she was beautiful and complimenting her cooking while patting her affectionately on the tush. After years of working to support us, my mother bloomed under Walt's caring and love.

Walter was also very fond of me and supportive of my dream to go to college. Mother often spoke of how important it was for me to have an education and graduate from college. This dream, plus Mother and Walter's support, gave me a great sense of inner strength and optimism for the future.

My Chinese amah and me

A proud Mother and me at my UC Berkeley
graduation ceremony, 1942

College Years and the War

There was never a question in my mind that I would go to college; I knew it would open countless doors to a fuller, more rewarding life and enable me to explore what the world had to offer.

As the Depression dragged on into its eighth year, Mother and I were faced with the challenge of how to pay my tuition at the University of California, Berkeley. The cost, twenty-seven dollars a semester, was a fortune in those days relative to the two dollars and eighty cents a day I was making at the Emporium and the eighty dollars a month Mother was earning selling corsets at Aunt Agnes's shop. We had been struggling living on that amount! Mother always said we'd do whatever was needed—take out a loan, sell whatever we could, even the piano—but that I would indeed go to college. We scrutinized our expenses and found ways to streamline even further. We finally decided that, between what I could make that summer, what Mother could contribute without jeopardizing rent and household expenses, and a sweet offer from Walter to help, we could swing it. I would have to live at home in San Francisco to avoid paying rent, but that was no problem. I was determined to take advantage of all a college education had to offer.

In September 1937, giddy with anticipation, I walked through Sather Gate to register for my first semester. Thumbing through the course catalog was like looking at a long, exotic menu and wanting to try every dish. Greedy for knowledge, I was drawn to everything: modern literature, Shakespeare, political science, psychology—anything having to do with learning and culture.

Unable to decide what to major in, I went along with Mother and my piano teacher, Mr. Windemeir, who urged that I major in music. Though I had studied piano for many years and was considered talented, I was intimidated when thrown in with top musicians, some of them the leading composers and performers of the day. In my piano duo class, the meticulous Madame Pietré presented us with scores, expecting us to play them by sight. I had learned to play the piano by ear and memorize the music, so I needed to take the scores home before I could play them. Madame Pietré's arrogant displeasure with my playing made me anxious. Unable to perform in her class as flawlessly as everyone else, I began to feel a nagging sense of incompetence.

Yet there were parts of the music program that I loved. Professor Edward Lawton, Jr., my music professor, taught solfège (singing musical scores by sight) and composition classes, which were strenuous and demanding. Underlying his gentle demeanor was a passion for helping students develop the skills needed to hear the intricacies of sound and melody in individual instruments. Without him I might never have been aware of the rich nuances and dimensions of music. My joy in classical music to this day is due to that thorough training.

It was a privilege to study contemporary music during the summer session with two visiting professors that year: the great composer Ernest Bloch, known for his uncanny ability to express deep, exquisite emotion through his music, and his protégé Roger Sessions, also a composer of profound feeling. My own musical compositions were passable but not outstanding. Because I held myself to such a high standard, I felt disappointed in my work. Though I delighted in hearing and understanding musical composition, if I was going to major in music I needed to perform, and I quickly recognized that I was not as competent a pianist as my peers. As the semester continued, I became increasingly discouraged, so I cut classes and my grades plummeted.

But there was another reason I cut classes: I had fallen in love. Or thought I had. A few weeks after classes began, I met Sid at a dance at Hillel House to welcome entering Jewish students. Walking up the steps, I could hear those luscious big band sounds spilling out the windows and couldn't wait to dance. The place was jammed and jumpin'—a sea of swirling dresses, baggy pants held up by suspenders, and jackets tossed to the sidelines, with a live orchestra generating such energy that there wasn't a still body in the room.

I had barely walked in the door when an adorable guy with

a warm smile pulled me onto the dance floor. As he tossed me out and quickly pulled me in to the beat of the music, he blurted out, "I'm Herb from Brooklyn." Next thing I knew, a handsome student who appeared to be an upperclassman cut in. Sid could jitterbug better than anybody I'd ever seen, but I kept up with him. Breathless by the time a third young man, Martin, cut in, my spirits and confidence were soaring. The whirlwind of partners made me feel like the most popular girl on the floor—no longer the plump, pimply-faced wallflower of high school.

At the break Martin led me across the dance floor, eager to introduce me to his three roommates, all from his hometown of Revere, Massachusetts. I was especially drawn to Mel, with his curly black hair and timid expression. When the music started up again, full of confidence and uncharacteristic bravado, I said, "Let's dance," as I pulled him onto the floor. "I don't dance ..." he protested, but I showed him how to hold me and sway back and forth while the band played a smooth swing. He was thrilled, calling to his astonished pals, "I'm dancing!"

Little did I know then that Herb, Sid, and Mel would play important roles in my life.

Sid kept cutting in, and, hours later, when the dance was over, he walked me to the train on Shattuck Avenue. I learned that he was twenty-one, an entomology major working toward his Ph.D., and an avid tennis player who had been in tournaments since he was a boy. We made a date, and a few days later we were on the courts playing a vigorous game of tennis. We soon became formidable doubles partners, taking on all the other players on the university's Bancroft tennis courts. Sid and I began meeting regularly on campus for lunch, sitting on the grass or inside the Hillel House, now almost a second home, and sharing homemade sandwiches.

I was attracted to Sid's thin, handsome face, which was framed by his wavy brown hair. I loved to watch his face and eyes as they changed, reflecting what he was thinking. His high forehead seemed to emphasize his intelligence, and I found myself riveted when he talked, especially when he spoke about his passion for one of the escalating issues of the day—Russia and the Communist movement. A neophyte in the world of international politics, I was fascinated, not only because politics was a new, exciting world to me, but also because of my Russian roots.

We were terrific dance partners, attending weekend dances at the student union, where there was always music—maybe not a live band, but at least a jukebox or record player. Occasionally the university held a large dance in the men's gym, where the melting pot of UC Berkeley students from all over the country and world danced to the greats—Benny Goodman, Count Basie, Glen Miller, and Artie Shaw. The floor was always packed and the bleachers filled with people sitting out until they got their second wind. When the tempo slowed and the lights dimmed, couples danced so close they almost made love on the dance floor. Sid and I took full advantage of the low lights!

Some evenings we'd take in a movie or go out for coffee.

Sid worked two jobs but, always a gentleman, insisted on paying for our dates. The magnetism between us was palpable; whenever possible we found a place to neck, careful not to "go all the way." Mother, like the mothers of most of the girls I knew, had indoctrinated me to believe that "nice" girls saved themselves for marriage, and in those days we listened to our mothers. I was only seventeen, and the extent of my experience with the opposite sex was a kiss or two. Here was this "older man" with whom I had entered serious territory ... not to mention that I had been intensely devouring the diaries of Anaïs Nin, which fueled my desire to experience sex.

When Christmas vacation rolled around, Sid drove me to Los Angeles to meet his mother and sisters. I had just turned eighteen, and on the way back to Berkeley we impulsively took a detour to north Lake Tahoe, Nevada, where we were married by a justice of the peace. Finally we could have sex, the most important thing on our minds and my reason for getting married. I admit I was totally complicit and had no thought for the consequences.

Predictably, Mother was outraged and immediately went about finding a way to undo the situation. It didn't take long for me to realize that marriage while a freshman wasn't as romantic as I had imagined. Sid and I were both busy working jobs and going to school; we were strapped for money, barely able to pay the rent on our cramped apartment on Euclid Avenue. Coming home after a day of classes, then shopping and preparing dinner, certainly wasn't the life I had bargained for. I secretly longed to be unattached again, free of obligations.

The marriage lasted a few months, until Mother got my cousin Harold, recently graduated from UC Berkeley's law school, to annul it, claiming it had not been consummated.

What a relief. After the annulment, my passion for Sid diminished. We tried to remain friends but he was terribly hurt, claiming he still loved me. Toward the end of my freshman year, my grades were down and I'd been blatantly absent from many music classes. I was required to see the dean of liberal arts, Guy Montgomery, who also happened to be my favorite professor; I'd taken his Shakespeare class, the only class in which I received an A. He listened attentively as I told my sad tale—feelings of inadequacy in music classes, failing grades, even my impulsive marriage—and asked me what I would really like to major in. Without a second thought I blurted out, "psychology." "Psychology it is," he said as he entered this new major into my records.

Ever since I was a little girl I had been fascinated by human behavior, my own included. I recall watching people, finding their actions perplexing and wondering why they behaved as they did. Why were some people optimists and others pessimists? Why had I often felt different from the people around me, sometimes even estranged? Now I was being given the chance to enter the realm of self-discovery and excavate the psyche for deeper insight.

Questions about who I was and what I really wanted were surfacing. Most glaring were the inconsistencies and complexities of growing up with polar-opposite parents. How could I reconcile my feelings for my father, whom I adored as a child

31

and who seemed to love me dearly, with the fact that he was totally irresponsible and unethical, and had abandoned me? Mother, who dedicated her life to me, was practical to the core and lacking in spontaneity, but she was my rock. I had never for a moment doubted her love, and in turn I loved her and felt grateful that she was there for me.

A Hard-Working Student

By now I had switched from working at the Emporium on Saturdays to working at the H. Liebes & Co. department store, an expensive, fashionable boutique on Grant Avenue, the most upscale street in San Francisco. In addition to selling on the floor, I offered to coordinate clothes and colorful accessories for display. Soon I was invited to dress the mannequins and arrange the window displays. I took on this new role wholeheartedly, running around San Francisco to find special props and painting background sets to make the windows absolute show-stoppers. I hadn't explored this artistic side of myself before and found I had a real talent for creating atmosphere and a sophisticated sense of fashion.

Working at Liebes was a unique learning experience, expanding my knowledge of fashion and style. During summer vacation following my freshman year, I worked there six days a week, earning sixteen dollars and eighty cents a week at thirty-five cents an hour—a fortune for me at the time—which paid for my room and food. My supervisor hoped to train me to become a buyer when I graduated from college, which I appreciated but knew was not the direction I wanted to follow in life. However, I did manage to save enough money for the next year's tuition, and also enough to live in Berkeley instead of commuting from San Francisco.

By my sophomore year I was happily ensconced in the Psychology Department and completely absorbed in my coursework. I appreciated my professors, who were not only knowledgeable but approachable, encouraging us to meet with them. I joined the Psychology Club and spent many happy hours doing research in the psychology library. I had returned to my "carefree" student life, studying hard and making almost all A's, not only in psychology but also in my minor, public administration.

Some of my favorite classes were in applied psychology, taught by the astute Professor Ghisseli. He was so inspiring that after lectures I eagerly joined other students gathered around him for long, impromptu discussions. One of Professor Ghisseli's classes, called Time and Motion Studies, taught us how to write job descriptions. He thought my work thorough and perceptive, and offered me a paying job with the City of Berkeley writing job descriptions for the personnel department. Though other students were interviewed as well, I was chosen for this coveted position, working part-time on the mornings I was not in class.

Other boyfriends came along, but I had learned my lesson well about spur-of-the-moment commitments or jumping into bed casually. After my impulsive brush with marriage, I began to explore the meaning of sexual desire versus real love and commitment. I was careful never again to tell anyone I loved him unless I truly meant it and knew there was deep commitment underlying sexual desire.

Mother and Walter got married, and Walt's daughter, Florence, also a student at Berkeley, became my stepsister. Our parents decided that we could save money by sharing an apartment, so in my sophomore year we moved in together. It was disastrous. Florence, resentful and jealous of sharing her father's attention and financial support, was callous and nasty to me. When I was in the campus hospital for a week with the flu, she lied to my friends who called, telling them she didn't know where I was. I was outraged, but when I confronted her she just shrugged her shoulders and turned away. After that disturbing experience I decided not live with her for another semester. For many years my relationship with Florence was cool and distant, but thankfully Walt understood what was going on between us and didn't take sides. As we grew older, married, and had children of our own, Florence and I came around to an amicable relationship.

I moved into a well-maintained women's boarding house on Durant Avenue. The monthly costs were more than I could afford, but Walt offered to pay part of the rent. In this harmonious atmosphere, quite by accident I developed a thriving little side business. Because my dresses and blouses were so perfectly pressed, my housemates asked if I would iron their clothes, so at thirty-five cents for a dress and twenty-five cents for a blouse I enjoyed a nice, steady cash flow. I purchased a special small ironing board for the ruffles and puffed sleeves but could hardly keep up with my new business. Within the first week I had covered the cost of the ironing board. I was thrilled with the extra money, which helped pay my living expenses.

Glorious Summers in Yosemite

During my sophomore year, I learned about jobs for college students through the National Park Service. Having spent the previous summer indoors at Liebes, dressed in stockings and high heels six days a week, I longed for an outside job and eagerly applied to work for the National Park Service the coming summer. After an interview by the representative who came to the campus, I was assigned to Yosemite National Park to work as a bus person at Curry Village, one of the visitor accommodations run by the park concessionaire.

Four girls from different colleges in the United States became my tent mates. What an amazingly exciting and adventurous time we had! We were on our own, responsible only to report to work five days a week and do a good job. There were plenty of young men from all over the world working in the park for the summer, so we had a full social life. On our days off we were free to go anywhere as long as we signed out to the Park Service and let them know exactly where we were headed, with whom, and when we would return.

Spellbound by Yosemite's magical quality, I chose to remain in the park on days off, eager to explore as many of its wilderness treasures as possible. The other girls and I often hitched a ride up to Tuolumne Meadows; from there we'd set out with our packs and sleeping bags for overnight trips to high Sierra lakes and passes. Each new meadow, each rock face, each waterfall I discovered was more exhilarating than the one before and I began my joyful, lifelong love affair with Yosemite.

Two idyllic summers at Yosemite not only gave me valuable experiences within a large government organization but also ignited my passion for hiking, exploring mountains, and my dedication to Yosemite and the environmental movement. To this day, whenever I crave spiritual rejuvenation and sustenance, I head for my beloved Yosemite National Park.

Hiking in Yosemite

Mother, Walt, and Good Friends

Mother, happy to be out of the world of selling undergarments, was finally enjoying some leisure, while Walt worked for a chemical company close by in San Francisco. They had moved into a lovely apartment on Anza Street off Geary Boulevard, always graciously opening their doors to the friends I invited home. Like all college students, my friends never passed up a home cooked meal, especially Mother's marvelous pot roast, but the food was really just the delicious accompaniment to the spirited conversation we all relished.

Mother and Walt loved young people and were interested in their views on anything—music, art, and current events. Mother, particularly fond of Mel, was impressed by his gracious manners and insights into music and literature. Herb, whom I had been dating, fit in perfectly with his high energy and infectious enthusiasm. Walter was still a bit of a socialist, his ideas sparking many multifaceted discussions as we all bounced political ideas back and forth. After dinner, we gathered around the piano to initiate my friends into my family's long tradition of singing after dinner.

I am forever thankful for friendships made during my student days at UC Berkeley. Anaïs Nin wrote, "Each friend represents a world in us, a world not possibly born until they arrive, and it is only by this meeting that a new world is born." This exactly describes my deep friendships, some of which began in high school, many in college, and have enriched my life for more than seven decades.

Ever since I dragged Mel onto the dance floor at that first

Hillel dance, he and I had remained friends, getting together regularly for coffee, to study together in the library or to swap East Coast/West Coast stories. Mel, a serious student, wanted to follow in the footsteps of his uncle who was a famous mathematician. I found his determination and commitment to scholarship admirable. Our friendship remained easygoing, without confusing romantic undertones. I was flattered when he asked me to help him buy a bracelet for his new girlfriend, Betty. After Mel treated me to lunch in San Francisco's Chinatown, we went on a search for the perfect bracelet for the girl he clearly was crazy about. Shortly afterward, Betty and Mel became a twosome and would eventually marry.

My good friend Ann from Lowell High transferred to UC Berkeley after her first year at Reed College in Oregon. Her overprotective mother wanted her to attend a college as far away as possible from her new boyfriend, Jim. When Ann and I decided to become roommates for a semester, little did her mother know that Jim had followed Ann to Berkeley and was living nearby, though he was always at our apartment! It was great sport covering up for them whenever Ann's mother called. If Ann's mother came for a visit we scurried around to hide all signs of Jim's presence. The next semester Ann and Jim married. The three of us would remain lifelong friends.

A year after the Hillel dance, I spotted Herb in the library and we picked up where we had left off. I liked his looks, high energy, and his thick Brooklyn accent that made me smile whenever he opened his mouth. In addition to my bringing him to Mother and Walt's on weekends and holidays, he invited me to campus events and pizza dinners with his fellow optometry friends. Most of these young professionals were from Brooklyn and New York City and I looked forward to hanging out with them, hearing their wild tales of life in the Big Apple.

I was eager to show Herb all of my favorite places. We hiked on Mt. Tamalpais, took long walks on Stinson Beach, and drove along the dramatic coasts of Santa Cruz and Carmel. A true city boy from the heart of Brooklyn, he found California's natural beauty spectacular and was unable to contain his enthusiasm wherever we happened to be. Herb's high spirits and ceaseless wonder were contagious. He and I frolicked like a couple of puppies, rolling down the grassy hill at the Tilden Park or down the sand dunes at Point Reyes.

When other students attended football games on Saturdays, Herb and I both worked, but neither of us felt left out. We were grateful that we had jobs in those still-hard times. Proud to be working my way through college, I admit I scoffed at the unabashed enthusiasm of the sorority girls and fraternity boys for football, the frenzied pre-game rallies and after-game drinking celebrations, all of which I thought were frivolous.

Through Herb's job working at the 1939 World's Fair on Treasure Island, he was able to get us free tickets and entrance to numerous events, such as dances and music concerts. Wandering through the pavilions and exhibits from all over the world whetted my appetite for exotic travels.

We dated throughout college, but I was also seeing other men as my social circle widened and became diverse. Herb invited me to our senior prom where we jitterbugged until the last "Goodnight Sweetheart." There he asked if I would marry him after we graduated and the war was over, when he envisioned starting his optometry practice in New York. I was evasive, letting him know I liked him very much and wanted to remain his friend. Although a wonderful person, I knew then that I wanted to spend my life with a man who thought more deeply about life and the world.

Disquieting News from Europe

In late 1937, I knew of several courageous male students who had gone off to fight Franco in Spain. It seemed so noble that I wanted to join the Abraham Lincoln Brigade to fight fascism, but as a freshman at UC Berkeley I knew of no women who had joined. I was also hesitant because my mother insisted I was too young and must continue my education. Later I was glad that I attended a large university with such a diverse population and was exposed to many viewpoints.

When war spread throughout Europe, many students at the university were actively engaged in politics. There were isolationists who claimed we had no business getting involved, and others who felt what was happening in Germany was ghastly and reason enough for the United States to step in to help the Allies. We had known that Jews and other minorities were being rounded up and sent to camps, but we didn't learn about the genocide until much later. It was difficult to learn what was really happening because of heavy censorship of news from Germany, but by listening to BBC at night on shortwave radio and receiving reports from refugees and those who were lucky enough to escape Hitler's creeping fascism, we were able to have a glimpse of the horrors.

One day during a loud Sproul Hall anti-war rally, I hurried to see what was going on. There was Dave Bers, a Trotskyite and isolationist acquaintance, who believed the war in Europe was an imperialist war and the United States had no business being part of it. He handed me a sign that read "U.S. STAY OUT!" I took one look at it, banged it on the ground, and broke it. I was appalled at my friend's slogan on the Trotskyite sign and the aloof role of the U.S. in not becoming involved with what was happening in Europe. Neither my local Jewish friends nor even Hillel, the Jewish cultural center for students at UC Berkeley, were acknowledging or taking a stand against Hitler's propaganda. Though Dave and I vehemently argued about politics, we became friends, enjoying stimulating conversations over coffee.

In spite of my anger about what was happening internationally, I was still having a good time at school, enjoying stimulating, diverse activities and new or deepening relationships. My friendship with my high school pal Bernice, who had taught me how to dance, continued through our university years. She too worked on Saturdays in a department store because her father had recently died. She was a good student with an appealing gift for conversation. She continued to be as popular at UC Berkeley as she had been in high school, and was never without an entourage of boyfriends. Sometimes we double-dated. In my senior year, when I was living in a small, cheap room with one electric burner to cook on, Bernice and her roommates invited me to share meals with them at their spacious apartment on Bancroft Avenue. We put money into a kitty, took turns shopping and cooking, and competed to see who could whip up the best meals for the least cost. A tablecloth, a few candles, an elegantly set table, a home cooked dinner and the easy company of other women with good conversation made this semester a particularly happy time for me.

In the winter of my senior year at the university, on the night of December 7, 1941, I was studying for finals with two male friends when we heard on the radio that Japanese bombers had attacked Pearl Harbor, catching Americans by surprise. In that instant, my generation was called to war. My study companions slammed their books shut, stayed up all night talking, and waited for the enlistment offices to open first thing in the morning.

For months we had read in the newspapers and listened on the radio to reports of the German invasions in Europe— of Denmark, Norway, France, Belgium, Luxembourg, and of their subsequent surrender. With the Blitz, the night-bombings of London and other cities in Britain, we increasingly feared that fascism's threat could reach our shores.

Since my freshman year I had followed news of the growth of fascism in Europe. Friends who had left college in 1937 to volunteer in the Abraham Lincoln Brigade to fight the fascist invasion of Spain wrote to me regularly and kept me posted about the state of affairs in Spain and Europe. By late 1941 before Pearl Harbor, they had sent alarming letters with news from the Polish underground of the extermination camps and mass murders by the Nazis. Those reports were well believed by my veteran friends who had already witnessed Franco's atrocities during the Spanish Civil War.

Many in my generation felt that our participation in the war was absolutely crucial to defeat Hitler and the oppressive regimes that threatened democracy. By serving in the armed forces, we fervently believed we were helping save our world for democracy. We were proud of our patriotism and serving our country. I use the word "we" because when close male friends signed up to put their lives on the line, it affected me deeply, and I, too, enlisted.

Young men went in droves to the enlistment office, almost as a rite of passage, and by the following week there was a complete drain of male students at school. One-third of the men of the class of 1941 would not return home from the war.

Deeply affected by what was happening in the rest of the world, I wanted to do my part. I signed up too, but with only one semester to go, Mother insisted that I graduate from college before going off for my training.

For me, joining the war effort meant going into the women's branch of the navy called WAVES, which stood for Women Accepted for Volunteer Emergency Service. We WAVES took over jobs in the continental United States and Hawaii so that navy men could go overseas. Mildred McAfee, the president of Wellesley College, became the first woman commissioned officer in U.S. Navy history and the first director of the WAVES.

I recall proudly wearing our blue and white WAVE uniforms designed by Mainbocher, a well-known French design-er. I wore that chic uniform, with a curvy fitted jacket and gored skirt, for three and a half years—feeling patriotic and feminine. I found a soft navy blue wool fabric that draped perfectly for a custom-designed uniform that I had made up with extra darts at the waist and the skirt a little shorter than regulation. The navy regulations required that we keep our hair above the collar, but I figured out a way I could roll my hair up over a rat (a hair bun) so that it would be short in the daytime, yet when I went out in the evenings I could remove the rat and let my hair down to my shoulders. While the government issued white cotton blouses we were to wear under our jackets, some of us ordered soft silk blouses for evenings and special occasions. Since I knew well how to hand wash and press silk blouses I was able to avoid huge cleaning bills. Through this skill I endeared myself to roommates who didn't know how to press at all, and for the favor I was taken to dinner and given gifts in appreciation.

During my last semester, government representatives came to the university to interview us for jobs related to the war effort. With my major in psychology and minor in public administration, I felt I was qualified to take the civil service exam for a junior administrative assistant, passing high on the list. I was soon offered a position as a junior interviewer at California State Employment Services in Los Angeles. While waiting for my navy assignment, I began this job, using all the testing techniques I had learned at school. I administered psychological and manual dexterity tests to prospective employees, mostly women seeking work in the burgeoning aircraft industry. These women were replacing the men who had vacated their jobs to enlist in the war. These few months working on my first job out of college and living in Los Angeles were an incredible time for learning.

A college friend, Jan, was already in Los Angeles working in the aircraft industry. She and I rented an airy, two-bedroom apartment near the Miracle Mile off Wilshire Boulevard. Every day, I hopped the bus a block from our apartment arriving at my downtown office within twenty minutes. Jan and I joined a political left-wing group that gave us news of the Spanish civil war and also inside reports of Hitler's vicious campaign against the Jews not only in Germany but in Czechoslovakia, Poland, Holland, Hungary, and other nearby countries. At that time we had not yet heard reports of the camps. We were living a double life of inward anxiety and outward hedonism. On weekends we headed for the pristine beaches of Santa Monica, or I spent my days playing tennis.

Most of my friends were either in the service or working in jobs to help the war effort; but no matter what we were doing, we were caught up in the progress of the war and followed the news avidly. Wherever we went there were men and women in uniform, on the move, about to ship out or walk into the belly of huge troop-carrying transport planes. We were living in frightening times, with a sense of urgency underlying each moment. The horror and uncertainty of a world gone mad left us no choice but to live every moment to the hilt. We danced a little later, laughed a little louder, and hugged our young men in their navy blues a little tighter, wondering if they'd come home whole, maimed, or in a body bag when the nightmare was finally over.

Ninety-Day Wonder

Although I liked living in Los Angeles, my job there was not as stimulating as I had hoped, and I eagerly awaited my new assignment in the Naval Reserve. Six months after graduating, I received my orders to proceed immediately to the U.S. Naval Midshipmen School at Smith College in Northampton, Massachusetts, for intensive officer training to become a "Ninety-Day Wonder." The navy believed that we college graduates could be trained as naval officers in a mere three months.

My first assignment as an ensign at the Bureau of Naval Personnel in Arlington, Virginia, was to analyze officers' backgrounds, qualifications, and education in order to match them to specific assignments in the navy. Using the training from my applied psychology classes and my work experience for the City of Berkeley, I sifted through files containing the applicants' college coursework, prior work experience, psychological tests, personal interests questionnaires, letters of reference, and other relevant information. After a complex analysis of all this information, I hoped that I had judged well in assigning officers the best-fit job given their background.

Although I knew I was doing important work, sitting at a desk all day analyzing endless tests and questionnaires became monotonous. It was tolerable because of my intelligent, supportive commanding officer, Lieutenant Lowell Hattery, who believed that any job within the Office of Navel Personnel, regardless how routine or seemingly unimportant, was a worthy contribution to the war effort. His wise words sustained me yet I longed for a position where I could physically move about, influencing the public on the importance of civilian participation and support in the war effort.

Another issue contributed to my unhappiness. I was experiencing anti-Semitism from Southern women officers who had never met a Jew before and who were assigned as I was to live in the Bachelors' Officers' Quarters of the Raleigh Hotel in Washington, D.C., which had been converted into living space for female naval officers. Whenever I entered the dining room or joined the other women officers at one of the long communal tables, the other women would stop talking and ignore me or their conversations would shift to small talk. If I sat at an empty table, other WAVES did not sit next me. I didn't know how to respond. I felt rejected when I was excluded from their lives, daily worlds, and evening outings. Lonely and depressed, night after night I would stay alone in my room crying. I was miserable living in the hostile environment of Officers' Quarters of the Raleigh Hotel, and in desperation I applied for a transfer out of Washington, D.C.

When I discussed my unhappy living situation with Lieutenant Hattery, he assured me that he valued my work and didn't want me to leave. He recommended that I call his friend, Marian Hoffman, a civil servant and older woman of about thirty who might have a room in her two-bedroom apartment near Dupont Circle. Marian welcomed me into her sunny apartment, offering me a choice of her larger room or the second bedroom, which I was delighted to move into. She welcomed me into her life, cooking and leaving prepared food in the refrigerator. She bought tickets for both of us to concerts, and introduced me to the Corcoran Gallery of Art. We talked far into the night about our careers, the war, our hopes for the future, and became close friends. In turn I introduced Marian to the joys of hiking in the outdoors through a membership in the Appalachian Trail Club. Together we purchased her first sturdy hiking boots and small backpack for our outings in Shenandoah National Park not far from Washington, D.C. I also invited her to be my guest for dinners and to the Officers' Club gatherings and dances at the aristocratic, old Mayflower Hotel. The club turned out to be a friendly spot where we two met local hostesses and handsome young officers eager to make friends and dance.

One of the perks of being a WAVE during World War II in Washington was that naval officers were invited to join the exclusive Chevy Chase Country Club, which before the war had admitted only white males as members. But during the war it patriotically opened its doors to officers in the services. When I invited Marian to lunch in the staid country club's grand dining room, two women—one in full naval uniform—must have been an unusual sight. Because I was a good tennis player, playing regularly in college and since I was ten years old, I was sought after as a tennis partner and made diverse new friends through tennis. Within a few months of moving out of the WAVE Officers' Quarters, I developed a lively social life in Washington circles and was happy again.

Just as I was beginning to feel comfortable and at home in Washington, D.C., almost hoping they had forgotten my request, my transfer abruptly arrived, with orders to report within ten days to the Twelfth Naval District Headquarters in San Francisco. With a mixture of sadness and excitement I packed and bid farewell to Lieutenant Hattery, Marian, and other newly made acquaintances. I will always be grateful to Marian for offering her home, friendship, and unequivocal acceptance at one of the lowest points of my life, giving me the support I needed to carry on with my job.

"Personal initiative . . .
Free enterprise . . .
It's the American Way."
Help preserve it by—
Supporting the Fifth War
Loan Drive with War Bonds!

Be a blood relation to a
fighting man. Let blood
ties bind you . . .
Give more blood and
Save more lives . . .
Send your blood to War!

U.S. Naval Training and Distribution Center

THE MASTHEAD

Vol. III—No. 16   TREASURE ISLAND, S. F., CALIF.   June 3, 1944

V-Mail Exhibit at Treasure Island

* CONTENTS *
PHOTOGRAPHIC SAFETY FILM
NOT DANGEROUS

WAR & NAVY
DEPARTMENTS
V...-MAIL SERVICE
OFFICIAL BUSINESS

PENALTY FOR
PRIVATE USE TO
AVOID PAYMENT OF
POSTAGE. $300

V····-MAIL
STATION

V····-MAIL

RUSH

Exact size of V-Mail box when folded to its original size 4"x4" contains 1750 letters in 16MM film form, weighing four ounces.

Top this band is a part of the precious cargo destined to bring "rays of state de-light" and pilfering smiles to those fighting Bluejackets who are delivering the Mail that will eventually spell doom for all foes of democracy. Judging from the beautiful smiles of these two winsome WAVES, Sp(M)c Cecilia Simon and Sp(M)2c Millie Vito, find it a distinct pleasure to serve in their capacity at the Fleet Post Office in the V-Mail division.

1750 V-MAIL LETTERS WEIGH FOUR OUNCES; GOES BY FAST PLANE

PHOTOGRAPHED IN YOUR OWN HANDWRITING BRINGING A PERSONALIZED MESSAGE

Open skies . . . and the drone of an approaching plane stirs the silence. Below an "Operations—", men watch tensely as they wait to identify the roaring craft. This may be it! Watchers relax as the steady hum becomes a roar overhead. Broad smiles are suddenly the order of the day and figures dash from all directions, spreading the news . . . cargo planes! . . . Supplies desperately needed, necessities for a little more than mere existence . . . and mail! For mail is the ever growing link between the men in that isolated spit point on the map and his folks back in Everytown, U.S.A.

A constant stream of supplies is being sent to those outlying stations and space is so vitally important now . . . important because every beachhead must be held by equipment from home. Thus the line leads directly to that small brown V-Mail envelope . . . V-Mail providing precious connection from one side of the world to the other . . . exchange of "news and views" from you to me . . . and vice versa!

Each V-Mail letter is a perfectly reduced photograph of the original. Johnny out there is pretty pleased when he sees that familiar writing. He probably doesn't stop to consider the process that makes precious his letter available . . . much less how. However, when the first miniature V-Mail letter from Johnny was placed in the box at home, it created a lot of notice and his dad, being of an inquiring mind, started a bit of an investigation.

Result—John, Sr., discovered the whole idea to be . . . "solid"

John Sr. was right. A letter written on a V-Mail form in any one of the following:

Dark ink
Heavy pencil, or
Typewritten.

Is easily photographed . . . Imagine 1750 letters only weighs four ounces of film; it carries an A-1 priority and goes by fast plane to the war areas. The V-Mail negatives are then printed and swiftly delivered . . . and another blue-jacket knows he is not so far away after all.

The original letters are kept on file at the Fleet Post Office until delivery of the V-Mail prints has been assured. Then the old forms are destroyed to maintain security.

This very process will be demonstrated in a complete and highly interesting exhibit sponsored by the V-Mail division of the Fleet Post Office through Lt. (jg) Cecilia Rosin, officer in charge of V-Mail publicity in the Fleet Post Office, is to be shown in the lobby of Main Ship's Service daily, June 3 through June 8. The hours are 1000 to 1630. WAVES and specialists, trained in the postal school at Sampson Naval Training School, Sampson, New York, for positions in the V-Mail department, will be present. Experts each, they will be on hand to describe the details of the amazing program and to answer any and all questions.

The whole exhibit is worth "a bit of an investigation" so don't forget the time and place. Bring a friend . . . we'll meet you there . . . at Main Ship's Service. Free . . . V-Mail stationery.

Don't need schooling to know how to handle these Bluejacket—seven lovely WAVES plus seven mail bags full of letters for the fighting Bluejackets everywhere equal two thousand something. Holding one V-Mail bag of V-Mail letters which contains all the letters eventually to be sent from home. Shown holding the mail bags are (left to right) Sp(M)2c Helen Roberson, Sp(M)3c Molly Nora, Sp(M)1c Genevieve DeLuny, Y3c Bonnie Wanigas, Sp(M)2c Vickers Cameron, Y1c LaVonne Cobble and Y3c Edith Worthen. Holding the V-Mail bag of letters are Lt.(jg) Cecilia Simon and Millie Vito, Sp(M)2c.

I helped the war effort by promoting V-Mail

Wartime in San Francisco

1943–1946

The whole military was on the move. Young men in fatigues and bell-bottoms packed Union Station in Washington, D.C., catching trains that would take them to their assigned posts and from there to their destiny in the "war to save the world." I boarded my train for San Francisco with a suitcase, a touch of trepidation, and much excitement. In Salt Lake City, I noticed a handsome naval pilot walking down the aisle. He introduced himself as Ensign Glen Kitchen and told me he was headed to meet his squadron at the Naval Air Station in Alameda where he'd be deployed as a fighter pilot. We talked about our respective assignments and flirted as the train rolled west.

When I arrived in San Francisco I stayed briefly with Mother and Walt out in the Sunset District while I looked for an apartment, which would be paid for by a generous housing stipend from the navy. San Francisco was different from the beautiful, peaceful city I lived in before the war. By day life went on as it always had; people going to work, shopping, getting their hair cut, meeting friends for lunch. But at night the city was a dark reminder that these were potentially dangerous times, that perhaps we were a target for a Japanese bomb. A curfew, strictly enforced by police, sent people rushing home before nightfall and streetcars stopped running early. People whispered as streetlights were dimmed, turning the city into a dark, eerie place except for hundreds of little points of light—flashlights helping people find their way to homes darkened by blackout shades.

Along the San Francisco and Marin shorelines, protecting the Golden Gate, huge guns were poised to defend the bay. There were no Japanese people to be seen. Japanese Americans living on the West Coast had been ordered to relocate, for our government was convinced that given an invasion, Japanese Americans would choose to be loyal to Japan rather than to the United States. There were no known acts of espionage or sabotage by our Japanese American citizens, only hysteria and racial prejudice against them. Japanese families were rounded up from their homes and swept off to internment camps (euphemistically called "relocation camps") in remote areas of California. There, behind barbed wire, they lived in tarpaper-covered barracks that, when they arrived, lacked plumbing or cooking facilities. They lost their rights as citizens and they were not allowed to speak Japanese to each other.

I hated these unjust acts by our government, yet I regret I didn't speak out about their civil liberties being violated.

Trusting President Roosevelt's handling of the war, and about to become a naval officer, I reluctantly went along with our president and government.

I began my job in the navy as an ensign at the imposing Federal Building in the heart of the civic center of San Francisco. My assignment as public information officer for the Fleet Naval Post Office was to promote the patriotic use of V-Mail, just the kind of stimulating assignment I had hoped for. The navy soon found a large building, at Fifth and Bryant streets, where the huge stacks of letters being shipped to and from the Pacific could be processed. My commanding officer, Officer McDermott, was a wonderful man, eager to hear my ideas and supportive of how I carried them out.

When Glenn, the pilot I had met on the train, invited me for a spin in his fighter plane at the Naval Air Station in Alameda, I didn't hesitate. Fearless and excited, I stepped up into the tiny two-seat, open cockpit F4 fighter plane. Buckling me up, he handed over goggles, a head protector, and into the blue sky we soared. He proceeded to perform daring stunts— flips, stalls, and even flying upside down—maneuvers I found scary, yet exhilarating. I liked his adventurous spirit and we began to see each other on a regular basis.

Justine Jones and the Casbah

I needed to live closer to my job at the Fleet Post Office and search for a roommate to share the expensive costs of housing in San Francisco. Officer McDermott was the ideal person to ask for suggestions; he was a great partier and knew many navy people. Throughout the day he drank his cokes enhanced with a shot of gin from a flask he kept in his top drawer. I asked him if he had any ideas for a roommate, emphasizing I wanted a liberal WAVE, because of my devastating experience of anti-Semitism in D.C. "I just met just the WAVE you are looking for last night at a party," he said, "and I am sure you and Justine Jones will hit it off."

I called Justine Jones's office; we made a date to meet for lunch in front of the Federal Building. We discovered we both worked there but on different floors. Since she was in the same uniform as all the other WAVES coming out of the building for lunch, she wore a red carnation so that I could recognize her.

Standing in front of the Federal Building, Justine was impossible to miss, but not because of the carnation. Not only was she tall and willowy, but strikingly beautiful, with a fresh complexion and auburn hair. She exuded the kind of energy that made men stop in their tracks and stare.

Officer McDermott had it right; we instantly connected. Although we came from different backgrounds—Justine grew up in a coal-mining town in Mormon-dominated Utah—we had both arrived, amazingly, over our twenty-one years, at similar political and humanitarian beliefs. By the time lunch was over we knew we wanted to live together.

I answered an ad in the *San Francisco Chronicle* for an apartment at Washington Street and Taylor, clinging to the side of Nob Hill. A tall, sculptured entrance gate hid green shrubs and trees, with stairs winding to the manager's apartment.

Hearing music from the manager's apartment, I rang the bell. "Welcome to the Casbah," he said as he opened the door, a paintbrush in one hand and a glass of wine in the other. Farwell Taylor, artist and manager, offered me a glass of wine. We were off to a good start.

Roommates at the Casbah
Back: Jean Broadbent and me. Front: Justine Jones, Winnie Lair

The apartment for rent was up eighty-seven stairs on the top floor and fabulous! It was spacious—not one, but two living rooms with panoramic views of both the Bay Bridge and the Golden Gate Bridge, two small bedrooms off an airy kitchen and a third large bedroom with a fireplace. The patio, with its round outdoor table, umbrella, and chairs invited guests to a view of the entire city. Farwell asked if I wanted to meet Margaret, the woman living in the apartment who had advertised for roommates. I trusted that living with Margaret would be fine and would meet her later, but I knew immediately that I'd take the apartment. Asking Justine if she wanted to come see the apartment, she said, "If you like it take it. I'll move in with you." Her unquestioning trust in my judgment touched me. I felt even closer to her than the day we met.

Justine and I enthusiastically moved into Apartment 1230B in the Casbah, named for its North African feel, with a plaster exterior, an outdoor winding staircase, and breezy open landings. Margaret, the hard-working woman in residence, was thirty, an old maid in our young eyes. She must have regretted her ad, because shortly after we moved in she moved out. We often came home late, bringing people to 1230B to continue our many parties. Crowding into the kitchen, friends came and went at all hours, leaving bottles and dishes all over into the next day, or taking over both living rooms for music and dancing until dawn. Poor Margaret would poke her head out of her room and cry, "Can't you be quiet? I have to get up early for work tomorrow!" We found another WAVE to move in. Although our new roommate was a proper New England

Wellesley graduate and a Republican, her easygoing attitude fit in with the gestalt of 1230B.

Every morning I ran down the eighty-seven steps to catch the Washington Street cable car that took me to Market Street and from there I walked to the Federal Building. If I wasn't outside at the moment the cable car stopped in front of the Casbah, the good-natured driver would impatiently clang his bell but kindly wait for me.

Justine and I lived at the Casbah until the end of the war, packing joyous times and friends into that apartment. Whenever we went out together we created a stir. We were a dramatic duo attractive in our neatly fitting uniforms, both exuding confidence, with Justine standing a full foot taller than I, even in my high heels. Men waved and whistled at us and we loved it. Our favorite spot, a few blocks walk from our apartment, was the Officers' Club in the Tonga Room of the Fairmont Hotel. As soon as the two of us entered, army and navy officers swarmed around, eager to meet us and dance.

Victory Mail

Letters from home bringing comfort and news were lifelines for our men overseas. Besides the obvious terrors the soldiers confronted, loneliness and homesickness were relentless. Mail boosted morale like nothing else. Reassurance was also desperately needed for those at home—families wanted to hear the thoughts and feelings of their sons, husbands, and fathers on the front.

Lieutentant junior grade working at
Fleet Post Office, San Francisco

Hundreds of bags of mail, weighing tons and taking up valuable cargo space, could not be shipped because crucial medical supplies for our men in the Pacific had priority. This delay of mail demoralized our troops. The military decided to implement a system, originated in Britain, that would unfailingly get mail to our men without compromising precious space—V-Mail. V-Mail stood for Victory Mail. Its bright red logo, eventually becoming synonymous with frequent and rapid communication that made the war bearable, showed three dots and a dash—Morse code for the letter V.

I took great pleasure in my job promoting V-Mail. We asked the public and naval personnel to write their letters on a one-page V-Mail form. These letters were then photographed onto microfiche and airmailed as a small roll of film to fleet post offices throughout the Pacific. The film was developed back into letters on a V-Mail form and delivered to our troops eager to hear from home. The same process was repeated with the letters that our sailors sent to their families in the States.

Convincing the public to use V-Mail was difficult. Many people worried that navy personnel might read their private letters as they worked on feeding the V-Mail letters into machines for photographing. But the naval processors were warned that the letters were, by law, confidential. And the truth was that they fed so many hundreds of letters into the machines at a time they could not possibly read them.

Officer McDermott gave me full responsibility to carry out this important assignment as I saw best. With help from a Hollywood writer who was in our Public Information Department, I produced a short film demonstrating the entire V-Mail process from the time the letter was written to the time it was delivered. Our pitch was that writing V-Mail letters was one of the most patriotic acts that Americans could perform. Letter writing was of the utmost importance but so was space on the carrier ships and planes. V-Mail was the solution to both issues. This compelling film was then shown in movie theaters on spots of "News of the Day." In addition, we promoted "V-Mail is Patriotic" on radio, news announcements, billboards, interviews, and newspaper articles.

I introduced the idea of exhibits, which could be prominently displayed in public buildings or locations where people gathered. The windows of the Emporium on Market Street in downtown San Francisco were a perfect place for a pilot exhibit. Although I was comfortable writing press releases, articles for newspapers, and radio spots, rendering the designs for the exhibits was difficult for me. I had met an enlisted Seabee, Emile, stationed at Santa Rita, who in civilian life was a well-known architect from Los Angeles. Emile, captivated by the challenge of working on designing exhibits, offered to help if I could arrange his temporary transfer to our fleet post office in San Francisco. Officer McDermott finessed his transfer. Emile drew up the specifications to have the exhibits built.

The exhibits turned out to be so powerfully convincing that we were requested to take them on tour of the Twelfth Naval District, which included northern California, Utah, Nevada, and Colorado. Two enlisted WAVES accompanied me to demonstrate V-Mail use, answer questions, and assure the public that their letters would remain confidential. I worked on this assignment with great dedication; the impact of our media blitz soon became apparent. The public stopped resisting V-Mail and embraced its use.

Rudy

On an evening when Glenn and I were to have a dinner date, I got an unexpected telephone call from his roommate, Rudy Hurwich, informing me that Glenn's squadron had suddenly received orders to depart for the Pacific. Glenn had asked Rudy to take me to dinner in his place. Squadron movements were highly classified, therefore Glenn was not allowed to contact me before he shipped out.

Not wanting to commit to dinner before we met, I invited Rudy over to 1230B for coffee. When he arrived, Ensign Hurwich stood in my doorway in his navy uniform, blonde and boyish, looking barely out of high school. He had curly hair and sparkly blue eyes that crinkled when his broad smile lit up his face. Wanting to appear nonchalant, I was ironing my bras to sharp points when he arrived. As he entered the living room, he glanced at my ironing board and I saw a slight flush creep over his face. Months later, when we were closer friends, he confessed in a rare moment of openness that it had been a major turn-on.

Rudy had just graduated from MIT in mechanical engineering and he, too, was a "Ninety-Day Wonder." He was stationed at the Naval Air Station in Alameda, waiting for his assignment as an aircraft maintenance officer on the carrier *Intrepid*. I wondered if he was scared, or just not thinking about what lay ahead.

I didn't take him seriously for he seemed so young and boyish, yet I was drawn to his sweetness and innocent charm. He was reserved and only spoke when he had something to say. I discovered he was interested in many of the same things I was—politics, the progress of the war, and music. When I initiated a subject, he was articulate and a good conversationalist.

Rudy received word that Glenn, along with most of his squadron, had been tragically killed in one of the early battles in the South Pacific. Suddenly there was an immediacy for Rudy and me to spend as much time as possible together, wanting to live each moment fully.

We often walked to North Beach to listen to jazz, sometimes with Justine, whom Rudy found easy to talk to, interesting, and with a similar sense of humor. If we felt like dancing we walked the few blocks to the Officers' Club where we danced to a live trio around the huge pool in the middle of the Tonga Room. Rudy wasn't a terrific dancer but was willing to get out there on the floor instead of hanging on the sidelines. He liked to stop someplace later in the evening to have a drink or ice cream. I didn't know the first thing about drinking booze. Rudy suggested a Cuba Libre—rum in Coke—which became my drink of choice during the war years.

One afternoon on a walk in Golden Gate Park, Rudy told me he thought I'd make a good mother. "Is this a proposal?" I asked. Rudy replied that he'd like us to be engaged before he shipped out to the Pacific theater. He was baffled when I boldly asked how could we get married if we had not yet slept together; we needed to know if we were sexually compatible first.

We made love one afternoon. I felt Rudy was without sexual experience (but he wouldn't admit it) and I led the way, making love to him. His response was spectacular; he loved it and so did I.

By the time Rudy boarded the USS *Intrepid*, I feared I might not see him again. He shipped out before I agreed to the engagement but each time the *Intrepid* was hit—at least three times—the damaged carrier limped into the Alameda or Vallejo shipyard for long repairs, allowing us more time to get to know each other. During one of these periods, Rudy presented me with a beautiful square cut diamond engagement ring. By now I had realized how responsible and trustworthy he was, traits I admired and wanted in a man—those that were absent in my father.

My feelings for Rudy had grown, and I felt I was in love with him. I accepted the ring but we kept our engagement secret, except from Justine. Although I would have liked him to be more emotionally demonstrative, I focused on what I loved about him and that certainly included his engaging smile, blond curly hair, and eyes that crinkled when he laughed. He was attractive in a boyish way. Everyone said, "What a good-looking guy!" Rudy was devoted to me, reliable, possessed a great sense of humor, and we had lots of good times together.

We decided that on his next leave we'd travel to Chicago to meet his family. He had assured his mother that I was Jewish, an important factor in her accepting me as a daughter-in-law. I didn't know what to expect as we drove cross-country in the Lincoln convertible loaned to us by our now good friend, my landlord, Farwell Taylor. I liked Rudy's mother, Diana, and his fourteen-year-old brother, Saul. Diana hosted a gracious evening at their home to introduce me to the extensive Hurwich family, who viewed me curiously in my navy uniform but welcomed me warmly.

After our return from Chicago I was transferred back to the Twelfth Naval District Headquarters at the Federal Building. The navy wanted the public to hear wartime stories while they were fresh. My new assignment as a public information officer was to get those stories out to the public. Naval ships were returning to San Francisco shipyards for repairs after months in the Pacific. As soon as a ship docked at the Naval Air Station in Alameda, I received permission to board, along with my talented cameraman, Andre. The men returning from the Pacific were so thankful to be home on American soil, out of danger, and talking to an American woman, that they readily shared their stories. The articles that I wrote about our fighting men and their experiences were very moving to the folks back home.

Public relations officers received word of where and when ships would return for repairs, just a few days before they docked. Though the personnel stationed on these ships knew they were headed to the West Coast for repairs, they were not informed about which port or naval shipyard they would be assigned. When the *Intrepid* returned for repairs, I was waiting at the dock to see Rudy.

Justine and the Shadow Side of War

In stark contrast to my positive work experience, Justine became severely depressed by her job. Her assignment as Communications Officer was top-secret. She often came home after midnight disheartened, but unable to talk about anything except that the day had been long and exhausting. Aware that her work was confidential, I did not pry.

Justine adored jazz and the music became an antidote to her depression. We often wandered over to North Beach to hear groups at San Francisco's well-known clubs such as Enrico's or the Jazz Workshop. She also spent many evenings at her favorite club, where she became friends with Johnny Cooper, a black Stanford graduate and jazz pianist. After the club closed in the early hours of the morning, he'd walk Justine home to 1230B. One day Navy Military Police showed up at our apartment to ask if I had a roommate, a naval officer, who was seeing a black man. I deplored the implications of the question but, holding back my anger, I replied in order to protect Justine: "I don't know. We work different shifts; she has many friends coming and going." Several weeks later she was formally reprimanded by her commanding officer for walking home with a black man.

That incident left her feeling personally invaded, and the confidentiality of her work became an unbearable strain. She spiraled into a nervous breakdown and entered Mare Island Naval Hospital. When I first visited her I was shocked to see her collapsed in a chair in the common room, staring at nothing. Her hair, usually neatly rolled in a rat, hung halfway down her back in dull, scraggly strands. The nurses told me she wouldn't let them wash it, but when I visited her she let me do so.

Soothed by my brushing her damp hair, she began to talk in a subdued voice of the unspeakable messages she received as an officer in the communications room. Day after day she decoded tragic reports coming from ships in the Pacific—the rhythm of the short and long taps that inevitably spelled disaster: "Enemy ship near; send help, about to be torpedoed…" a foreboding message from a nearby ship unable to arrive in time, gruesome in its simplicity: "All personnel lost." Justine put her head in her hands and wept for the boys drowned; she said she could see them going down into the dark, cold, terrifying water. Another message, the code paraphrasing the complex results of a well-planned Pacific island landing maneuver: "Walked into disaster, send help."

Justine couldn't get the images of the dead and maimed out of her head and wondered how their mothers would cope. No longer able to filter the emotion or hold her feelings in, she just cried. She was also angry and disillusioned by the navy. I vividly remember her indignantly saying: "How dare they send black men to the front lines, but they're not to associate with officers. Fine for them to die in battle, denied the rights and respect of the freedom they're fighting for on behalf of others. Who is the navy to tell me I can't be seen with one of the most honorable men I've met?"

We both lamented as she talked—Justine for the devastation she absorbed, I for my dearest friend's broken spirit.

Justine came home to 1230B depressed. She reminded me of a magnificent bird whose wings had been clipped, no longer the buoyant, humorous person who could tell a funny story and make everybody laugh. She was a mess, drinking and not taking care of herself. Not much of a housekeeper, Justine let go of the bare minimum. The piles of clothes on the floor of her closet were larger than before. She didn't have the energy or motivation to do her laundry and would stay in bed all day. She made cynical remarks about herself as well as others. As her sense of humor faded, she'd ask me, "How long is this going to go on?" which broke my heart. I worried about her but did not believe she was suicidal.

She had begun therapy in the hospital and continued after discharge. Jungian therapy transformed Justine. She came out of therapy serious and more responsible. Formerly carefree and easygoing, she now chose her words carefully, anticipating the outcome before she spoke. She was still spontaneous, brilliant and lovable, but she seemed less innocent and trusting.

Justine's and my contrasting experiences in the navy in World War II left us both pacifists. My years in the navy were an expansive coming-of-age experience. I traveled, met people from all over the world, had responsible positions, gained confidence in my abilities, and implemented my college training. Yet I came away with a sadness for all who had lost their lives in the war. Not just U.S. military, but all those who were killed in Europe and the Pacific. As soon as I was discharged I knew I never wanted to participate in another war again. I would do anything I could do to oppose war in the future. And for the rest of my life I did.

Wars on Two Fronts End: The United Nations Is Founded

On May 8, 1945, Victory in Europe Day, the world finally saw the unconditional surrender of Nazi Germany and the end of Hitler's Third Reich. Six weeks after V-E Day, on June 26, the original charter for the United Nations was signed at the San Francisco Opera House by fifty delegates representing

150 nations. I was thrilled to be assigned by the Twelfth Naval District to cover and publicize this momentous occasion.

Sitting next to me at the ceremony was an attractive navy lieutenant. We shared the excitement of the momentous occasion, spoke of our mutual commitment to world peace. I had no idea who this articulate lieutenant might be until he introduced himself as John F. Kennedy.

When I stood up and looked around, I was surprised to see there were no women delegates and, except for secretaries, translators, and staff accompanying delegates, I was one of the few women present and the only one in uniform. This was unforgivable given the widespread and heroic participation of women during the war, not only from the United States but the courageous women in European countries.

The proceedings were simultaneously translated into five languages: English, French, Spanish, Chinese, and Russian with the notable absence of German, Italian, and Japanese. My story was prominently featured in the local press and picked up by numerous news services. Radio stations called to interview me about my participation in this historic occasion. Though I was thrilled for the United Nations' quest for peace, as a WAVE officer I was appalled that no country sent a woman to represent them. If we were going to have peace in this world, it seemed to me both sexes needed to be involved in the decision making.

On August 6, 1945, the *Enola Gay* dropped the first atomic bomb on Hiroshima, indiscriminately killing its citizens; three days later a second bomb killed at least 75,000 more and blew Nagasaki to smithereens. By the following week, Japan had surrendered and Emperor Hirohito accepted the terms of the Potsdam Declaration. World War II was finally and officially over. A great day, although clouded for me by the news of the bombs' devastating effects.

San Francisco, and cities throughout the United States, celebrated with wild joy in the greatest moment of collective inebriation I have ever seen. As I stepped out of my office onto McAllister Street, I joined the hordes of people who had spilled onto the streets—strangers hugging, singing, and dancing. Champagne corks popped and bottles were passed around as radios blared the incredible news over and over. Strangers weren't strangers any more. I was proud of my contribution to the war and joined in celebrating that we had given the world a chance to become a better place.

Marriage and Second Crossing to China

In November 1945, Rudy and I were married in our navy lieutenant junior grade uniforms in a civil ceremony at San Francisco City Hall with Justine as our witness. During a later visit to Chicago, Rudy's mother invited Mother and Walt to be guests in her home for our Jewish wedding ceremony officiated by a rabbi. Rudy's young brother, Saul, acted as our best man.

Rudy had already moved into 1230B with Justine and me. He and I remained in the navy another six months before our discharge in May 1946. Rudy commuted to the U.S.

Rudy and I signing our marriage license

Naval Air Station in Alameda, while I worked at the Naval Discharge Center for Enlisted Personnel in San Francisco. There I helped WAVES prepare for civilian life, educating them about the GI Bill, home loans, and other military benefits. Most of these young women had joined the navy directly out of high school. As a counselor, I provided information about colleges that suited their interests and walked them through the mechanics of how to gather their records in order to apply for the GI Bill. If they were looking for a job, I helped them research how they could go about finding or training for a job. I found deep satisfaction counseling these young women about their future plans.

About this time I received a message through the International Red Cross that my father had been released from the Japanese internment camp where he had been detained during the Japanese occupation of China during the war. We heard from Father that he longed to see me and meet Rudy. I heartily looked forward to our reunion since I hadn't seen my father since I was eight years old.

Rudy agreed to visit my father in China. After visiting my father, I hoped to take advantage of the GI Bill to study in Europe, but Rudy had no interest in more travel or schooling. He wanted to get back to civilian life in Chicago and join his mother in the family business. I was disappointed and felt we were giving up a chance of a lifetime, and yet, as a dutiful wife, I went along with my husband's wishes.

Remarkably, Father had made money while interned by the Japanese during the war and was able to send us the tickets to travel by ship to Shanghai. While awaiting the arrival of our visas, Rudy and I took our delayed honeymoon.

After three years in navy uniforms, we reveled in our comfortable civilian clothes and the freedom to explore the West in our Mercury convertible, top always down. First stop was my favorite place in the world, Yosemite. I couldn't wait to introduce Rudy to this breathtaking national park and the pleasures of skiing. As luck would have it, on our first day out Rudy fell and broke his leg. The ski patrol helped him into the car, but there was no way he could drive. Never having had a car in our family, I neither knew how to drive nor had a driver's license. Nevertheless, I gingerly sat behind the wheel as Rudy, in excruciating pain, instructed me step by step how to shift the gears and use the brake. Mindfully, I managed to drive down the winding, two-lane mountain road from Badger Pass to the hospital in Yosemite Valley where orthopedists set his leg.

Happily spending our honeymoon in Yosemite

For the next three days I timidly drove from my tent at Camp Curry to visit Rudy in the Yosemite Valley Hospital. When I arrived at the two concrete gates leading into the hospital grounds, I stopped the car, got out, and eyeballed whether I was in an OK position to navigate the narrow space between the concrete gates. Not yet having polished my parking skills, I parked the car as far from the other cars as I could, for potential damage control.

Rudy was discharged, with a full cast on his leg, unable to drive. After I drove 260 miles from Yosemite to Santa Maria, I was ready to take the test to get my driver's license. I passed the test easily thanks to my intensive mandatory driving "class" from Rudy. For the next six weeks of our honeymoon I was at the wheel until Rudy's cast was removed.

With the top down, the wind in our hair, and Rudy's cast propped on the dashboard, we drove to the Grand Canyon. There, the park rangers showed a film of a group rafting down the Colorado River. Beside myself with excitement, I grabbed Rudy. "Wouldn't a raft trip be fabulous when your leg heals?" His reply, "Why would we want to do anything like that?," made my heart sink. I felt a disturbing glimmer that I might have chosen the wrong man, one not the least bit interested in adventure.

Heading to Santa Fe and Taos, then south to Mexico through El Paso, we stopped in Monterrey, Mexico and sleepy towns along the way. In Mexico City we picked up Rudy's brother, Saul, who had flown in from Chicago to join us, and set out for Acapulco, driving at night to avoid the heat of the day. I drove in the balmy night air, boisterously singing at the top of my lungs, as Rudy and Saul slept soundly in the back seat.

Acapulco in 1946 was a quiet fishing village where we settled into the small, friendly Hotel Montserrat on a hill overlooking Caleta Beach for a few weeks. We made friends with the manager, Antonio, who went out of his way to make us feel at home, taking us out in his motorboat to small islands in Acapulco Bay and showing us the wild, undeveloped coast. It was Mexico's monsoon season and during a torrential downpour one afternoon, the roof of our room at the Montserrat collapsed on my suitcase, which was filled with all my beautiful new clothes. As was the custom then with clothes bought from specialty stores, each item had been carefully wrapped in black tissue paper. When the black dye ran on all over my trousseau, my clothes were ruined beyond repair.

Fuming about the low standards of Mexican buildings, I reasoned that if I hadn't worn civilian clothes in three years, what difference did it make if I lost them? Antonio, full of apologies, offered to pay the cost of my wardrobe out of his own salary. Thanking him, I figured this was good chance to buy the inexpensive, colorful clothes that I admired on the local women. At the outdoor market, with Antonio, Rudy, and Saul voicing their preferences, I purchased a new, brightly colored wardrobe of Mexican skirts, blouses, and sandals. With my recently acquired tan, my hair grown shoulder length and braided, I was taken for a Mexican woman married to an American for the rest of our trip!

When word of our visas finally arrived in October 1946, we drove directly back to Chicago from Acapulco to arrange our passage from San Francisco to Shanghai by ship.

In 1946, for the second time in my life, I set forth on the trans-Pacific voyage to China, this time with far more complex feelings since I was but a baby when I first made the trip.

I looked forward to reuniting with my father after so many years, but not knowing what to expect, I was also nervous.

When our ship docked in the port of Shanghai, we found that Father had hired an accordion player to fill the air with music for our arrival, and he was standing on the dock with his new wife, Pana, waving a huge banner that read "Welcome Cecelia and Rudy." I could feel Rudy's dismay—whatever was he about to encounter? Pushing aside my embarrassment, I rushed to throw my arms around my welcoming father.

Father had lost his slender good looks, had grown a little paunch, and was balding, but he still exuded the charm and affection I remembered as a child. He hugged me, his arms tightly around me, then while looking directly into my eyes he announced, "Cecelia, you've become a very beautiful woman."

Father owned a thriving import/export business, belonged to the Russian Club, and lived in grand style in a flat in a gracious building in the French Quarter on Avenue Joffre. He had recently purchased a sleek, black car, employed a chauffeur, a cook, and two servants. He continued to lead the high life that he had led in China before the war. Pana, a blonde and voluptuous Russian, was a good match for him. They enjoyed an active social life, liked to drink and dance, and seemed to get along well in their open marriage.

Father, master of the lavish gesture, had bought a new grand piano in honor of my arrival. The piano sat huge and looming in his living room. For years as I was growing up he had heard from my mother that I'd been taking piano lessons and assumed I was an accomplished pianist. Unable to receive letters from us during the years he had been interned, Father didn't know I had dropped my music major and was not pursuing a career as a pianist. I had not touched a piano in five years.

In the middle of a big dinner party Father and Pana hosted in Rudy's and my honor, he proudly announced to his guests that his daughter Cecelia would play the piano. Aghast, I replied that I hadn't touched a piano in years. In typical fashion, Father insisted. Reluctantly, I sat down and tried to play a Haydn sonata. I faltered after the opening passage and was obliged to start again twice. Unable to remember the notes, I banged the piano keys with both hands and ran crying from the room. The next day, Father quietly apologized and that incident was not mentioned again. The piano sat there in his apartment, ignored, for the duration of my visit.

Rudy and I found Shanghai to be exotic and turbulent. Extremes of wealth and poverty were evident everywhere, triggering a flashback to my childhood in Harbin: a big house next to a hovel, a sleek chauffeur-driven car passing a malnourished man pulling a rickshaw. Chinese families huddled together shivering in the cold. It was sad to see these extremes had not changed in twenty years.

For years China had opened its doors to refugees from Russia and around the world. In the 1930s many Jews escaped Hitler's Europe, finding their way to Shanghai and China where they were given refuge, settled, and formed close-knit communities. My father's family was part of a Russian-Jewish contingent that left Russia following the revolution. Most of these Jews became successful businessmen and merchants founding their own private clubs.

We remained in Shanghai for three months, living in Father and Pana's flat, taking side trips to learn as much about China as we could. We traveled by train to Peking, and with special permission visited the Great Wall and the Forbidden City and emperors' palaces, which had just been opened to the public after being closed during the Japanese occupation.

Rudy and I were affectionately welcomed and entertained by uncles, aunts, and cousins whom I had not seen since I was five. In Tsingtao, Uncle Henry, Father's younger brother, and my first cousins Bobby and Mark opened their home and hearts to us. In Tsinsin, my Great Uncle Abrasha, Grandpa Gregory's younger brother who was now an old, but vigorous man, couldn't do enough to make our stay comfortable. He knew everyone in town and gave a grand party in our honor.

Father finally spoke of his internment by the Japanese during the war—the crowded, squalid conditions, the daily bowl of soup that looked and tasted like dirty dishwater, and the overwhelming heat and humidity in Shanghai that killed a number of internees. He related how prisoners were subjected to extortion, trumped up charges, false arrests, torture, or forced to make large payments for their release. Despite Father's hardships, he managed in his inimitable fashion to wheel and deal with both the Chinese and the Japanese during his internment, so that when the war was over and he was released, he came out a wealthy man.

I decided that with all the big meals and drinking it was

time for me to begin exercising seriously. Near my father's office, I found a Russian professor of physical aesthetics and culture with a small studio dedicated to exercise. Twice a week I took a rickshaw in the morning to the studio where I went through a rigorous routine of calisthenics with the well-trained professor. I came away from each session invigorated and feeling wonderful. This physical training in Shanghai was the beginning of a devotion to disciplined exercise that has continued throughout my life.

After my workouts, I met Father at his favorite spots for lunch in the busy International Bund area. Wherever we ate, he knew the maitre d' by name and greeted his business friends in Mandarin, Russian, English, or French. I hoped during these meetings to get to know my father better but our con-versations were warm yet limited to his business dealings and his bragging about influential friends and parties he attended. I was unable to draw him out about his feelings about Mother and me during those years we had been apart. I told Father how I missed him as I was growing up and of our struggles and hardship during the Depression. Father responded with his usual declarations of love for my mother and me but did not directly address my feelings. It was evident that deep dis-cussions were not my father's way of relating.

Before leaving Shanghai, Father's departing grand gesture was a fur coat as a wedding gift. When I protested that I didn't want a fur coat because I was opposed to wearing fur, he in-sisted, "What do you mean? Nonsense. Every woman wants a fur coat. I'm giving you a mink and that's that." Nothing I said could convince him. I gave in to his wishes by visiting the furrier for numerous fittings under Father's personal supervision. My coat of Russian sable was copied from the latest designs from Paris. Father had carefully chosen each pelt and proudly showed them to me one by one, stating emphatically, "I chose each one myself, and they're A-1 quality." After three or four fittings, the coat I didn't want became mine.

That ill-fated coat would reluctantly travel to Chicago with me. Friends had advised me that I would certainly use a fur coat in Chicago's cold winters. Because it was insured, I tried desperately to lose it. I left it at jazz clubs draped over my chair when I went to the ladies' room. I took it to Grand Central Station in New York, laying it over my suitcase while I walked into the telephone booth for five minutes, only to return to find it still there. I couldn't lose that fur coat or have it stolen no matter how hard I tried. Finally I gave it to my mother, who was delighted with its style, color, and quality and wore it happily for the rest of her life.

My father was a businessman and an Old China Hand who loved his lifestyle of servants and private clubs, never believing that the Communists would take over China, although we could hear the gunfire as their armies approached Shanghai. In our travels from Peking to Shanghai, Rudy and I had observed Communist soldiers already patrolling this important railroad line. Having read Edgar Snow's *Red Star Over China* on our voyage to Shanghai, I was alerted to the Communist takeover and warned Father to get out of China while it was still possible. He stubbornly refused to leave, insisting there had always been fighting and warlords in China and he wasn't worried. Father eventually lost his home, business, cars, jewels— everything. He and Pana were two of the last foreigners to leave Shanghai in 1956. Rudy and I were obliged to pay bribes to debtors who claimed he owed money, because his name had to be cleared before he could secure an exit visa. A Jewish agency helped Father immigrate to São Paulo, Brazil, where numerous Russians from China had already settled. In São Paulo he worked diligently to learn Portuguese, one of the few languages he did not speak. In order to survive his early days there, he taught English to Brazilians. With his proclivity for making money, he eventually made another fortune dealing in gems from the mines of Brazil.

In January 1947, Rudy and I bid Father and Pana an affectionate goodbye, boarded a ship in Shanghai, and began our journey back to San Francisco. My reunion with my father had helped me accept his many sides—the crook, the philanderer, the gambler, the businessman—along with his generous, loving, and charismatic traits. Still, I was unable to accept that he hadn't been there as a father.

Our wedding portrait

Demonstrating the wonders of Wonder-Foil
in a department store

Partners in the
American Dream

1947–1962

In August of 1947, two years after the war ended, life appeared to be getting back to normal—at least, on the surface. Women had returned to their roles as wives, mothers, helpmates, and homemakers; to what society believed was our rightful place. It seemed a distant memory that during the war years so many of us, with no hesitation, tossed off our aprons and our schoolbooks and picked up tools to help build the ships, planes, and tanks needed to feed the voracious war machine that finally defeated Hitler and the Japanese empire. Patriotic women dedicated themselves to vital non-combat jobs in the army or navy. Courageous nurses joined American troops and helped many of the injured come home alive. With ten million men in the armed forces, women capably took up needed roles on the home front, overnight becoming wage-earners, authority figures, decision-makers, fix-it girls, bill-payers, and even pitchers or catchers for their children's baseball practice.

Yet after the war, men reclaimed their traditional roles, uncomfortably aware that women had had a glimpse into the "larger" world. Most women didn't complain, thankful to have their men—their breadwinners and protectors—back home. For some it was a relief, but for others, a subliminal discontent was brewing. Although the seeds of the second wave of feminism had been sown in these war years, it would take almost two decades for those seeds to sprout, when Betty Friedan's transcendent book *The Feminine Mystique* finally burst onto the bestseller list. *The Feminine Mystique* would change forever the way women thought about themselves and the way society thought about women. In it Friedan described aptly the feeling of so many women of her time: "A strange stirring, a sense of dissatisfaction, a yearning that women suffered. Each suburban housewife struggled with it alone . . . afraid to ask even of herself the silent question—'Is this all?'"

Life in Chicago

Upon our return to Chicago, Rudy began working with his mother at the Hurwich Department Store. His father died when Rudy was sixteen, leaving his mother with two young sons and the family store to run. Helping his mother manage the business was not the career Rudy had envisioned for himself after his years in the navy and marriage, yet he felt obligated to return to Chicago to help her.

During the two years that Rudy and I lived in Chicago, I grew to admire and love his mother, Diana Hurwich. Industrious and smart, she managed the family business with more success than her husband. Following his death she began acquiring real estate, constructing apartments and commercial buildings. In addition to being an astute businesswoman she was also a fine homemaker and devoted mother. Ever since Rudy had enrolled at MIT, she assumed he would return to take over the family businesses. But after the war he had other thoughts.

While Rudy busily worked at the Hurwich Department store, I attended a graduate program in psychology at the University of Chicago, studying with Carl Rogers. Rogers's graduate class argued that a person's nature is essentially positive, and that by accepting a person without negative judgment one could take a humanistic life approach that is based on listening non-judgmentally to one's experience. Roger's humanistic approach that human beings are inherently good resonated with me and confirmed what I had long felt—a belief in people's potentials. Over time, I have come to realize how studying with Rogers deeply influenced my positive views of the world, of the human race, and myself.

After a year living in Rudy's mother's home, we moved into our own two-room apartment in Hyde Park on the South Side near the University of Chicago. The neighborhood was an interesting place to live, with modest small houses alongside stately old homes and flats and different ethnicities and classes intermingling peacefully and thriving amongst each other. It was a time of intense intellectual excitement for me. Mortimer Adler, the president of the University of Chicago, had initiated a rich undergraduate curriculum that emphasized breadth of learning. He started the Great Books series and invited social and political activists to be on the lecturing faculty, giving us a chance to discuss ideas with authors such as James Baldwin, Richard Wright, and James T. Farrell.

To round out my understanding of political science, I enrolled in a class with Hans Morgenthau, the erudite and world-renowned scholar of political science. Morgenthau's lectures introduced me to his theory of questioning the moral significance of political actions. Morgenthau argued in his famous book *Politics Among Nations* that morality was applicable in relations between individual people but not between states. After Dr. Morgenthau's lectures, we grad students, many of us WWII veterans on the GI Bill, would gather around Professor Morgenthau with questions about the morality of bombing of Hiroshima. Years later came Vietnam and Morgenthau changed completely. He said the war could not be won and that the slaughter was immoral.

Rather than agreeing with Professor Morgenthau's theories that the more military power and arms a nation had, the safer it was, I believed otherwise and opposed military buildup and war, reasoning that if you built an arsenal of arms they would certainly be used. To this day I fervently support the Ploughshares Fund, which works to stop the use of weapons of war, prevent the spread of nuclear, biological, and chemical weapons, and the ending of their development and production. Supported by citizens and peace groups around the world, the Ploughshare Fund is increasingly successful in building national and global support for security policies that promote regional and international cooperation for a more peaceful world.

This year in Chicago could hardly have been more intellectually stimulating, studying at three different schools, meeting writers, artists, dancers, attending lectures, concerts, and political rallies, and having deep conversations and debates about how our generation could make a difference. Then, in the midst of this renaissance, was the joy of learning I was pregnant with our first child.

At the same time that I was student at the University of Chicago, I also pursued a budding passion for contemporary architecture, interior design, and color at the Institute of Design, headed by the well-known Bauhaus designer/architect Ivan Serge Chermayeff. I studied, read, and lived the mantra of the aesthetic that "form follows function." All objects of everyday use must be not only beautiful but useful. The Institute of Design taught the principles of space and light and how to incorporate them into designing environments. Since then I have integrated these principles of form and color in creating environments for clients from the San Francisco Bay Area to Mumbai. To this day, I apply these aesthetic guidelines in our home and life.

During our two years in Chicago, Rudy and I each developed distinct interests. Helping his mother run the family department store, he entered the world of business, construction, and real estate while I returned to school to study psychology, design, and modern dance. We learned to appreciate our differences and strengths and decided that we would like to be and were ready to become parents. We were thrilled when, two-and-a-half years after we married, our first daughter, Barbara Joy (BJ), was born in Chicago on July 2, 1948.

While pregnant with BJ, I had been drawn to campaign for Progressive Party candidate Henry Wallace in the 1948 presidential elections, despite the fact that I was also a full-time student. Henry Wallace embraced the civil rights struggle and advocated full voting rights for blacks. During his campaign, Wallace would not allow segregated audiences or eat or stay in segregated settings. His campaign gave a sense of hope and inclusion for minorities. Universal government health care was a top priority. Wallace believed in world peace, supporting friendly relations with the Soviet Union and an end to the Cold War. Ringing doorbells in Hyde Park and telling neighbors about Henry Wallace's platform spurred what would become my lifelong commitment to progressive politics.

Rudy and I explored our budding political beliefs and shared a new interest in politics. In our search for like-minded people, we discovered the American Veterans' Committee, where we met other veterans who became our new friends. This group also became our introduction and education in liberal politics and activism. Some of our members had fought in Spain with the Abraham Lincoln Brigade, an experience that solidified their left-leaning consciousness. Many brigade veterans returned questioning our capitalist system, believing communism might be a viable alternative. Within the thriving intellectual environment of our veterans' committee chapter, bitter debates erupted over the possibility that some members might be communist. It became a disruptive element that tore apart our good work on behalf of veterans' issues and broke the spirit of our close-knit group. It was long before the coming McCarthy era that we learned the sad lessons of how devastating a hunt for communists could be.

Our life in Chicago was a period of immense personal growth and ripening for me. In addition to my courses in psychology, political science, and design, I was exploring another world of creativity through art and dance.

One of my life-changing mentors in Chicago, a member of the avant-garde in dance, was philosopher/dance teacher Anne Rudolph, a free spirit in flowing gowns who also taught movement and nutrition. It was synchronicity that led me to Rudolph on a cold winter day in 1947. As a Californian, I missed exercising outdoors year-round. "I think I'll join a health club," I told Rudy. Hearing of an upscale club on Michigan Avenue, I visited their site and expressed my interest. "We only let in the finest of people," said the manager, by which he meant no blacks or Jews. Coming down in the elevator I met Eleanor, a woman who was also turned off by the elitism of the club. "I really need a place to exercise," I told her. "I know just the place," Eleanor said. "A few blocks away from here there's Anne Rudolph's studio in the Fine Arts Building where you can learn dance and body movement." That day I went to meet the creative, quirky, and outspoken Anne Rudolph.

The moment I entered the Anne Rudolph School of Modern Body Education and Dance at the Fine Arts Building, I sensed I had found a niche in an exciting new world. The first words Anne uttered were, "Why are you wearing a brassiere and high heels?" as she reached around my back and energetically snapped the elastic of my brassiere. She did not believe that the human body should be constricted by unnatural supports. She never wore a brassiere, yet her breasts remained firm through her eighties. Her trademark attire consisted of loose tunic dresses with flat open sandals, even during Chicago's frigid winters.

As a student of Anne Rudolph's, I danced and floated and learned strengthening movements and body relaxation throughout my pregnancy. To be part of the Chicago dance world, moving effortlessly and participating in studio performances, was an exciting, ethereal experience. Anne believed that dance was not only an activity of the body, but of the mind and spirit. One beautiful spring day, Anne spontaneously moved us all outside to perform barefoot in colorful flowing tunics on the steps and lawn of the Art Institute of Chicago. Before we knew it, a *Chicago Tribune* reporter was snapping photos that appeared the next day in the newspaper. During my pregnancy with BJ, I moved and danced at Anne's studio until the day before my daughter was born. I attribute my healthy pregnancy, easy delivery, and natural childbirth (without drugs) to my regime there. Ten days after BJ's birth I elatedly returned to movement classes, with my beautiful new baby snug in her little basket, resting nearby on the studio floor.

Chicago's rich intellectual and cultural milieu spilled over into our married life. I returned home from classes enthused with fresh and stimulating ideas to share with Rudy. While I was enriching my personal life, Rudy worked diligently at the Hurwich Department Store, frustrated that his talents and training as an engineer were not being challenged. Although Rudy loved his mother, he felt working with her on a daily basis was not leading to the entrepreneurial independence he had gone to school for.

I urged Rudy to strike out on his own, telling him, "You are smart and can do anything you set out to do." I reminded him of our good times, and the sense of adventure and freedom we felt when we lived in San Francisco. I had complete confidence in his abilities. We both agreed that he needed to build his own career and distance himself from the family business. Remembering California's mild climate and our stimulating life in San Francisco, we grappled late into the night with heated discussions about our options.

Finally, with reluctance, Rudy admitted to his mother that the family business wasn't fulfilling and that he wanted to return to California to pursue the engineering profession he had trained for at MIT.

This was a hard blow for Diana, who had assumed that Rudy would take over the Hurwich family business. She wanted us to make Chicago our home. Diana had fallen in love with BJ, her first grandchild, and hoped we would remain near her. When she heard of our plans to move to California, she vented her anger and disapproval at our proposed move. Most painful was that she accused me of taking away her son and granddaughter. I had grown to respect and love her. I hoped that over time she would come to understand our move and Rudy's need to follow his career path.

The war years, our navy experience, and our two years of growth and blossoming in Chicago had given Rudy and me complete confidence in our abilities and our role in society. With a baby and a happy marriage, we felt we could conquer the world. We didn't think about money, or the big risk we would be taking in giving up the security of our comfortable income from the family business. Neither did we consider the downside of leaving our life in Chicago, where our apartment, family, and friends were all there to support us. We saw only the upside, the benefits of striking out on our own, and the infinite possibilities that awaited us. With this enthusiasm, we eagerly prepared for our move back to California.

Breaking with Tradition: Move to California

In early 1949, I flew to San Francisco carrying six-month-old BJ in my arms while Rudy drove in our Mercury convertible. With $2,000 to our names and heady dreams for our new life, we moved into Mother and Walter's comfortable bungalow in the Sunset District. While Rudy searched for a position as an engineer, I found a temporary job as a teacher in a nursery school. Although we were living rent-free, our meager savings were dwindling fast.

After three months of searching and interviews, Rudy did

not find the job he wanted. He considered all his options as an engineer and arrived at an important decision—he wanted to start his own business using his engineering training plus his business know-how.

We had noted the lack of aluminum foil for kitchen use on the West Coast, though it was widely used in Chicago and the eastern United States. We looked for it all over the San Francisco Bay Area in grocery, department, and hardware stores, to no avail. Rudy decided he would fill that hole in the market by finding a source for aluminum so he could produce and sell aluminum foil on the West Coast. As the idea evolved, Rudy initially set up shop in Mother's garage. Quickly outgrowing the garage, he needed room to design and build a machine that would roll the foil, so he rented a space in a nearby machine shop.

Sending letters and telephone calls and using all his connections to make contact with Kaiser Aluminum, Rudy eventually met with the company's top executives. After numerous meetings with the Kaiser team, Rudy skillfully negotiated a contract with Kaiser to supply the aluminum for our new product. The contract with Kaiser Aluminum was a coup for Rudy and he worked diligently to set up our fledgling aluminum foil business. Together Rudy and I kicked around ideas for a product design using a colorful red-and-white oblong box with a distinctive logo for "Wonder-Foil."

We wanted to first try out Wonder-Foil on San Francisco consumers, but first we needed to convince retailers that they should carry our product. We took a portable broiler lined with Wonder-Foil to Macy's in San Francisco and other department and hardware stores in our area, where I demonstrated the various uses of aluminum foil in the kitchen. I showed how wrapping in foil kept meat, produce, and baked goods fresh in the refrigerator or freezer, and lining stoves, broilers, ovens, and pans with foil kept them clean. For the first two years we were barely able to pay the rent on the company.

A rapt audience watches my Wonder-Foil demonstration

As Rudy and I pushed and promoted Wonder-Foil, our business slowly grew thanks to our demonstration and advertising efforts all over the San Francisco Bay Area. A free and unexpected blurb appeared in local newspapers such as the *San Francisco Chronicle* and magazines such as *Sunset*, and in radio interviews I explained the uses of Wonder-Foil. In time Wonder-Foil became accepted as an indispensable household staple in California and the entire West Coast. Energized by all the possibilities, Rudy and I worked side by side, true partners, enjoying the rewards of doing business together, completely believing in the American Dream.

Within a year, we moved the business out of Mother's garage into a modest, low-rent building on Hearst Avenue in Berkeley, where R. Hurwich Company was born. With one-year-old BJ, Rudy and I found a small, inexpensive bungalow to rent on the quiet one-block-long Bateman Street in Berkeley. When BJ was almost ready to attend a cooperative nursing school, we began talking about our eagerness for another child.

About a year after our return to California, Rudy's mother gracefully forgave us and accepted our move. She admitted that she missed each of us. I tearfully told her we missed her too. She told us how she wanted to visit us, see our home, and look at Rudy's new plant. With much anticipation we prepared for her stay in our home. When Diana arrived, she inspected the premises of R. Hurwich Co., showing her astute interest in Rudy's packaging business, and letting Rudy know she was indeed proud of him. Her biggest joy was playing with and getting to know her granddaughter, BJ. She thought Berkeley was a marvelous place to raise a family and admitted to finding California's weather and casual lifestyle most agreeable. During her visit, we hosted small gatherings in honor of Diana to introduce her to our circle of close friends. My mother and my stepfather, Walter, who knew and liked Diana from their earlier visit to Chicago, enjoyed visiting with her and taking her on outings to see local sites. With great relief and happiness, we returned to our close and loving relationship following her visit to Berkeley.

Our business had finally started to make money when the Korean War broke out and severely restricted the supply of aluminum, which was needed for building airplanes. By 1953 we were out of the aluminum foil business. Rudy and I were disappointed that after so much effort and hard work our burgeoning company had been nipped in the bud by world forces beyond our control. Yet we knew many possibilities still existed out there. We were not deterred from exploring new directions for the R. Hurwich Company and focused our energies on the next step.

With Rudy's experience in engineering and packaging and research into new possibilities and avenues for diversification, R. Hurwich Company expanded into other areas of the packaging industry. R. Hurwich received an order to package a new product for sun protection called "Sea and Ski." Other packaging orders from the cosmetic and food industry trickled in.

Our new business grew little by little. During the first years of R. Hurwich Co., I brought Rudy his lunches from home because we carefully budgeted our living expenses. One day when the company had grown from a one-person to a three-person operation, Rudy asked if I would make my lunch deliveries shorter; with three employees looking up at me and away from their work for three minutes, nine minutes of production and costs (which Rudy quoted in an exact dollar amount) were lost. This type of exacting quantitative analysis was typical of Rudy Hurwich.

R. Hurwich Company grew and diversified into new products. Rudy and I continued our into-the-night discussions on possibilities and ideas for expanding our business, striving toward making a living and a home for our family, which now welcomed our second child, Robbie, born September 11, 1950.

Wife and Mother

The night before Robbie was born I had sporadic contractions; by morning they were coming regularly at ten-minute intervals. At each contraction, I practiced my natural childbirth exercises by breathing deeply and expanding my belly to counteract the pain. When my water broke, I knew I would soon be heading for the hospital. As Rudy left that morning to open R. Hurwich Company for his employees, I reminded him to hurry back so he could drive me to the hospital. When the contractions intensified to five minutes apart, I telephoned him to rush home and get me to the hospital. He replied, "I'm working on a packing machine but will be right over." After another ten minutes passed, I got anxious. I knew I couldn't wait any longer and called Rudy again, telling him the contractions were coming closer and that I needed to be off to the hospital.

Terrified that the baby could arrive any minute, I asked my elderly neighbor, Mrs. Davis, to look after BJ while I drove myself in our beat-up old car to Kaiser Hospital, about ten minutes away. At each contraction, now coming faster and stronger, I moved over to the side of the road, breathing deeply until it subsided. When I pulled into to the emergency entrance of Kaiser Hospital in Oakland, the nurses took one look at me and wheeled me directly into delivery, without a moment to spare. Robbie was born twenty minutes later.

The hospital called Rudy, informing him that he was the father of a baby boy and that, by the way, his wife had driven herself to the emergency room. Rudy replied with pride, "Congratulate my wife." Happy to have a son, Rudy bragged about how I had driven myself to the hospital while in labor.

Instead of confronting Rudy at the time for not being present at our son's birth, I buried my feelings of anger. I reluctantly went along with the accepted belief of the 1950s that a husband's career took precedence over all else. I didn't tell Rudy then how sad and disappointed I was by his absence and lack of support while I was in labor. The thrill of our new baby boy was tempered by a sense of loss—my trust and devotion for Rudy. I buried these feelings and did not voice them until years later, and then with a vengeance, as I erupted in a torrent of anger—"And you didn't even drive me to the hospital when Rob was born"—when I asked for a divorce. Looking back, I'm astonished that I accepted Rudy's boasting about me driving myself to the hospital to give birth to our son without screaming out my grief.

I had always hoped for three children. Our third child, Lyn, was born four years later on February 15, 1954. In the years that followed, I was greeted in the grocery store or the bank, with "Oh, hello. You're Rudy Hurwich's wife, aren't you?" or "You're Robby's and Barbara's mother." I nodded and smiled.

The women's magazines all proclaimed that I should be happy and fulfilled in the role of wife and mother. Why, then, did I feel a huge weight in my psyche? I wondered where was that strong independent girl who grew up during the Depression; the young woman who worked her way through college, spent summers working and hiking in Yosemite; the college graduate who enlisted in the navy to fight for her county; the young newlywed who attended two graduate schools simultaneously, became politically active, and danced throughout her first pregnancy until the day before her daughter was born—where had that woman gone?

With Rob and Lyn in cooperative nursery school and BJ in kindergarten, I carpooled to and from school in the old jalopy bought for $100 from a neighbor, now full of children. We were living on a small budget so I volunteered by helping the teacher one day a week and exchanged babysitting with other mothers whose children were too young for nursery school. The daily tasks of caring for kids, grocery shopping, cleaning, loads of laundry, hanging clothes to dry outdoors, ironing, cooking, and talking almost exclusively with children became my way of life. I began to feel like a robot, moving from one task to another, without space for creative or intellectual thought. I recall making a rule that when I went to the bathroom and closed the door, the children were not allowed to come in. This was the only quiet time I had to myself. I longed to read a good book and hoped that I might find a moment some evening.

Like other veterans of World War II, Rudy and I were

struggling to make a living. We were not alone, for our friends of the "Greatest Generation" were in similar situations. We had married during the war and after discharge from the navy started our family and new business. We felt a responsibility to "make it" on our own—a tough goal, though it encouraged our strength and creativity. We were highly dedicated and worked hard. We believed in our country, our government, and ourselves.

Our generation eventually did succeed: we created new science, art, literature, industry, and helped bring economic strength and security to the country. There was a huge surge in the construction and auto industries and groundbreaking research and development that led to the computer industry. New home appliances gave families modern conveniences to make their homes more comfortable. In the San Francisco Bay Area, Nathan Olivera, Elmer Bishop, Roy De Forest, Manuel Neri, and Richard Diebenkorn burst on the art scene. Writers such as Arthur Miller, Norman Mailer, Phillip Roth, and Betty Friedan were highly influential voices in our generation. We and our liberal friends, many of us veterans, recognized our common purpose and values—equality of opportunity, civil liberties, a sense of security, peace, and family that guided us through this historic stage of our lives.

By 1956 we had outgrown our tiny two-bedroom bungalow. The children, ages eight, six, and two, needed more room to roam. With the aid of a Veteran's Administration loan, we purchased our home on Hillegass Avenue in the Elmwood neighborhood of Berkeley for $19,800. Our furniture consisted of an old sofa, our beds, our kitchen table, and chairs. The children delighted in running around the empty house, playing ball and chasing each other. Family members felt sorry for us and gave us their used furniture. Little by little, a sofa, chairs, and dressers made their way into our house, which began to look and feel more like a home.

In December 1957 an inventor approached Rudy for ideas about what to do with his invention, a handheld device that printed embossed plastic labels. Rudy instantly recognized the potential of the product. He quickly began promoting and demonstrating this handheld label-making puncher to potential investors. He highlighted the machine's diverse uses for industry, home, retail, museums, and many aspects of business. In partnership with his attorney, Leo, Rudy brought together a group of investors made up of classmates from MIT, local business associates, and professional acquaintances to finance the development, manufacture, and marketing of the product they called the Dymo Label Maker.

Rudy became the president of Dymo Industries, Inc., in early 1958, and put together a creative group of employees to help develop and perfect the labeling system. The company started operations in the original R. Hurwich Co. plant, which it soon outgrew as employees in the fields of engineering, business management, computers, and sales were recruited.

As the wife of the president of Dymo, I was expected to entertain colleagues and business associates visiting from all over the world. We employed a full-time housekeeper during this period and a catering staff for the elaborate parties we hosted in our home. I created menus with delicious recipes and set an elegant table. It was a job that I dutifully performed but didn't relish. We often started the evening with cocktails at our home followed by fancy dinners at San Francisco restaurants. The one spot in San Francisco that I did like to return to was the elegant yet understated World Trade Club in the San Francisco Ferry building, with its breathtaking views of the bay and bridge. This excellent club was invariably relaxing, with a pianist playing quiet jazz in the background. Through Dymo's business membership in the World Trade Club, we grew to feel comfortable there, with its gracious waiters serving excellent continental cuisine.

Another aspect of my role I did enjoy was dressing up and being able to afford beautiful clothes. A small boutique, Obika, opened on Sacramento Street, featuring unique designs by local designers. Wearing these local designers' clothes, I dressed not as the *Vogue* portrait of a corporate president's wife, but creatively, with color and individuality. Almost every week Rudy and I were obliged to attend dinners and social events. The demands of maintaining the role of corporate wife became an unwelcome chore. I deeply resented this intrusion into our personal life.

I despised the prescribed language that permeated these dinners—business talk about increasing sales profits and money. I found myself wanting to shock these conservative corporate types by blurting out liberal proclamations about the sorry state of our materialistic society. Rudy would nudge me under the table to hush up. He didn't want to rock the boat despite the fact that he shared my liberal beliefs. I began to dislike who I believed Rudy was becoming. I sorely missed the sweet, unassuming man I had married. He seemed to have chosen to put principles aside to get ahead. Clearly I wasn't cut out to be the agreeable corporate wife.

In the late 1950s, Dymo built a striking, architect-designed, modern manufacturing plant and suite of offices in Emeryville. The company employed sales representatives to market its products in the United States and later in Mexico, Canada, South America, Europe, and the Far East. Business magazines touted the success of Dymo, with Rudy featured on the cover of *Time* in November 1960. Rudy became famous overnight as the youngest president and CEO of a company at age thirty-nine. With advanced publicity and hype, Dymo would eventually go public in 1961 and make its debut on the New York Stock Exchange in 1963. But as Rudy became more and more committed to his business, our marriage began to fall apart.

Creating a New Role

With my children still in elementary school, I found myself looking for an identity that was more than just mother and wife. Interested in the creative arts, I thought I could find a career in the field of design. Yearning for a creative outlet, I followed up on my enlightening studies in design, color, and contemporary architecture at the Institute of Design in Chicago. Hoping to develop a career of my own, I applied for further study under the GI Bill at the California College of Arts and Crafts (CCAC) in Oakland.

After two years of rigorous training and studio work at the CCAC, my design instructor offered me an incredible opportunity—the job of furnishing and coordinating the interiors of three model homes for a builder in Walnut Creek. I had to find local resources for furniture, textiles, accessories, floor coverings, and other materials in order to completely furnish these model homes. At about this time San Francisco was opening a design district featuring dramatic showrooms in refurbished old buildings in Jackson Square and the Showplace, a block of old brick warehouses gutted and rebuilt south of Market where manufacturers and representatives of furniture, lighting, carpets, fabrics, products, and accessories for interior designers and architects exhibited their beautiful and diversified wares from the around the world. Within a month of accepting my CCAC assignment, I printed my first business cards, which read "Interiors Cecelia Hurwich," received a resale license from the State Board of Equalization, and opened for business as an interior designer! As a professional interior designer, I was invited to become a member of the newly opened Design Centers in San Francisco.

The model homes I created were identical in structure and layout, yet with the completely different color schemes, textures, materials, fabrics, and styles I specified, each home took on a separate and individual flavor. They proved to be a big hit! Prospective buyers loved the colors, furniture, and ambiance of these model homes and wanted to purchase not only the home, but also all the furnishings and accessories I had selected. My business was launched. As an interior designer, I particularly enjoyed the creative challenge of researching new materials and products.

Although I would have worked at this exciting project without remuneration, I needed to pay in advance for materials and furnishings, so I set a nominal fee structure for my services and time. Rudy cautioned that making money at my profession might put us in a higher taxable income bracket. It didn't occur to me at the time to challenge him about this. I went ahead with my interior design business but, because of Rudy's admonitions, I refrained from charging the higher fees I might have received.

As I helped people design the interiors of their homes, I found problems in the lives of many of the couples who were my clients. I discovered that in many cases they were attempting to fix their relationship by redecorating their house—redoing externally what really needed exploring internally. It was not surprising that after we redesigned the entire house, they often divorced. It was not too long before it became clear that internal exploration was needed in my marriage with Rudy.

On Shaky Ground

In 1958 I met Don Ross at a gathering of the Berkeley Liberal Democrats that Rudy and I attended. Don later told me that when I walked into the room, he said to himself: "I've got to meet her. She's the most fantastic woman I've ever seen."

As Don wove his way through the crowded room toward me I was struck by his handsome, classical good looks. He had dark hair, blue eyes, strong facial features, and was tall and slender. He introduced himself shyly, saying he was a teacher of industrial arts in San Francisco. We talked for only a few minutes, but it was clear there was a strong attraction between us; I wondered if Rudy, on the other side of the room, or Don's wife, Rosalie, in another room, noticed how absorbed we were with each other.

Following our first meeting, I made sure Rudy and I attended future Liberal Democrat events because Don and Rosalie might also be there. During this period, both of our marriages were experiencing troubling times.

Rudy and I were essentially leading separate lives, meeting in the evenings over late dinners and occasionally for Sunday outings with the children. I felt Rudy was more married to Dymo than to me, and more engrossed in his business than in what was going on in his children's lives and school. One Saturday when we were preparing for Rob's birthday party and Rudy left for work, I remember following him to his car with tears in my eyes, saying: "Go! Go to your mistress, Dymo." Sometimes he didn't see the kids for days at a time—he left early for work and returned home long after they were in bed. He was obsessed with fulfilling his mother's prophesy of becoming a millionaire by forty. In the beginning I was sympathetic with his long hours and absences from home, but as the years wore on I felt as if I was a single parent and I resented his lack of presence in our lives.

My days were full of arrangements for our children: dancing, violin, and swimming lessons, helping with their homework, listening to their accounts of day-to-day happenings, shopping with them for clothes, supporting them in their daily needs, driving carpools, and organizing birthday parties and activities with their friends.

I wanted to offer our children as many diverse travel experiences as possible. Though Rudy assented to vacations I suggested, if I hadn't planned them, there wouldn't have been any. One year we went to a dude ranch in Palm Springs where he and the children learned to ride horses in the desert. On a Christmas vacation trip to Kauai, they swam in the warm ocean, learned to body surf, and tried out boogie boards. Their first experience with another culture was in Acapulco, Mexico, where they loved the open markets, talking with the vendors, and eating Mexican food. I remember their excitement watching the clavadistas de La Quebrada as they said a solemn prayer at a small shrine and then gracefully dove from the top of a high cliff into a narrow chasm with ocean swells rising and falling.

It was mostly during these vacations that BJ, Robbie, and Lyn had time with their father. But while he relaxed and read, he didn't seem to enjoy himself or our joint activities as much as we did. The children and I loved the outdoors but, regretfully, Rudy did not. He joined us out of a sense of duty. On one family vacation, he confessed that he couldn't help thinking about what was going on at the plant.

The most disappointing summer vacation was our weeklong trip to the Lair of the Bear, a UC Berkeley family alumni camp near Pinecrest where the five of us shared a tent. Rudy found the tent cramped and uncomfortable, the wood floor dirty, the camp surroundings dry and dusty. Although I later recognized that Rudy's obsessive cleanliness prevented him from having a good time camping in a tent, I had hoped he might find the coziness of our family sharing a tent fun and an adventure. He particularly disliked the loud family dining hall, where I had hoped he might connect with some other couples. After spending only one day and night he decided to drive back to Berkeley to work and come back the following week to pick us up. We were all terribly sad and disappointed that he would not be with us for the week.

Together these factors added up to problems in our marriage. When I spoke about my feelings of missing him in our lives, Rudy remained silent. I goaded him to say something, to respond to me, to talk about his feelings; I wanted him to show something, anything emotional. As I pushed for a more intimate connection, he retreated further. I pleaded with him to help make changes to save our marriage. I wanted him to spend more time with the children and me, for us to feel we were important to him. He defensively replied: "I'm working hard for you and the kids. You let your emotions rule; you are not logical." I replied that I wanted a relationship where we could talk about our feelings and connect emotionally. He wanted me to be linear in my thinking. I didn't know what it meant to be linear. He didn't comprehend my need for emotional intimacy. In retrospect, I believe that at that time in his life he did not know how to express his emotions or value being in touch with his feelings. We didn't seem to understand each other, and our discussions deteriorated. We could not reach a resolution. In despair we uttered the scary word . . . separation.

Representing Dymo in Lausanne, Switzerland,
with Rudy (right)

Learning to climb in the Swiss Alps

A Transformative
Experience

Sometimes a single event inspires us to discover who we really are and to create a new life for ourselves. For me, it happened on the road to Yosemite National Park.

I was driving BJ and her friend Crissy to Yosemite as a special treat for their junior high school graduation. I wanted to share Yosemite with them and have them love it as much as I did. I was looking forward to breathing the mountain air; things with Rudy were strained, and, under stress, I had erupted into a troublesome case of hives all over my midsection. The doctor had prescribed an antihistamine to lessen the itch but had neglected to tell me that it might make me drowsy.

Desperately trying to stay awake and keep my eyes open, I told the girls to roll down the windows and said we'd stop in the next town, Tracy, for a cup of coffee. That's the last thing I remember before we crashed into the metal railing along the side of the road. I felt my arm shoot out instinctively to protect the girls as we flew through the air until the car hit the water and plunged sixteen feet into the muddy Mendota Canal.

"If we get out of this alive, my life is going to be different," I thought.

The water seeped rapidly through the floor of the car, reaching our waists. I knew both girls were good swimmers and yelled: "Get out. Hold on to me." I opened my door and felt Crissy clinging to me, but as I reached for BJ she wasn't there. I panicked—did she already get out? Crissy and I surfaced. Looking frantically for BJ, I screamed her name over and over, but she was nowhere to be seen. I dove down to reach the submerged car but couldn't see anything through the murky water. Resurfacing, I could feel the current rapidly carrying us downstream.

Suddenly I heard two men yell: "Get out of there. You're headed for an underground tunnel around the bend." I saw them climb to the edge of the canal and point madly to a ladder on the side. Using all our strength, Crissy and I swam upstream toward the ladder. "My baby's in there. I can't come out," I shouted, hysterical, looking around and screaming for BJ while I helped Crissy get to the ladder.

One man held the other, dangling him by his feet so he could reach Crissy and pull her out of the water. After what felt like an eternity, BJ surfaced and I watched her swim toward the ladder. The men pulled both of us out of the rushing water.

Gulping to catch her breath and shaking as I held her, BJ

told us that just before we hit the railing she had unfastened her seatbelt to reach into the back seat for a peach. When the car hit the railing, the back of her head slammed into the dashboard, knocking her unconscious. When she came to, her head was touching the inside roof of the car with the water seeping up to her chin, only a slight air pocket left for her to breathe. Unable to open her door, she had the presence of mind to grope around underwater until she felt the open door on the driver's side, maneuvered her way out of the car, surfaced, and swam to the ladder.

I hung onto my frightened daughter and reached for Crissy. What if I had lost the girls...how could I possibly live on? Slowly, the previous minutes of terror dissolved into the deepest gratitude I could ever imagine. That we lived through this accident was nothing less than a miracle.

The next day local newspapers reported the objective facts about the accident: the air bubble allowed me to open the door against the rushing current; it also allowed fourteen-year-old BJ to breathe until she regained consciousness. Two men driving from the opposite direction saw a red car disappear, stopped to investigate, and saved our lives by helping us reach the ladder to climb out of the canal.

I never had hives again. Shortly after the accident, I dreamed that I was holding back my tears because if I cried my hives would become huge bumps, evident to all who saw me. I took our survival as a signal, giving me the courage to begin making significant changes in my life.

Jungian Analysis

My best friend Justine had embarked on a Jungian analysis following her devastating experiences in the navy, and it transformed her after an emotional breakdown into a highly functioning person. With her analysis as my inspiration, I decided it was the propitious time for me to seek Jungian therapy. My marriage was troubled; I was unhappy and in my forties. I wanted a more fulfilling personal identity than that of mother and wife.

On Justine's recommendation, I chose Dr. James Whitney, one of the most respected Jungian analysts in the Bay Area. Justine, now married and a therapist herself, knew the Jungian community well. Dr. Whitney's mother was a Jungian analyst who had been analyzed by Jung himself. I was also drawn to Dr. Whitney because he was active in Berkeley politics and had run for city council. It was a plus for me that Dr. Whitney was a friendly, extroverted person with an inviting office that looked out at a colorful garden.

Recognizing that I had been holding in my emotions and anger during my marriage with Rudy, I held nothing back from Dr. Whitney. In my first session I blurted out, "I have three marvelous children, a lovely home, and everyone tells me I have a wonderful husband, yet I cry all the time." Over the next few months, Dr. Whitney listened to stories about my anger at Rudy not being physically and emotionally available for the children and me.

I told Dr. Whitney about my parents and their divorce, my unusual childhood in China and growing up in the San Francisco Bay Area, my education, service in the navy, marriage, motherhood, and ultimately, my loneliness in my marriage. Together we examined my past. Dr. Whitney encouraged me to discuss my dreams. Often, as I sat down in the easy chair opposite him, he asked simply, "Any dreams?" Through keeping a dream journal, drawings of my dreams, and deep reflection, I began to unearth glimmers of my unconscious feelings and emotions. My journal remained by my bed. I taught myself to wake up as soon as I dreamed, grab my journal, and write down my visions; if I waited until the morning they were lost. My dreams became an exciting source of delving into my unconscious. I could hardly wait to go to sleep to see what I might dream.

One memorable dream was about our family's parakeet, Tweetie, a favorite in the house. We often worried that Tweetie would fly out the door and be lost forever. In my dream, Tweetie had escaped outdoors into the open. The children were fearful and concerned for the bird's safety, since she had always been indoors. I was happy for Tweetie in her freedom to fly where she wished. I calmly reassured them: "Tweetie will be OK. She can take care of herself."

In another dream I found myself in a room with all four walls stacked with books from the floor to the ceiling. Looking around, I thought: "Oh my god, what a gift. I can read all these books." In contrast to my restricted life as a mother and wife, this dream offered renewal and vitalization.

One day when I arrived at Dr. Whitney's office, heavy art books were spread all over his desk with my dream drawings superimposed on them. Dr. Whitney recognized the significance of archetypal symbols, noting that some elements of my dream drawings were similar to Indian motifs and carvings in ancient caves and on temples in India. He looked at me seriously and asked, "What do you think of the similarity between your drawings and these archetypes?" I was baffled yet impressed by Dr. Whitney's findings. When I came home from that session I announced to Rudy, "I am going to India some day!" He responded quizzically, "Why would you want to go to India?"

My interest aroused, I checked out books from the library on the art of Indian temples and the drawings found in ancient Indian archaeological sites such as caves. Dr. Whitney lent me books from his extensive library and scholarly research of ARAS, the Archives for Research in Archetypal Symbolism, at the Jung Institute in San Francisco. Drawing upon Jung's work on the archetype and the collective unconscious, ARAS is a pictorial and written archive of mythological, ritualistic, and symbolic images from all over the world and all epochs of human history. The collection probes the universality of archetypal themes and provides a testament to the deep and abiding connections that unite the disparate factions of the human family.

Determined to learn more about India, I enrolled in a class at UC Berkeley on Indian art taught by the eminent scholar Dr. Joanna Williams. She showed hundreds of slides of Indian drawings and mythology, an inspiring introduction to the arts and crafts of India, which one day I hoped to see firsthand.

A Transformative Experience

My sessions with Dr. Whitney shaped my thoughts, behavior, and emerging identity over the next few years. Together we honed my awareness of how real-life events relate to the unconscious elements of dreams. Looking inward, I learned to recognize and acknowledge that my feelings from within held answers if I was willing to listen.

Through my hours of analysis with Dr. Whitney, I learned to verbalize what had been a growing, painful, and difficult realization. Rudy and I had been partners for many years, creating three wonderful children, but our marriage had changed and so had Rudy and I. I was questioning if our marriage could go on. Externally, I worked hard to be the good wife and mother. Internally, my stomach was in knots—I felt emotionally alone in my marriage, and unfulfilled as an individual in life. I felt that, despite my longing and demands for emotional intimacy, Rudy just didn't know how to connect and respond to my pleas.

In 1965, I asked for a divorce. In doing so, I was bucking the mores of our society, which valued marriage and children as the most fulfilling roles for a woman. In anguish and despair, we decided to take a first step toward divorce.

This was the most difficult decision of my life and took five years to reach.

How distressing it was for us to tell our children about our plans to separate. Rudy and I had purposely kept our quarrels private, so when we told the children of our impending separation they were surprised and devastated. BJ was fifteen, Rob thirteen, and Lyn ten. We assured them that although Rudy was moving out, we both loved them dearly and would always be there for them.

I had not foreseen the emotional and psychological consequences of divorce for my children. The scars remained for years. Nor had I realized the social fallout of a divorce for a single woman. I was no longer included in social gatherings, except for a few close friends who were there for me then and remain my friends to this day. Later, when I asked certain people why they didn't call me or invite me over, their reply was "We did not want to take sides."

Our separation became a reality when Rudy moved out of Hillegass in 1966. After two years of separation, Rudy and I worked out an amicable agreement for our divorce. We even hired the same lawyer, who, impressed by our amicability, recommended that the two of us write a book on "creative divorce." We agreed in advance that I would receive the Hillegass house and Rudy would get the business. Our other assets were divided in half. To help me learn how to handle my newly acquired finances, I reached out to my old college friend Mel Gladstone, who was now running his own investment management company. Until his retirement at age eighty, Mel and I met regularly to review my portfolio and afterwards would lunch at the most "in" places of the Bay Area. Concerned that I be economically secure for the rest of my life, Mel gave me books and articles, taught me financial jargon, took me to shareholder's meetings, and opened up a whole new world of investments.

Interlude with Don

After my break with Rudy in 1965, Don and I began to see each other regularly. By this time Don had divorced and moved to San Francisco, and had been living alone for three years. I was still adapting to life with three children—two teenagers and one preteen—without Rudy.

From those first days, ours was an intense relationship, tempestuous and volatile. As soon as we saw each other, our excitement was hard to contain; we wanted to kiss and touch. With my children around, Don and I were constantly plotting ways to get away from the house so that we could be alone.

Exploring ruins in the Yucatán with Don

Don and I enjoyed a busy social life. Through my interior design connections, we received invitations to museum and gallery openings. We attended parties and get-togethers with lots of music and dancing. Other casual gatherings in friends' homes focused on liberal politics. After a few martinis, Don felt more comfortable and outgoing. It became the norm for him to drink to feel good, and I joined him. Fueled by our drinking, these parties often ended in terrible arguments. I loved to dance and flirt with dance partners, which made Don jealous. My own jealousy flared when I felt Don was dancing too closely with an attractive woman. After too many martinis, I once threw a glass with ice cubes at him in a fit of anger. Drinking intensified our jealous quarrels, which we resolved by going to bed.

Our flare-ups occurred time and time again. For three turbulent years, I was torn between wanting to remain home as a good mother and craving to go out with Don. My children disliked Don; they thought he was taking their father's place, did not like his drinking, and resented the time I spent with him rather than them. The children's disapproval added to the stress and guilt that I felt about our relationship. On the evenings he came to our home for dinner, I fed the children first and cleared the kitchen before he arrived. Though we were happy to be together, the martinis inevitably got the better of us, triggering quarrels and loud talk. The children, upstairs in their rooms trying to do their homework, viewed our behavior with disdain, adding to my discomfort and self-condemnation.

A Transformative Experience

I felt like a bad woman, torn between the euphoria I felt with Don and my remorse and guilt for the volatility of our relationship. Going out with a woman with three children was not easy for Don. Although Rudy had moved out of Hillegass during the two years we were separated before our divorce was finalized, having an affair with Don felt adulterous.

Rudy and I had joint custody of the children as per our divorce agreement, but they rarely went to his home, only four blocks away. He didn't invite them for dinner and seldom took them out. Rudy wouldn't agree he was an absentee father, but he was usually not available.

Despite our struggles, Don and I loved each other fiercely. Yet neither of us felt satisfied with the relationship as it existed. After six years of living alone, Don couldn't understand why I wouldn't marry him. During the months he waited for me to make up my mind, I found out that he had been dating another woman, Shirley, a home economics teacher at his school.

On Christmas vacation, Don told me he was driving to Mexico with his friend and colleague, Tony Sims. While he was away, I was welcome to take my children to use his cabin in the Sierra. It sounded fishy to me that Don would go off on vacation with a male friend. I suspected he and Shirley were really taking off on a Christmas fling together. All I knew was that she taught at the same school as Don, she had invited him to her house for dinners, and that she was a single woman in her thirties.

While at Don's cabin with the children for Christmas and skiing, I was compelled to find out the truth. I located Shirley's phone number in the directory at his cabin. I called her house in San Francisco, telling the woman who answered that I was an old classmate of Shirley's and how could I reach her? The woman said Shirley was visiting her parents in Texas and gave me the number. I called Texas and asked to speak to Don Ross. When Don came to the phone I commanded, "You get yourself right back here!" He was astonished and guilt-ridden. The next day Don and Shirley left Texas for the drive back to California.

Don and I had a tearful reunion, with both of us proclaiming our love, but neither of us changing positions. He wanted to marry. I wasn't ready. After twenty years of marriage and with three teenagers to raise, I didn't feel comfortable jumping into another marriage when we already had significant problems. I needed time to grow. I wanted to be on my own to pursue a career other than marriage. I hoped Don would see me through this time of self-exploration without the demands and distractions of marriage, yet we could not come to terms with each other's needs and desires. After months of thought, deliberation, and endless talking, we decided to go our separate ways. Our breakup was heart-wrenching.

Not long after Don and I broke up, I was devastated to hear from him that he was marrying Shirley. The week after Don married, he told me he already realized he had made a mistake, but he was going to stick with it. He wanted to be married and taken care of. All through his marriage we stayed in touch, meeting for lunch around our birthdays. It was exciting to see him and remain connected. From his description of his marriage, life with Shirley was dull and unfulfilling. He missed the excitement, adventure, and mutual friends that I had brought into his life.

In 1966, near the end of my analysis, while still grieving over my breakup with Don, I received a call from Dr. Whitney's son telling me that Dr. Whitney had suddenly died of a heart attack. It was a terrible loss when he died. I knew that I had Dr. Whitney to thank for having helped me make major breakthroughs in my life. My mother and I were working on some challenges in our relationship. Through Dr. Whitney's sessions, I had learned to reinterpret her behaviors as coming from a place of love, rather than manipulation or control. From this evolved viewpoint—it's not what happens to you but how you view what happens to you—my emotional responses shifted from anger to love and acceptance.

I remember my mother once telling me when I was eight, not long after she and Father had divorced: "I am twenty-nine years old. I am young and have my own life. Do you know I don't need to take care of you? Unless you are a good girl and mind me, I can put you in an orphanage." After my father had already abandoned me and left for China, Mother's threat scared the hell out me and loomed in my mind for years.

One day, after Dr. Whitney had died, Mother and I reran an episode that formerly would have been explosive and left me exhausted, yet I handled it with great finesse. Mother had again brought up my spending too money much on clothes, traveling, and what she thought of as a no-good relationship with Don, who to her was just a schoolteacher, while Rudy was a successful businessman. As I closed our front door after giving Mother a hug and kissing her goodbye, I whispered gratefully, "Thank you, Dr. Whitney." Through his guidance I made a lasting peace with my mother. It was a tremendous turning point for me. I let my past anger toward Mother go. From then on, we became closer friends—calling and seeing each other regularly, listening to and appreciating each other's stories, shopping and vacationing together. After she retired, we attended the same health club and took the same classes.

Spreading My Wings

After my divorce in 1967, I checked out the human potential movement. Excited and feeling liberated, I found myself savoring the experience of driving Highway 1 alone, the top down on my convertible, as I headed to Big Sur to attend a workshop on "abundance of life" at Esalen. With its dramatic location on cliffs overlooking the Pacific, Esalen, an alternative education and growth center, offered myriad workshops addressing the unrealized capacities of humankind. Participants from all over the world converged at Esalen, seeking courses in personal enrichment and growth. Adding to the wonder of Esalen were its natural hot springs overlooking the Pacific, therapeutic massage and bodywork, organic gardens producing delicious food, and lodging in small rustic cabins scattered about the glorious grounds.

Other weekends, when the kids were with Rudy, I took off to Yosemite for rock climbing classes offered by the Sierra Club. Joining such groups, I made new friends remarkably different from my former social circle. My new outdoorsy friends, predominantly single or divorced, seemed adventurous and open to fresh thoughts, risks, and novel experiences. By contrast, the married women friends of my post-war generation were homemakers and raising children. Though they might have graduated from college, they were not pursuing careers. Their husbands were focused on getting ahead and making money.

Throughout this fertile period I remained fascinated by my dreams and kept a dream-journal. Eager to learn more about Indian symbolism and archetypes, in March 1968 I attended an exhibition at the de Young Museum called "Unknown India: The Art of Tribe and Village." It was so compelling that I visited the museum almost every day for six weeks and purchased the colorful catalog and map of India showing where these artworks originated. This catalog became my talisman. I believed that I would one day visit these villages to learn more about the beautiful handicrafts and so, on the last day of the exhibit, I told the Indian curator traveling with the exhibition that, "One day, I plan to visit this 'unknown India.'" He handed me his card with his name, Haku Shah, and said, "If you come, please look me up!" About three years later, I did exactly that when my travels brought me to Ahmadabad.

Haku Shah introduced me to master craftspeople and crafts-centers in Gujarat. He accompanied me to the world-renowned Calico Museum of Textiles in Ahmadabad with its distinguished and comprehensive collection of textiles and artifacts. Haku introduced me to the museum's founder, a good friend of his, Gina Sarabhai. Made wealthy in the cotton industry, the Sarabhai family were friends of Gandhi who became committed followers of Gandhian principles, funding many institutions of arts and culture in Ahmadabad. Gina invited me to her family's tasteful home, designed by the Bauhaus architect Le Corbusier, set elegantly and naturally into the gardens of their verdant estate. Before leaving Ahmadabad, Haku Shah invited me to his home to meet his family. The next year when I returned, I was welcomed as a family guest.

With Robbie and BJ off to college, and Rudy in his own home, Lyn, now thirteen, felt lonely with just the two of us living at Hillegass. Very headstrong, she argued that she didn't want to keep going to school in Berkeley. Her wish was to return to a school in the Swiss Alps for a year to become fluent in French. Two years earlier she had taken an educational trip there to study French and explore Switzerland for a month. Lyn remembered fondly the small village in the mountains, where she had stayed in simple Swiss chalets, eaten delicious cheese, and was lulled to sleep by cowbells during the night.

After much research into Swiss French schools in the mountains, we felt we had found the perfect school. Rudy and Rob had visited it on an earlier trip to Europe. In the fall of 1967, I accompanied Lyn to the school, located in Montana, Switzerland. When Lyn and I first entered the building, I was taken aback to see an austere interior with bare walls and the most basic furnishings—a table, chair, and desk in the foyer. The library held few books and posters were not allowed on dorm room walls. I was further surprised to notice that most of the young girls were wearing makeup, though only about age twelve. My instincts warned that this place might not be a good match for Lyn. Some girls were daughters of affluent American executives stationed overseas, and others the children of wealthy Middle Eastern families.

The school had advertised itself as coed, but we learned after arriving that the boys' school had recently moved to a separate building after one of the girls became pregnant. Though classes were coed, living and eating quarters were separate. Visiting days were restricted to Sundays. I didn't feel comfortable departing for California, leaving Lyn in this cold, unfriendly environment, so I decided to stay and give the school a few weeks' trial to see if Lyn felt comfortable and made some friends.

With Lyn busy in school that first week, I decided the best way to see the Swiss countryside was by hiking in the mountains. Calling around, I found a rock-climbing program with an English-speaking guide in Andermatt, the German-speaking region of Switzerland, about a two-hour train ride from Montana. Upon arriving in Andermatt on an early Monday morning, I was met at the train station by a Swiss guide, Martin, who brought me to a cozy family hotel and loaned me knickers and a warm jacket for hiking. After he introduced me to the town, the two of us studied maps and planned our week of hiking and rock climbing lessons.

Walking together in the mountains the next morning, we came to the edge of a cliff. Martin needed to know if I was afraid of heights. He tied a rope around my waist, his waist, and anchored it around a big boulder. Then he asked me to walk to the edge of the cliff and look down. It was a huge drop, but I didn't waver or draw back. Looking down over the edge without being afraid, I passed the first test for a rock climber. I spent a week in the Alps around Andermatt learning to rock climb. Being in the high mountains was spiritual and invigorating. I had not realized before that I could have a good time traveling alone. It was a real breakthrough!

The following Sunday, Lyn and I were happy to be together for the day wandering about Montana, eating meals in small restaurants and shopping in the village. We found Lyn a portable combination phonograph and radio that she loved and eventually brought home to Berkeley. Two weeks in, she didn't feel that the school was academically satisfactory. She wasn't convinced that she would become fluent in French because all of the girls spoke English outside of class. Just before I was to return to the United States, Lyn asked if I would visit her again the following Sunday. I was happy to do so, eager to see her settled in a school that she liked. After a pleasant last Sunday together at the museum in Lausanne, it was time for me to go back to the United States. I told Lyn that she had to stay the full year if she wanted to become fluent in French. Although not completely satisfied with the school, she assented.

Upon returning to California after my Swiss climbing exposure, I joined the Sierra Club and enrolled in its beginning rock climbing class. As the oldest person and one of only two women in this group, it was with determination and great effort that I got better at the techniques of climbing, this time practicing on the towering peaks of Yosemite. We climbed Yosemite's Cathedral Peaks and practiced at the base of the Royal Arches. As always, the high mountains were an environment where I felt a spiritual connection to this natural world of earth, sky, and rocks; to something greater than myself.

To keep up with the younger rock climbers, I embarked on a running regime in the Berkeley Hills. Starting with one mile on the track near my home at the Deaf School (now Berkeley's Clark Kerr Campus), I moved on to two miles on a trail and eventually four miles of trails in the hills, about four days a week. It was a kick for me to go shopping for sports equipment at REI. I also loved learning to read topographical maps and use a compass to find our routes.

Through my rock-climbing classes I met hikers who told me about the wonders of hiking in Nepal. I attended a Sierra Club slide show of a hiking trip to Nepal given by Alah Schmidt, who was leading another trip to Nepal the following spring. Alah and I spoke about the possibility of Lyn, now sixteen, and I joining his trip. He urged us both to sign up, claiming that the group would love to have us along.

Lyn had learned to speak French pretty well while in Switzerland. She was glad to get back home, away from the affluent children of foreign diplomats in the Swiss school in the Alps, to return to her circle of friends at Berkeley High School. But after a year at Berkeley High, Lyn was disenchanted and cutting classes, hanging out in the MLK park next to her school, claiming she didn't want to go to college and getting in trouble with the school administration.

Because of Lyn's dissatisfaction with life at Berkeley High, and because I felt she needed a change of scene from the bad influences of her friends at school, I felt that a Sierra Club hike to Nepal would be a good experience and destination for us. From an early age Lyn loved to travel, and when she found out that pot was legal and easy to get in Nepal she became enthusiastic about our proposed adventure. I viewed our trip as an opportunity to become closer to my teenage daughter, and as chance for Lyn and me to experience a third-world country and come away with a broader outlook and a deeper appreciation for other cultures and environments.

We arranged with Berkeley High for Lyn to take a leave from school for a springtime trek in Nepal. On her return, she would need to turn in papers to receive credit for geography, history, English, and photography. I looked forward to time with Lyn away from Berkeley and so, excitedly, we prepared for our adventure in Nepal.

Springtime in Nepal

Nepal in 1970 was a land of exquisite peace and beauty, timeless in its remoteness from civilization. Other than two flights a week in and out of its capital, Kathmandu, the country was essentially cut off from the outside world. Kathmandu sits in the heart of a gentle valley, surrounded by the towering snow-capped Himalayas. A series of trails emanating from this bustling city led far into the remote countryside.

The leader of the trip, Alah Schmidt, was a robust seventy;

A Transformative Experience

Lyn was the youngest member of the group. Al graciously imparted his knowledge to Lyn about the mountains, the flora and birds, the people, and Buddhism. Two fellow hikers, Anthony Russo—Tony, as we called him —and John Goodwin, would become lifetime friends. The four of us quickly became close companions early on in the trip when we shared a cab to tour the Kathmandu Valley. Our taxi driver, thrilled with Tony's generous tip, offered to take us around anytime without further charges. Three years later, when I was in Kathmandu alone to climb Everest, I looked up the driver who, true to his promise drove me everywhere. Remembering how he had been fascinated with Lyn's and my Timex watches, I brought him one as a sign of my gratitude.

Our month-long trek, along the gorge of the Kali Gandaki River, took us through seldom-traveled regions of the Himalayas. We crossed rivers roaring far below us on swaying, unstable suspension bridges made of wooden planks with heavy rope handrails. We slogged along muddy trails, finding leeches crawling on us and inside our hiking boots, our legs bloody from their bites. We bathed in magnificent waterfalls along the rivers and icy-cold streams. Each night we slept in tents carried by porters who walked ahead, set up our tents, and kindled fires for cooking our dinner and for hot water to wash in.

Our days were long and tiring, but each ended with a delicious hot dinner served to us by considerate Sherpas and porters. They would purchase a chicken or a goat in a nearby village, carrying it over their backs until we arrived in camp, to cook over an open-fire for dinner. Dinners included lots of rice, chapattis, hot tea, and soup to prevent dehydration. After dinner each night, Lyn and I settled into our tent, where we rehashed the day's exhilarating events and giggled into the night wrapped in our cozy sleeping bags.

We learned about Buddhism from our Buddhist Sherpa guides. Occasionally we made our camp near Buddhist villages, relating nonverbally with the villagers. We visited gompas, Buddhist compounds, where we talked far into the night with priests and lamas who spoke some English.

Wherever we hiked we saw prayer flags suspended high along the trails of mountain ridges fluttering in the breezes, offering prayers for the Wind Horse to carry to all beings. For centuries, Buddhists have hung these flags, sure that they'll bring happiness, prosperity, and longevity to those nearby, and that the beneficent vibrations of peace and compassion will be blown into the farthest reaches of the universe for the benefit of all. I found it easy to share their belief as I stared up at the flags—in sets of yellow, green, red, white, and blue cloth representing the elements, each inscribed with symbols, prayers, and mantras—quivering against a sky so azure blue it took my breath away. According to Buddhists, the flags, sensitive to the slightest touch of the wind, sanctify the air and over time, as the cloth frays and the words fade from exposure to the elements, their messages become part of the universe. Life renews itself as bright new flags are suspended next to faded, tattered ones. Beneath those flags, surrounded by the majestic mountains, I felt I was a part of a vast ongoing cycle.

Our adversities were minimal compared to the hardships of village life at higher elevations. Villagers walked barefoot for miles with their sick children when they heard our group was traveling with a doctor who had medicines. Diseases such as tuberculosis, eye infections, skin rashes, stomach troubles, and goiters were prevalent and medical help scarce. The villagers lined up as our doctor carefully examined them. Through a Sherpa interpreter she listened to descriptions of their ailments and dressed wounds, suggested treatments, or dispensed the necessary medicines.

Nepal was our first exposure to the third world. Lyn reacted emotionally to the sights about her. She was struck by the young, exhausted women who walked for miles to a clinic, carrying their infants in blankets, accompanied by children with weepy eyes that attracted flies; women with big round balls of goiter; small wiry Nepalese men lugging huge slabs of wood on their backs up the steep trails from Kathmandu to build their homes, the mountains having been stripped of trees; the lack of running water in their homes. Over the course of the trip, Tony and John kept telling Lyn: "You're crazy not to go to college! Your parents are willing to pay your way and you're not interested?"

The whole Nepal experience subtly influenced Lyn's decision to graduate from Berkeley High School. Before the Nepal trip she hadn't acknowledged any reasons for going on to college. But after witnessing the environmental destruction and human destitution in Nepal, she decided a college education would be her best bet for getting in a position to contribute to the betterment of the poor countries and people in the developing world.

Her choice eventually brought her to the College of the Atlantic in Maine, a small alternative college with a rigorous program and highly qualified faculty, where she majored in human ecology. From the College of the Atlantic, Lyn went on to receive her law degree from UC Berkeley's Boalt Law School in international environmental law. Today she heads the Circumpolar Conservation Union in Washington, D.C., where she was one of the early advocates fighting against global climate change and its disastrous effects on indigenous populations.

The Wonders of Synchronicity

My dream drawings kept India at the forefront of my thoughts and increasingly I felt compelled to visit. I particularly wanted to study the village arts and crafts that had been passed down from masters for generations. Amazingly, my desires became a reality when two synchronistic events sent my life in an extraordinary direction. It became clear that I was meant to go to India.

The first event had happened the fall before Lyn and I left for Nepal, when I attended a lecture on landscape architecture and design by a well-known landscape architect at Stanford University. Two women in beautiful saris were sitting in the row ahead of me. We introduced ourselves and exchanged cards. The older woman's card read: "Princess Maryan, Sister of His Holiness," with addresses in Cambridge (Massachusetts), Bombay, and Oxford. Whoever heard of a Sister of His Holiness? I thought to myself, What a phony.

When Princess Maryan saw from my business card that I was an interior designer, she declared that she wanted to redecorate her palace in Bombay and requested a meeting with me. She telephoned twice to set up an appointment but, disbelieving the truth of her card, I claimed I was too busy preparing for our trek in Nepal. The following week, her son-in-law drove from Fremont to my home in Berkeley to personally deliver a gift of beautifully embroidered appliquéd caftan with a note reading "Compliments of Princess Maryan."

Obliged to thank her for the gift, I invited the princess to my home for tea. I found her imperious, yet charming. In a pronounced British accent she informed me she was a Bhori (Dawoodi Bhora) Muslim, part of a special sect with around a million followers throughout the world. She referred constantly to "His Holiness," her brother who was head of the Bhoris.

Responding to her request to redecorate her palace, we pored over my interior design books all afternoon. I taught her some basic principles about the use of design, color, and space. Her interest in my life led me to tell her about the Indian art exhibit at the de Young Museum and to confide my wish to travel to the regions of India that had been featured in this exhibition. She warned me that a single woman must not travel in India alone and that I had to be accompanied by my daughter or a close friend. She insisted that, if asked, I must reply that I was a widow, not divorced. Divorced women were looked down upon, whereas widows were respected. I found out that people would give up their seats on buses to widows, easily identified by their white clothing or saris. If asked where was my husband, I would lower and shake my head, "no."

When Princess Maryan heard that I didn't know anyone in India and had no "connections," she was aghast, insisting that I must have formal introductions. "I have a plan," she announced, "Let us see what we can do for you at the Indian consulate in San Francisco. Make an appointment with him!" she commanded. She became my advisor and mentor for my dreamed-of India trip.

The day of our appointment at the Indian consulate in San Francisco, Princess Maryan arrived dressed to the nines in a silk sari, complemented by gold, diamonds, and an emerald necklace and earrings. At the consul general's office she imperiously announced: "I am Princess Maryan, daughter of His Holiness, and this is my friend Cecelia Hurwich. She wants to go to India and must have introductions."

Three assistants interviewed us before we were finally admitted to the sanctum of Mr. Josi, the consul general, who carefully examined the princess's card and bowed. She looked aside at me, smiled and nodded as if to say, "See?"

Princess Maryan emphatically told the consul general that I was planning to travel to villages in India alone to study their crafts and certainly needed letters of introduction. Baffled, he asked, "Whom shall we write the letter to?" Confidently, she replied, "To the Minister of the Interior." Mr. Josi diplomatically suggested that he write the letter later, to be addressed to the All-India Handicrafts Board.

Princess Maryan stepped right in, offering to dictate the letter then and there. Unable to say no to her, he nodded and introduced us to his secretary. Princess Maryan dictated the letter, including my typed proposal plan along with her request for the appropriate introductions. In the letter, I proposed to visit the villages that were listed in the catalog of the "Crafts of Unknown India," to help the master craftsmen design for a contemporary international market. I made it clear that I felt it was essential to keep the basic integrity of the original work of art or craft.

Princess Maryan insisted that the consul general sign the completed typed letter before we left the room, and that he place it into the diplomatic mail pouch labeled "Confidential," which she spotted sitting in his office.

Ten days later, after our visit to the consulate in San Francisco, I received a telegram from the All-India Handicrafts Board (AIHB) in New Delhi requesting that I report to them upon my arrival for an interview. The government was seeking overseas designers to help rejuvenate local crafts.

All of the events leading to my telegram from India were synchronistic, meaningful, and pivotal coincidences—from my dream drawings and Dr. Whitney's perceptive research of their Indian motifs, my unexpected meeting with Princess Maryan at a Stanford lecture, to her interest in securing letters of introduction for me in India, our visit with the Indian consul and the letter he sent on my behalf to India, and then this telegram to report upon my arrival in India to interview at the AIHB.

The AIHB had just initiated a program to encourage young Indians to learn the art of their forebears, consummate artisans. Instead of learning their ancestors' crafts, young people were leaving their villages and migrating to cities, only to find themselves unemployed and destitute. By studying ancient crafts techniques from older experts, these young villagers could pursue fulfilling careers and continue their artistic lineage. My proposal coincided with, and complemented, what the AIHB had recently initiated, namely, seeking design assistance from foreign designers to help revitalize the crafts of the villages. The government saw us as catalysts to help bring a fresh perspective. We were to maintain the integrity of the designs while suggesting modifications that would help the crafts sell in international markets, therefore providing ongoing employment for the craftsmen and a means to keep the crafts alive.

India Sojourn

After our month of hiking in Nepal, I headed for India and Lyn headed for home. I hugged Lyn goodbye at the small airport in Nepal, feeling that painful pull of wanting to hold onto her and letting her go. Arriving later that same day at a hotel in New Delhi, I took a walk outside and felt animated despite being alone in a city with more people milling around me on the streets than I had ever encountered. Temperatures were over a hundred degrees with extreme humidity. Surprisingly, I was comfortable among the crowds of Indians about me. For the rest of my India sojourn I would hear time and time again, "You must have been an Indian in another life." I would nod in agreement, almost believing it.

On the first day I arrived in New Delhi, I signed up for an American Express half-day tour on a much-appreciated, air-conditioned coach. The meeting place was the lobby of the Janpath Hotel, one of a well-known government-run hotels in Delhi. In the window of a lobby art shop, I recognized a batik as the work of an Indian artist named Mawasi Ram. I had one of his batiks hanging in my home in Berkeley!

Entering the shop, I pointed to the batik and announced, "That's a Mawasi Ram!" The young Indian proprietor asked in amazement, "Do you know him?" I replied that I had purchased one of Ram's batiks from a shop on Telegraph Avenue in Berkeley and hoped to meet the artist while in India. The store owner, Jeet, said: "He lives right here in Delhi! He's my friend! Please come back after your tour and see me."

When I returned to the Janpath Hotel, hot and tired after the tour, the shop owner, Jeet Anand, showed me his vast collection of Indian folk art while we sipped the gin and tonics he poured. Two hours later, he remembered that he was due at a family dinner party at Modi Mahal, a restaurant in Old Delhi frequented by locals, and impulsively invited me to join him.

The Anand family was celebrating a farewell dinner for Jeet's sister, who was moving to Kenya to join her husband. Animated conversations with Jeet's family and Delhi locals gave me a memorable introduction to India, along with the opportunity to taste an array of spicy Indian dishes. The next day, I was so sick with dysentery that I couldn't function. I learned that first evening in Delhi how Indian foods could affect my Western stomach, and to carefully watch what I ate.

It was three days before my stomach was back to normal and I was well enough to keep my appointment with the All-India Handicraft Board. There I met Iola Basu, head of the board and one of the top designers of India. Iola and I discovered that we were both fifty years old and shared a passion for art, literature, and design. I described how the Indian art exhibit at the de Young Museum in San Francisco had captured my imagination, and how I intuitively knew I was destined to visit these villages and crafts. Nodding her head, Iola exclaimed that I was just the kind of person they wanted! She outlined the AIHB program that provided grants to foreign designers to study and help revitalize the crafts of the villages. I mentioned meeting Haku Shaw, and Iola proudly told me he had won the Padma Shri award from India's president for being a national treasure.

We designers were to visit with the villages and work with the local craftsmen to help them keep the basic integrity of their art, while carefully modifying the object for foreign export. Iola arranged for letters of introduction to the villages where the All-India Handicraft Board had centers. In these villages I would be housed and fed but was otherwise responsible for providing my own transportation. Little did I know what "my own transportation" would entail!

It was considered an honor to be chosen as a designer for this innovative program. Many well-known designers from Europe were thrilled by this unique opportunity to travel and study in India. Iola helped put together an itinerary that only an artist who was well acquainted with the arts and crafts of India could. She suggested special areas rich in crafts and culture and gave me personal letters of introduction to craftspeople throughout the country with whom I could study local handicrafts in Behar, Ahmadabad, Baroda, Puri, Trivandrum Calcutta, Bhubaneswar, Patna, Kutch, Bikaner, Jaipur, Bangalore, Hyderabad, Madras, Cottoyam, and Srinagar. Her parting words, in her crisp British accent, were: "This won't be an easy trip. I wouldn't do it. I might have done it ten or twenty years ago, but not today. However, you seem quite hardy, so good luck." Iola remained my friend until she died in 2003.

For the next ten days I checked out Iola's recommended handicrafts centers in and around Delhi. There was such a vast and diverse array of crafts to be seen in New Delhi that I soon realized that my mission to study in remote villages would take much longer than the three months originally allotted. If I were to complete this program, I would need to extend my stay for another three months, which luckily I was able to do. The proprietor I had met in the art shop of the Janpath Hotel, Jeet, also took me about to meet many artists in New Delhi, and before I left for my trip, Jeet introduced me to Mawasi Ram, the artist whose batik I had purchased in Berkeley.

When I arrived in Ahmadabad Gujarat, I looked up the curator from the exhibit I had seen three years earlier in San

Francisco. I discovered that this small quiet man, Haku Shah, was the leading authority on Indian folk art, a painter, cultural anthropologist, teacher, author, and Gandhian. He offered to accompany and show me the tribal villages around Ahmadabad, taking me about to meet craftspeople on local buses. Haku Shah became my mentor, teaching me the fundamentals of crafts in Gujarat. As a Gandhian, Haku lived simply and frugally. Before I left Ahmadabad, he invited me to his home for an Indian dinner, where I met his wife and two small sons. On my subsequent trip to Ahmadabad, I was invited to stay with Haku and his family in their home as their guest.

With an introduction from Iola Basu, I met Johdi Bott, who taught photography at the University of Baroda. One day when Johdi took me to some Gujarati villages, acting as my guide interpreter, we happened upon a small hut with strikingly painted walls on all sides. An old woman appeared at the doorway. When Johdi queried her in the local dialect, she told us she painted from her dreams and the world around her. We asked if she would be able to do this on canvas if we brought it for her, and she shrugged, not knowing what canvas was. She had painted on the ground and mud walls all her life. We returned in a few days with painting supplies. She went to work with full intensity, so happy to paint that a week later all the canvases were vividly painted. She was a widow and her dreams were the source of her creativity. After we left, the old woman became a local celebrity because an American woman had purchased her paintings. Johdi returned and bought paintings from her, bringing visitors who appreciated her art.

A Transformative Experience

My travels to folk art villages were difficult and challenging. At times, the only way I could get to these remote villages was by oxcart, a local bus, or walking through swollen rivers and jungle, always in extreme heat. To reach larger cities I used buses and local trains. For longer distances, I took Indian Airlines. Often I was the only foreigner traveling by bus.

For example on a bus to Pipli, a small village in the southern Indian State of Orissa, medics boarded our bus to announce a smallpox epidemic in the region, lining up passengers for injections using the same needle for everyone on the bus. Vehemently I shook my head and loudly cried, "No, no, thank you!" I was ready to jump off the bus, but we were in a dense jungle. After heated back-and-forth gesticulations between the medics and me, with all the curious passengers gathered tightly around, the medics let me go without an injection.

Pipli is known for its colorful, one-of-a-kind appliquéd umbrellas, created by artists on old-fashioned treadle sewing machines and prized all over the world. With colored felt-tipped pens, I showed the Pipli craftsman the colors I preferred for my umbrella—red, yellow, orange, bright royal blue. Together we worked out designs. They showed me different cutout pieces of colored cloth in shapes of animals, birds, flowers leaves, gods, and goddesses. Lacking measuring tapes, they used pieces of string cut off at appropriate lengths; we chose the size of the umbrella. The artists were given free rein to either replicate a standard pattern, or create one-of-a-kind designs of their own, which took considerable time and painstaking detail to create. There were no means of shipping the umbrella from this small village, so I paid in advance for the umbrella and added money for freight. Luckily, an American man was driving by Pipli some weeks later, wanted to buy some umbrellas, and agreed to ship back mine with his.

The AIHB program to rejuvenate Indian crafts making was a huge success, both artistically and financially, for the Indian government, the villagers, and the craftspeople. From each village, the local crafts were sent to the nearest AIHB center where they were inspected for quality and packaged for shipment to their showrooms in Paris and New York. Other handicraft orders were shipped to sources such as Bloomingdales, Galeries Lafayette, Liberty House, and Takashimaya. Buyers and designers from all over the world flocked to purchase these fabulous crafts and goods. The AIHB received much praise and acclaim for a renaissance of Indian art and crafts. The program increased awareness of master craftsmen in India and spurred a whole generation of young artisans who design the tasteful beautiful Indian treasures that are eagerly received and coveted in the rest of the world.

For two weeks I lived with indigenous people in the remote village of Orissa to study their crafts. It took me eight hours to walk there from the paved highway where the bus let me off. The living conditions in the village were primitive, lacking running water, toilets, and electricity. The villagers washed themselves, their dishes, and clothes in the nearby stream, while others drank water from the same stream. I slept in my own tent and had brought my own food, which I ate within a week. The villagers generously offered to share their food and water with me. Though I purified my water with iodine and a filter, I was watching my stool for tapeworms, endemic in the village. And indeed, by the time I arrived in Madras, the next stop on my itinerary, I knew I was ill.

At the crowded Spencer's Drugstore on Saturday just before their midday closing, the pharmacist abruptly told me I needed a prescription from a doctor for the antibiotic I had requested. "Next person!" he called, effectively dismissing me. A voice behind me interjected: "Perhaps I can help you, Madame. I am a drug manufacturer and distributor." I turned to see a tall, white-haired Brahmin, with ashes on his forehead, dressed in a white, newly starched dhoti and kurta, who went on to say in excellent English: "My car and driver are outside. I will be happy to take you to my office to see if we can find your antibiotics." I felt I could trust this stranger and nodded my assent.

At his office, while he searched for the antibiotics, I grabbed onto his desk, feeling faint. He asked if I was all right and I shook my head. He took my temperature; it was 104.2°. "We must get you to a doctor!" He began calling all the doctors he knew, but on a Saturday afternoon it was difficult to reach anyone. Finally he reached his personal doctor at the golf course, insisting that he come immediately to take care of a sick American woman.

The kind man called the American consulate, arranged for a room in a small hospital for foreigners, took me to my hotel to pick up my bag, and waited at the hospital until his friend the doctor arrived. It turned out I had typhoid.

For the next ten days I rested in the hospital in Madras. Each day, my new friend Mr. Durairajan, his wife, or one of his four children visited me bringing flowers, candy, and books. When it was time for my discharge from the hospital, he and his wife invited me to stay in their home until I regained my strength. When I asked Mr. Durairajan why he had befriended a total stranger, he replied: "I happen to be blessed. I was there when you needed me." I found repeated demonstrations of this kindness and trust throughout my travels in India.

In Hyderabad, a large city in central India known for its handicrafts, a barefoot gypsy woman wearing a brightly colored ruffled dress walked by me on a street. I smiled and gestured my admiration, stopping her as I pulled out a photograph of my daughters from my backpack. I indicated that I would like her to sew the same outfit for us. She motioned for me to follow her. Without a second thought, I did.

We walked for over an hour, communicating by gestures and smiles until we were on the outskirts of town in a gypsy enclave of little huts by a river. One of the men spoke a few words of English. I gestured that I wanted an outfit such as my gypsy guide was wearing. Soon four women were measuring me with a string, cut off at different lengths for bust, waist, and hips. Continuing nonverbally with gestures, I indicated that my daughters' waists were smaller than mine. They jotted everything down on paper.

After I spent the day with the gypsies, they invited me to dinner. The entire village turned out for the huge feast of pig and chicken, which the women cooked over an open fire.

After dinner, as the men plucked stringed instruments and the women struck tambourines and castanets, we all danced in a circle with wild abandon. Three French tourists asking directions for Hyderabad drove by in a small auto and the gypsies promptly invited them to join our festivities. The Frenchmen later drove me back to my hotel in Hyderabad. I felt drawn to the gypsies' openness and communal living.

The following day, the gypsy woman, Nima, arrived at my hotel, but because she was a gypsy, the desk clerk refused to call my room to tell me she was there. Anticipating her visit, I came down to the lobby, where she was patiently waiting. I didn't pass up the opportunity to give the desk clerk a dirty look, shaking my head in disapproval. "Why didn't you call my room?" I asked. He just looked down and shook his head.

Nima and I walked to the nearby Government Cottage Industry Emporium. My gypsy friend agreed to deliver the finished dresses to the Emporium and the Emporium agreed to mail them to me in the United States. I strongly encouraged the Indian Emporium manager to carry these one-of-a-kind, hand-embroidered and mirrored outfits for tourists. The manager, who believed that the gypsies were not trustworthy and that they would not deliver the articles, told me I was a naive tourist to pay in advance.

A few months later, the package from the gypsies arrived in Berkeley with my entire order, even more beautiful than I had remembered, plus a gift of extra blouses from my generous gypsy friends. I wrote the manager of the Government Cottage Industry Emporium in Hyberabad telling them I had faithfully received my goods as promised from the gypsies, but I never received a reply.

During the India-Bangladesh war in November 1971, the U.S. State Department issued a warning to Americans that Kashmir was off-limits. The war was being fought on two fronts: in Bangladesh on the southeast, and on the border of Pakistan and Kashmir in northern India.

In my year of travels learning about Indian arts and crafts, I had heard that those in Kashmir—embroidery, weaving, wood-carvings, papier-mâché—were the ultimate in fine workmanship and design. I was eager to see them, yet apprehensive about traveling in a war zone. Undeterred by the State Department warning, I flew to Srinagar, capital of Kashmir, nestled among three lakes and the snow-clad Himalayas, to study with their local craftspeople.

Mr. Butt, my host and owner of the Butt's Clermont Houseboats on Dal Lake, had been highly recommended as honest in business dealings and knowledgeable about the area and its crafts. He picked me up at the airport and became my protector. Despite some bombs and air raids, in Srinagar it was business as usual. The Kashmiris warned me to stay away from crowded bazaars during air raids, because that was where the greatest casualties occurred.

The moment I stepped aboard Butt's houseboat, I was given a traditional greeting of flower petals sprinkled over my head. From that moment on, my stay at Mr. Butt's houseboat was unforgettable. I had a personal attendant who looked after my every need. He washed my laundry, kept the houseboat clean, and prepared whatever dishes I wanted. Each evening Mr. Butt arrived with a tray full of hors d'oeuvres and choices of drinks, from juices to gin and tonics.

The interior of the houseboat was warm and cozy, heated by a pot-bellied wood stove. Décor included wood-paneled walls, old-fashioned chandeliers, and comfortable chairs. From the picture windows in the bedroom I could see the many shikaras—a type of wooden boat common to the lake — silently gliding by. My personal boatman was available to take me on rides across the lake. With a colorful overhead canopy protecting me from the sun, I could lie back on pillows, covered by warm blankets, drink hot tea from a thermos, and happily enjoy the view as we moved quietly across the glassy waters. It was wintertime; the surrounding countryside was covered in pristine snow, and on the lake floated gardens of vegetables that grew year-round despite the snow-clad mountains that surround the valley of Srinagar.

As one of the few foreigners who risked traveling to Kashmir during the Bangladesh War, I was welcomed wherever I went—small artisans' workshops, handicraft stores, and even local restaurants. For six weeks I studied the unique arts and crafts of Kashmir and exchanged design ideas with artisans in their workshops. I worked with the individual artists in their workshops, homes, or small cooperatives. Their workmanship on handcrafted felt, crewel and silk embroidery, one-of-a-kind wool or silk carpets, hangings, papier-mâché products, woodcarving, silverware, jewelry, and handwoven baskets was even more beautiful than I had anticipated.

The friends I made during this initial trip to Kashmir who welcomed me so openly into their homes and houseboats would welcome me again and again on many return trips.

Travel, I found, can be a metaphor for internal growth. The Brahmin taught me the power of feeling blessed by being able to help another person. In Western thinking there isn't anything that remotely comes close to this attitude; in India, generosity of spirit and action is a typical way of displaying friendship to strangers. The gypsy taught me that when I assume a person is trustworthy it often turns out to be so or actually encourages that person to want to be trustworthy. I learned to not blindly accept others' opinions about a person or group but to use my own experience and perceptions. The danger in Kashmir taught me to allow my dreams to overcome my fear. By not giving in to fear, I was able to make friends in Srinagar, see the area's remarkable handicrafts, and meet the artisans. As a lone American woman, viewed as brave in Kashmiri eyes—I was blessed by warm, special treatment and lasting friendships.

Everywhere in India, from crowded cities to isolated villages, I saw older people integrated into daily life and treated with extraordinary respect. India's ancient tradition of revering elders may be its most powerful and cohesive social force. I experienced the power of the extended family, where elders were revered and looked up to for their wisdom. As an older woman, I was given a seat on crowded buses. Time and time again I saw children kneel down to touch the feet of their grandparents in love and devotion and in return receive a gentle hand on their head, a blessing bestowed. I learned it was the elders who united and guided the family, enjoying their special role as the teachers of family history and conveyers of cultural values. Strong family ties in India embraced elders as part of the family forever; and when they became infirm, they were lovingly cared for at home until they died.

It was during this year in India that the concept of old age as a rich and respected period of life magnetized me and planted the seeds for my future research.

A photo shoot in front of the Taj Mahal Hotel, Bombay, 1973

The Joys and Pains of the Emerging Self

1971–1978

According to Jung, the "path to Self" is particularly a task for the second half of life, a task that gives our lives renewed meaning. He believed that all people develop over their entire lifetime as they grow to know, accept, and integrate the various qualities that make up the self. The self is usually felt as an inner perception through which we are connected to everything else in the universe. Choosing a path with heart, making choices that lead to greater consciousness, involves being in touch with the process of individuation.

At the age of fifty-one, and recently returned from a long sojourn in India, I embarked on the "second half" of my life. Spending an extended time in India gave me the inner resources to grow as an individual.

My India Period

When I returned to Berkeley, inspired and energized by my exposure to all the spiritual, cultural, and social experiences I had seen and been a part of in India, I entered what my friends and family, lovingly but with slight bemusement referred to as "Cec's India Period." Our house and basement were overflowing with boxes and crates of fabulous Indian items that village artisans had asked me to sell for them when I returned to the United States. I had also gathered one-of-a-kind craft items from my work with master craftsmen. Robbie, who had a keen aesthetic appreciation for art, had written to me while I was in India about the possibility of opening a shop on College Avenue to show my one-of-a-kind imports. Excited at the prospect of introducing these high-quality arts and crafts, I scoured India for the most unusual items I could find. I also found an assistant who would take the crates of crafts through U.S. Customs to ensure their safe delivery to my home.

Hoping to bring the vivid colors and feeling of harmony I felt in India into my home, I draped my living room ceiling and windows with a profusion of colorful embroidered Indian saris and fabrics, hanging them so the room resembled the interior of a tent. Low, intricately handcrafted chairs from Iola Basu, the designer in New Delhi, sat by our fireplace. The rest of the house was decorated with paintings, embroideries, carvings, sculptures, and miniatures. My Indian-inspired clothes, made from soft, hand-woven textiles and saris, were fluid and exotic. I delighted in my India period.

Unfortunately, before our enterprise even started, Robbie realized he needed to pursue his career, and I was obliged to find another outlet for my goods. Choosing my finest textiles, I offered them to many art museums in California: the Los Angeles County Museum of Art, the Egg and the Eye Gallery in Los Angeles, the Museum of Contemporary Art in San Diego, and the de Young Museum and the Annenberg Gallery (a member of the American Craft Council) in San Francisco.

Traveling to meet the staff and curators of these prestigious museums and galleries was stimulating and taught me fresh ways to view my collection. As connoisseurs of fine textiles and art, they were thrilled to examine the delicate workmanship of the old, hard-to-find *phulkaris*—large embroidered shawls from northwest India—that I had collected. In the past, when a woman became pregnant, she began creating a *phulkari*. During her pregnancy she meticulously embroidered a three-by-five-foot cotton fabric, expressing her innermost feelings through the fabric, until it was offered as a gift to the newborn on the day of birth. The son or daughter wore the *phulkari* throughout life on auspicious occasions such as weddings, funerals and religious fêtes. The *phulkaris* in my collection were old and rare, for contemporary urban Indian women no longer embroider them.

When the Society for Asian Art in San Francisco saw the diversity of my collection, the curator decided to feature my crafts in a large exhibition, which took place in their stunning second-floor gallery on Sutter Street in San Francisco. The SAA provided all the publicity, mailing out hand-embossed invitations and notifying the *San Francisco Chronicle* and the *Oakland Tribune,* while I sent invitations to family and friends. The opening exhibition was wildly successful. During the two weeks of the show, we sold half the items, with inquiries for appointments to see the rest of the collection in my home.

How relieved I felt to receive a return for the money I had spent buying these items directly from the craftspeople. Though the profits were slim, the rewards of my India endeavor were many—visiting remote villages, handling the challenges of travel as a single woman and gaining confidence in my ability to weather what may lie ahead, becoming friends with the artisans, and becoming a better designer by learning age-old techniques from the masters.

With all this publicity, the de Young Museum called to view my exceptional collection of 16th- and 17th-century Indian miniatures—rich and colorful portrayals of scenes painted on small handmade paper—to purchase. I readily gifted the de Young the six miniatures they chose.

The Egg and the Eye, a prestigious gallery on Wilshire Boulevard in Los Angeles that specialized in crafts from around the world, was also eager to show the collection. Its owners offered to take on the publicity, while I was responsible for bringing all my crafts to Los Angeles to set up the display.

I was moved when Robbie offered to take a couple of days off to drive a U-Haul filled with my Indian goods to L.A. We talked and laughed all the way south, with Robbie sharing the difficulties of raising Jon Robin, his seven-year-old son, alone, making a living, and his desire to return to graduate school in business. This was a time of intimacy that I still cherish, sitting next to each other and talking in the big U-Haul. I recall the times when I traveled abroad whether it was to Peru, India, or Nepal, Robbie was always the one who wanted to drive me to the airport and was the first face I saw eagerly waiting for me as I exited the plane on my return. He worried about me traveling so far away from home and finally felt at ease only when I was home safe. Robbie has always loved Berkeley and wanted to stay here his whole life.

I spent the rest of the week setting up the exhibition with help from the gallery staff, along with my favorite cousin Meralee, with whom I was staying in Beverly Hills. On Friday that week, BJ and Lyn, glamorous in their new saris and Robbie in his Nehru jacket, flew in for the opening of the exhibit that was widely attended by an interesting array of locals. Meralee, who supported and encouraged my endeavors, hosted a brunch in my honor at her beautiful, art-filled Beverly Hills home, serving Indian food as delicious as the best in India.

Once the museums and galleries selected their pieces, I organized two weekend "Garden Happenings" in my home and garden, selling the many remaining crafts. Friends helped contact the curator of the Oakland Museum, Ted Cohen, who loved my Indian collection and graciously loaned display partitions, along with two of his staff to help set up my exhibition.

As visitors entered the garden, they were drawn to a large map of India with bright red dots identifying the areas where

I traveled to find these original crafts. Large black-and-white photographs of the artists creating their crafts surrounded the map with links to their specific areas. These photographs, shot by the gifted Baroda photographer Johdi Bott, were given to me in exchange for a few prized textiles.

Invitation to view my private collection of Indian art

Fascinated by the vision they encountered as they entered, viewers wanted to know about the individual artists, how I had found them, and would I describe their artistic processes. In museum-like fashion, I typed individual descriptions of the items on display. Later, some buyers began corresponding with the artists whose work they had purchased and loved.

In the garden, textiles were set up on movable racks and hung from fruit trees; hand carvings were laid out on long tables set up on the lawn, special cases displayed body adornment and jewelry. The visual effect was stunning; it looked like an exotic stage setting. Inside, the museum helpers draped the living room ceiling with fabrics and lanterns so that the house took on a striking ambience.

The Garden Happenings became events more than art shows, with strangers calling for invitations to the next show! Though I sent out only 150 invitations, many more visitors showed up the second weekend after hearing about it from friends. My family and I, dressed in Indian garb, served iced tea and white wine. As BJ, Lyn, and I assisted the customers, my mother and my good friend Dolores Bermak acted as cashiers.

The attendees left with their treasures, but much more was in storage in my basement and even more was arriving. The Indian artists, who had become my friends, were thrilled to receive acknowledgment and payment for their work, amazed that people in the United States wanted to buy their works of art.

This period proved to be an important one in my individuation process. It opened up a rich avenue of growth and friendship that continued in the years that followed. Not only had I followed my dream, a fulfilling and meaningful journey of its own, but I had also taken risks, traveled alone in remote areas of India, walked into the tribal regions, and learned to trust my inner voice and make decisions. I had no idea that the crafts would speak as eloquently to others in the United States as they had to me. Fortuitously, Californians were hungry for the exotic and ready to appreciate art they had not seen before. After all the journey had done for me, I felt proud that I had, in a small way, brought the "unknown art of India" back to the United States.

In India I had met travelers who were there on spiritual quests to learn how to meditate. Whenever possible, I visited ashrams and inquired about diverse spiritual practices. One meditation technique that appealed to me was Vipassana, which offered ten-day silent retreats. I spoke to both Indians and foreigners who had participated in these retreats and learned how this training had made a positive difference in their lives. I vowed that upon my return to the States I would check out Vipassana.

Vipassana, a simple yet highly disciplined practice, can lead to peace of mind and self-transformation through self-observation. The meditator learns to find the path to his or her non- judgmental, compassionate thoughts. Unlike most meditation techniques, Vipassana does not adhere to any particular religion or doctrine. It has been handed down from the time of Buddha to the present through an unbroken chain of teachers, with Satya Narayan Goenka considered the current authority.

Back in the Bay Area, I located a Goenka-type Vipassana group teaching a ten-day silent meditation retreat in the old-growth forest of Mendocino. We'd be using the facilities of an old Boy Scout camp, sharing bathroom and shower facilities with no hot water, and sleeping in rustic tent cabins with no telephones or connection to the outside world. Using our flashlights, it was a challenge to find the meditation hall through the thick tree growth, especially for the early morning session. Starting at five in the morning, we meditated twelve hours a day, with breaks for meals and rest from the grueling task of sitting all day on a meditation pillow in the lotus position. We were allowed no books, writing, contact with the outside world (except for emergencies), nor talking. During the breaks, I took off on a long run as soon as I got out of sight of the group (we were only supposed to do walking meditation). I needed to release some of my energy after sitting in lotus position for so long.

I did learn to slow down while eating the delicious vegetarian food cooked by volunteers. Instead of my usual gulping, we were instructed to mindfully chew each mouthful. This is when I first learned of the Moosewood Cookbook, which has become a staple of my recipes for the last forty years. Sometimes during meditation, I found myself dozing off but would then suddenly wake up and return to focus with a peaceful mind, feeling completely regenerated.

For the next retreat I chose a less rustic location, registering for a ten-day silent retreat at the Novitiate Jesuit Center in Los Gatos, California. The beautiful old buildings were a home for retired priests, who were famous for wines they made from the surrounding vineyards. I had my own sparsely furnished room: a bed, a chair, a lamp, and no mirrors except in the community showers. The views toward the Santa Cruz Mountains were exquisite, with lovely trails meandering through the acres of vineyards. Again, I meditated for twelve hours a day, ate wholesome vegetarian meals, and ran during the breaks (against the rules!).

I returned from the retreat clear in mind, and in lean physical shape. After these retreats, I moved and thought mindfully; I felt healthy and full of energy. At home after the Novitiate retreat my women friends believed I'd had a facelift because I looked so tranquil and refreshed! Since then, I've taken similar retreats in England, the rustic Santa Barbara mountains, and Spirit Rock Meditation Center in Marin County, invariably returning home renewed.

Chomolungma: Mount Everest Base Camp

Following my 1970 trip to India, I continued to exhibit and sell Indian crafts. By 1973, some of the original merchandise had been held up in Bombay customs and none of my efforts from home could release it. Customers were requesting more of specific pieces that I no longer had. Since these crafts were one-of-a-kind items, reordering them required a one-to-one meeting with the artists. It was time for me to return to India.

What better opportunity could there be than to combine a trip to India with my passion for mountains by joining Mountain Travel on their expedition to Mount Everest's base camp in Nepal? During my trip to Nepal with Lyn three years earlier, we had met climbers who raved about the wonders of climbing in Nepal. Because of Nepal's Buddhist culture and the ever-present snow-clad mountains in the distant horizons, I had hoped to return one day to climb to the Everest base camp. Returning home from that first Nepal trek, I embarked on a regime of gradually increasing my running from one mile to five miles, eventually running hills with a weighted backpack. My jaunts through the Berkeley hills gave me the energy, strength, and courage to tackle Mount Everest.

Climbing in Nepal to Everest's base camp is a rite of passage for most mountain climbers. At the age of fifty-three I felt uneasy but ready for the challenge. Although it is no longer the case, in those days only the highly trained climbers strove for the top. I knew that just reaching the 17,500-foot base camp would be a triumph for me.

What is it about the mountains that calls me back again and again? In the mountains I feel at peace and in harmony with the world; they are spiritual places for me. I find climbing a mountain comparable to reaching toward the heavens, moving toward the transcendent. Mountain climbers are courageous in their attempt to conquer the mountain and willing to take outrageous risks—from avalanches to falling rocks to extreme cold and exposure. High up, open to the elements, they share a common experience and kinship.

As I struggled on Everest with the air becoming colder and thinner, psychological challenges arose, forcing me to call upon new found inner resources. Our small group of hikers welcomed the silence as we walked in an unspoken intimacy. Without distractions, climbing becomes meditative. For me, problems dissipate as I connect with a larger presence, a higher power. Ultimately, there's joy in sharing the triumph of reaching our goal.

The hike to the base camp was a rigorous twenty-six-day trek, planned as a gradual acclimation to the increasing altitude. We started hiking in warm weather in shorts at 5,000 feet. Ten days later, we were in long pants and parkas, trudging through snow and ice. By day eighteen we could see our breath as we exhaled. By then, we were sleeping in our tents at subzero temperatures.

There were two twenty-eight-year-old women on the trip. Barbara was a marathon runner and accomplished climber. In top physical condition, she ran ahead of everyone when we began our hike and arrived in camp a few hours before the rest of us. But at 13,000 feet, as the air became thinner and colder, she slowed down. This upset her for she was used to being ahead of the crowd.

As the only two single women on the trip, Barbara and I were assigned as tent mates. During the long evenings, when the sun set around 4:30, our group retired to our tents to rest, read by candlelight or flashlight, write in our journals, or reflect on our day of adventures and commiserate on our aches and pains. Evenings cuddled in my cozy sleeping bag and tent reading and writing in my journal were a wonderful time for me. However, Barbara dreaded what she called "the long, dark, cold evenings with nothing to do." She cried most nights because she didn't like being stuck in the tent for so many hours. She was upset that her conditioning wasn't working at the high altitude.

With sympathy and concern, the group loaned her books and offered her writing materials to help her pass the hours in the tent. I encouraged her to talk about the psychological difficulties of the trip, so she could gain the inner strength and motivation to keep going. I asked that she consider the other rewards of the trip—the majestic beauty of the mountains, Buddhist culture, and the warm hospitality offered by the villagers. Despite our efforts, the challenges were too much for her, and at 14,000 feet she returned to Kathmandu to find a flight home.

Carefully crossing the Khumbu Icefall on my Mt. Everest trek

The other young woman, Karen, a strong walker but not a marathon runner, had the positive attitude to see her through the challenges to make base camp. Karen and her husband Jon had arrived in Kathmandu to discover that Pan Am had lost their luggage with all their hiking gear. They took the news in stride, shopping at the local market for tennis shoes and a few essentials to supplement what our trip members donated of their extra clothes. I admired their ability to readily adapt and their confidence that it would all work out. Three days later at about 8,000 feet, porters came running with Karen and Jon's lost duffels slung over their shoulders.

For three weeks, walking and talking on the trail to Mount Everest, Karen and I became close friends. We shared our life stories, finding our dreams and views of the world strikingly similar. Not only was she charming and beautiful—tall and slender with brown wavy hair—but she had a thoughtfulness and maturity about her that was both open and spiritual. Each evening over the campfire, after an exhausting day, we discussed our philosophies, our thoughts on Buddhism, poverty in the region, and the destruction of the environment around us. Since all the trees had been felled for housing and fuel, the porters were forced to return to Kathmandu—more than a day's hike—to carry up heavy loads of wood on their backs.

Though Karen was twenty-five years younger than me, her knees, like mine, ballooned at about 14,000 feet. In pain we limped up the trail side by side with the aid of walking sticks. Sharing our temporary infirmity with a sense of humor helped us persevere. Luckily, within a few days the swelling was gone and we were able to continue the trip unimpeded.

At about 16,000 feet, I developed a piercing headache. I thought I might be catching a cold, as other members of our group were coughing and sniffling. I plodded on. By early evening we reached base camp at over 17,000 feet. It might have felt like more of a triumph had I not been ill. That night, with no letup of throbbing in my head plus shivering in the freezing temperature, I found it impossible to sleep. Although I was grateful that I had climbed this far, altitude sickness and the possibility of pulmonary edema overcame me.

The next morning as our group prepared to climb higher to Kala Pattar, an 18,180-foot peak, I was so altitude-sick that Phil, our careful trip doctor, and I concurred that I needed to return immediately to a lower elevation. Ray, our knowledgeable trip leader, assigned a porter to accompany me down the mountain to a lower-elevation hotel where I might be able to spend the night to recuperate. The rest of the group would remain at the higher altitude of base camp another day, then hike down to the Lukla Airport where we would all meet to catch a return flight to Kathmandu. I would later discover that I had been hiking with pneumonia.

The day the porter and I descended happened to be Thanksgiving Day. As we trudged down 4,000 feet in the heavy snow to a hotel I had read about, I kept hoping they would have a room for me. The Hotel Everest View was perched in a majestic location with a panoramic view of Mount Everest. I had my sleeping bag and was willing to sleep in the hotel lobby or on the floor if necessary. I craved a roof over my head, a hot shower (we hadn't bathed in twenty days except in icy streams), and a warm bed. Synchronicity prevailed—one tiny closet room was available! The manager apologized that the hotel was fully occupied with a private group, but because I was a woman alone who had trekked from base camp, he wanted to accommodate me on our American Thanksgiving Day. The tiny room with a bath felt sublime. Throwing off my heavy, worn clothes, I jumped into a hot shower, washed my hair, and dressed in the last clean outfit in my backpack. Miraculously, my headache had vanished at the lower altitude.

Hosting the private group in the hotel was former Secretary of Defense Robert McNamara. Hearing that an American woman from California had walked with a porter from base camp, he promptly invited me to join his entourage of friends such as Rob Shapiro and Nigel Nicholson. They had flown in from Kathmandu with turkeys, champagne, and traditional trimmings for the adventure of a private Thanksgiving dinner at the highest hotel in the world at 12,729 feet. At the time, in 1973, I was ignorant of McNamara's role in Vietnam. Yet recovering from serious sickness and exhaustion, I was happy to indulge in delicious food and company. I was the sole woman attending this lavish dinner party, enjoying the dinner, French wine, and fascinating guests.

The next day, clean, fed, and revived, I hiked another 3,000 feet down the mountain to meet the rest of the group at the tiny Lukla airport at 9,380 feet. Since Lukla's short runway sits between two immense mountains, it's a dangerous airport for landings and takeoffs, so only planes with short landing and takeoff capabilities can use it. A few of our group, daunted by the danger of the Lukla Airport, hiked the extra week to return to Kathmandu. Although Lukla had been socked in fog for a week, a sudden break in the weather enabled the rest of us to fly out that day.

The Joys and Pains of the Emerging Self

In Kathmandu, our group stayed at the old-world Shanker Hotel, a former royal palace with beautiful gardens, only a twenty-minute walk outside the hustle and bustle of the city. For elite trekking companies, Shanker Hotel was the choice spot to bring their clients after arduous trips because of its tranquil surroundings, spacious gardens, good talk, and the camaraderie of the bar. Meeting in the cocktail lounge, warm, bathed, and rested, my fellow hikers and I celebrated our climb to the base camp of one of the highest mountains in the world. Although I was coughing uncontrollably, completing the trip left me feeling stronger and more confident.

The bar was the busiest spot in the Shanker Hotel, with blindingly bright lights and not a comfortable place to sit. It was very crowded, with old high bar stools that made it impossible to talk with other people. But I knew the lounge could be changed into a hospitable gathering spot and visualized a plan.

Kathmandu was an exotic, fascinating city in 1973, and I wanted to stay on to explore it further before leaving for India. Feeling up to anything after the Everest trek, I made an unusual proposal to the hotel manager: I would completely redecorate the lounge in exchange for all my expenses while I worked on the project—room, food, drinks, laundry, and incidentals. He readily agreed. We agreed that three weeks would be the maximum time to complete this project.

The complimentary stay at the grand old Shanker Hotel included dinner, which was a most nourishing aspect of my stay, as the waiters hovered over the single woman they knew was constantly coughing and temporarily working at the hotel. They offered me specialties not on the menu. New friends invited me for drinks and dessert while the bar was being transformed. My request for a car and English-speaking driver was readily granted. With a car and driver, I could get around Kathmandu to meet with the artisans who would fabricate the new furniture and lighting and weave the carpet and upholstery fabrics, .

Not knowing where to start, I made inquiries at the local bazaar—a busy, thriving area full of talented artisans who could fabricate anything with their hands. With the driver of the hotel car acting as guide and interpreter, I accomplished much in a few weeks. Showing pictures of the hotel and old cocktail lounge, I was able to explain my mission without speaking. We located artisans by networking and running about Kathmandu, asking each tradesperson where to find the next rug or build the furniture needed. One of the rewards of this project was becoming acquainted with the local Nepalese, meeting their families, and enjoying invitations into their homes.

When I finished my decorating project, the lounge had been transformed. The black-and-white room, with zebra prints woven into the textiles for the banquettes, bar stools, and carpeting, was dazzling. Splashes of bright reds and oranges covered two walls as a person entered, and large pillows carried out the color scheme with locally woven silks from silk farms just outside Kathmandu. The lighting was now soft and seductive.

The remarkable fabric of people coming together who

helped create the lounge was all pulled together in two weeks' time. Everyone who came to the cocktail lounge of the Shanker thought it was a huge improvement and the perfect spot to drink and meet. It became a haven where friends could intimately talk.

The Shanker Hotel invited the mayor of Kathmandu and other prominent officials to the opening champagne ceremony. Owners and managers of other hotels joined in the celebration. Their laudatory toasts left me proud and happy to have accomplished such a coup.

My Healing Hospital Stay

My Everest cough persisted after I left Nepal even though Kathmandu's local doctor had given me a tonic and a clean bill of health. I had fully expected it to disappear, but, unfortunately, by the time I arrived in New Delhi, I still had a cough that was now accompanied by yellow mucus. Another doctor ordered a chest X-ray and an antibiotic, finding nothing wrong. For a few weeks the cough seemed better.

Lulled into believing that all was well, I continued to travel and follow up on my grant of three years earlier, meeting again with the artisans I had collaborated with earlier. I was greeted like a long-lost family member in each village to which I returned. It was gratifying to see the fruits of our years of exchanges. Conditions in the villages were improved through the income the villagers received from their crafts sales.

Happily, Lyn came to visit me in India over her Christmas

break from college. I was tired of traveling alone. We stayed at the Imperial Hotel in New Delhi, and I introduced her to some of my close Indian friends. The joy of having Lyn along kept my mind off the persistent cough that still nagged me. Most of the time we traveled together I remained upbeat, but as the afternoons wore on I'd say to Lyn: "I'm exhausted. I have to go back to the hotel." I didn't recognize my lack of energy as a symptom; I just wanted to keep moving and sharing India with my daughter. In Srinagar, Kashmir, I introduced Lyn to the joyful experience of a houseboat on Dal Lake in winter. The snow-clad Himalayas encircled us and the boat was heated by a wood burning stove that my friend Mr. Butt, the owner of the boat, would light as the evening approached. When we wanted a shower he would start the water an hour before, because it took that long to prepare.

Mr. Butt told us that the Indian Army had winter troops stationed in the nearby mountains, patrolling the border to Pakistan. They had installed a simple rope tow in order to get up the mountain and ski down. When we arrived there they asked us if we knew how to ski, offering us their military-issued boots and jackets to use. They were astonished that two American women could ski as well as we did, for Indian women at that time didn't ski. This visit to Kashmir remains vivid in my memory for the warmth and loving time Lyn and I shared.

We spent the last week in Madras before Lyn returned to the United States. There in the extreme heat and humidity, the constant coughing returned, and I could hardly sleep. When

Lyn left, my spirits plunged and I felt tired. We had such a good time together that I attributed my low energy to her departure and to the prospect of traveling the rest of the trip alone.

As I made my way through Sri Lanka, still following the crafts, I grew more and more exhausted, until one day a month later in the mountain town of Kandy, I couldn't move or get out of bed. I called the American consulate in Colombo, who ordered that I find a car and driver and return immediately to Colombo. He arranged for a doctor and a room at the Joseph Fraser Memorial Hospital.

It turned out I had pneumonia and a damaged lung. The local doctors informed me that my condition was serious; I could fly home to be treated at a U.S. hospital or remain at Joseph Fraser. I chose to stay and be treated in Colombo. Alone in a strange country, I was frightened and thought I might die. On February 18, 1974, I wrote a letter home to my family with instructions to send a copy to my lawyer, Henry. The letter included the following passage:

As I lie here I am overcoming myself, affirming myself . . . time, fear, no longer exist. I am strangely calm. Not the calm of emptiness but of the heart. I know with certainty that there is something indestructible in me, which shall prevail.

I remained at the well-run private hospital for two weeks, receiving excellent treatment from a solicitous staff and under the care of an expert Singhalese doctor trained in Edinburgh. Joseph Fraser was a wealthy Englishman who had given his spacious home to the city of Colombo to be used as a hospital for foreigners. I was assigned a private room with the luxury of mosquito netting around my bed, and a window looking out onto a lush tropical garden. Upstairs, a library full of English and French classics and the most current magazines and newspapers coming daily from London were available to read. My treatment consisted of healthy food, vitamins, rest, and respiratory/pulmonary therapy to remove the secretions from my lungs. It was an old-fashioned, hands-on treatment of postural drainage, with my body hanging over the edge of the bed as the therapist vigorously thumped on my back to loosen the phlegm. We repeated the treatment every two hours. I have never experienced a more nurturing, healing hospital stay. The staff—room cleaners, therapists, cook, nurses, doctor— were all personally committed to my recovery. Amazingly, I was able to order any nutritious food I desired, with the chef visiting each morning to ask what I would like, so he could procure the local produce or whatever fresh fish I requested. Conscientious nurses brought coconuts from the trees in their garden for me to drink the milk, which they insisted was healing. The doctor visited at least twice a day to check my progress and make sure his instructions were followed.

On the second day of hospitalization, still feeling weak and fearful of what might happen so far away from home, I saw a handsome man poke his head in the door of my room to ask, "Is there an American woman here?" I nodded. Another American patient, who had just been discharged, told him I had just been admitted. He entered with a bag over his shoulders and showed me his treasure, a pet cobra! He handed me the three-inch-thick snake, and though terrified, I put my hand out, acting brave to make a good impression! The guest was Abe Blank, an American photographer in his thirties who was working for *National Geographic* on his way to New Guinea on an assignment.

Abe visited each day for the next few days with his pet snake, and we soon got to know each other. He was preparing to leave Sri Lanka the next week and asked if I could receive permission from the doctor to go out to tea. Since I was beginning to walk around and feeling considerably better, the doctor granted permission. In less then a week's time at Joseph Fraser, the seriousness of my condition had diminished.

Abe and I took a rickshaw to a nearby hotel café. During our tea Abe handed me a joint. When we finished our tea he asked if I wanted to go to bed. Stoned on grass, high on champagne, and enamored with his energy, I replied yes, and next thing I knew we were in a room. Afterward, we rushed back to the hospital. The doctor, on his evening rounds, pinched my cheek to tell me how much better I was looking and that the outing must have been good for me. For the rest of that week, I joined Abe for "tea."

Abe and I remained good friends long after we returned from our overseas travels. He visited my home with numerous lady friends, joined me on a Vipassana retreat in the mountains of Santa Barbara, traveled with Don and me on our trips to New Guinea, hiked with us in Wyoming, came with us to Hunza with his new wife, and joined us hiking in the Dolomites with his ex-wife.

After two weeks in the hospital in Colombo, my cough

was gone and my energy was returning. I was released with the warning to take it easy—no mountain hiking, stay only in good hotels, eat carefully, and see a specialist upon arrival in Bombay. I followed their advice and found a doctor in Bombay through my friend Gopi Mehta. Gopi drove me to each appointment. After appointments I would join Gopi, her husband, Madhu, and their two small sons, Nimai and Nitai, for home-cooked dinners.

I wrote the manager of the Taj Mahal Hotel there, telling him of my illness and hospital stay, and my plan to recuperate at the Taj. He gave me a special rate, offering me the use of all the hotel's healing facilities. For the next weeks, I lived at the Taj in an airy upper-floor tower room overlooking the Arabian Sea and Gate of India, as I swam in the pool each day, exercised, and attended yoga classes. After three weeks I felt rejuvenated and ready to return to the States. I look back at this experience as yet another reason to be grateful for being alive.

Reconnecting with My Jewish Roots

Although I am not a religious person, when I was away from my own country for extended periods, I sought reconnection with my Jewish heritage. Traveling alone for months in India, I was feeling rootless. I longed for a place where I'd be welcomed and feel at home, not the usual club or bar where foreigners gather, but a spiritual connection to my Jewish roots.

The Joys and Pains of the Emerging Self

While alone in Bombay, now Mumbai, I approached the front desk at the Taj Hotel and asked if they knew of a Jewish person who might accompany me to the synagogue. They gave me the name of Salome Parikh, a well-known half-Jewish feminist writer for the Times of India. Salome offered to pick me up for the Friday night service, held in a private home near the Taj. We learned that Jewish homes were being used in place of synagogues because most of the younger Jewish population of Mumbai had migrated to Israel. Mostly older folks remained.

It was Salome's first visit to this house. After the service, we were overwhelmed with dinner invitations from the appreciative congregation. Each time I return to India, I again see my good friend Salome.

After the heartbreaking terrorist attack on Mumbai in 2008, Salome wrote incisive and touching articles covering the horrible killing of innocent people and the damage to the Hotel Taj, the Oberoi Hotel, and the Chabad house, a Jewish outreach center.

With my connections to artists in India renewed by my 1973 trip, I returned to the States fired up and continued to show my Indian art and crafts to museums and private collectors. During the 1970s there seemed to be an endless interest in and appreciation of the beautiful work of Indian artisans.

When not working on my craft or interior design business, I was active in politics and environmental issues through groups like the Sierra Club and Save the Redwoods. It was a rich period of growth and excitement about the life I had created by myself, for myself. My "individuation process" was progressing. I felt healthy, vigorous, inspired, and more complete inside. I was eager for each day and passionate about my life. Glad to be single, I had no interest in marrying.

However, a meaningful relationship with an old acquaintance evolved. I had met Jack years earlier when he brought his daughter Debbie (one of Lyn's girlfriends) over to our house on Hillegass Avenue for a sleepover. As an architect, he found our home interesting, and we spent time talking about art and architecture. Jack came into my life again after he separated from his wife. He invited me out and we found we had much in common.

Savoring Machu Picchu with Jack Robbins

The Joys and Pains of the Emerging Self

We joined a group for a monthlong trip in the Andes, in-cluding hiking to Machu Picchu in Peru. I planned to stay on afterwards and continue to Bolivia and Ecuador. In prepara-tion for my trip, I enrolled in a language program in Guana-juato, Mexico, to study Spanish. There I lived with a Mexican family and steeped myself in Spanish for eight weeks, emerg-ing from the course with a basic grasp of the language. At the end of our trip to Peru, Jack returned to the States and I took off alone for Bolivia and Ecuador to visit craft and textile con-tacts provided by the World Craft Council.

Traveling alone, I spent most nights in the hotel planning the next day's activities scouting for crafts and textiles. It was a lonely period. Knowing I would be welcomed, I sought out a Jewish connection or synagogue for my sense of place. Again the American consulate helped me meet some Jewish people. I had heard that numerous Jewish families who escaped Nazi Germany had settled in Bolivia. What I didn't know was that the Jews in Bolivia were continually being spied upon by Nazis who had also migrated to Bolivia and were actively working against the Jews.

I called the Jewish family the consulate had recommended. They advised me to make sure the taxi drove to many differ-ent spots before arriving at their home, so that if my hotel had informed the taxi driver where I was headed we could shake anyone who might be following me. There were spies all over La Paz during this period.

As soon as I rang their doorbell, they looked through the peephole, whisking me in quickly. The family greeted me with open arms and a wonderful meal. I found out they had been wealthy in Germany and had luckily been able to bring limited funds to Bolivia. They were trying to establish a business but finding it difficult because of the anti-Semitism. Their funds were dwindling, and they hoped to leave Bolivia for another South American country with greater freedoms, perhaps Brazil, but it was difficult for them to obtain exit visas.

The family told me it was a harrowing time to be living in Bolivia because the right-wing government gave a "nod" to Nazis. It's no wonder to me that Bolivia is now Socialist and elected the first indigenous president, Evo Morales, because there was horrible fear and repression there in 1977. Toward the minority white European Bolivians, not only the Jews, but also the indigenous people were second-class citizens. By contrast, when I visited my father in the late 1960s in Brazil, Brazil had opened its doors to Jewish immigrants from Germany, China, and other parts of the world, offering religious freedom. In the large Jewish community in São Paulo there were numerous synagogues thriving. Now Brazil is a prosperous, democratic country.

From Bolivia, I boarded the rickety train to Guayaquil in Ecuador. For many years I had dreamed of sailing to the Galapagos Islands, 600 miles off the shore of Ecuador. I had read Darwin's *Origin of the Species* and believed fervently in his theory. It was in the Galapagos that he found an array of birds, reptiles, and plants that had developed in isolation from the mainland but often differed from similar species on neighboring islands. These differing characteristics, he theorized, could be explained only by a gradual transformation of the various species. As a believer in evolution, I wanted to see proof of this theory with my own eyes.

Spontaneously, I booked a flight to Baltra, the starting point for Galapagos trips. Usually reservations for these trips were made at least a year in advance. I figured if I went there alone, I would meet people on the flight from Guayaquil to the Galapagos and be able to make the necessary boat arrangements. I met some couples from Germany and France on the plane, mostly folks in their twenties and thirties, who were also hoping to locate a boat for a week. We decided to join forces. After much searching in Baltra, we found a boat, but there was just enough room for the couples, not for me. I had come this long distance to sail in the Galapagos Islands and now at this late moment was stranded alone on the dock. As the boat departed without me I waved bravely, but once it was out of sight I burst into tears.

My tears were momentary, however, as I pondered a solution to this latest challenge. I did have a name of a local boat outfitter tucked into my address book. Making some inquiries of locals on the dock, I found the outfitter's name and address and walked two miles on a trail on the water's edge of the island to reach the Angermeyers' bungalow on a promontory looking out over the bay. The Angermeyers were a couple in their sixties whose parents had left Germany during World War I to find a safe haven in which to settle and raise their family. They had made a business of showing tourists the Galapagos Islands. They were certified naturalists, sailors, and boat makers, who not only knew the islands well but were also reported to be wonderful cooks.

The Angermeyers told me that their sailboat with auxiliary motor was promised to a German client arriving in Baltra the next day. Perhaps he might be willing to share the boat with me. Fortunately, the client, a scientist and photographer, agreed to share the boat if I paid part of the cost. He turned out to be an easygoing and knowledgeable traveling companion for the six-day trip, later sending me many photos of our journey.

On my return from the Galapagos, I stopped over in Quito, the capital of Ecuador, to check out its famous handicraft markets. Without an itinerary, I let the few days in Quito unfold. As I meandered through the city streets on the cold September day, I found a welcoming bookstore on the ground floor of a private home. An inviting fire burned in the fireplace as I entered, and the first book my eyes focused on was *The Bar Mitzvah Book*. Surprised, I asked the proprietor whether there were Jewish people in Quito. "Oh yes, and I think it's their high holiday today," he replied. My datebook told me it was Yom Kippur, the Jewish New Year. I asked if there was a synagogue in town, jumped into a taxi, and headed to the address the proprietor gave me. Synchronicity again!

I arrived at a synagogue while the congregation was singing Kol Nidre, the prayer for those who have died. Tears welled up in my eyes as the familiar aria filled me with thoughts of my grandmother and sitting next to her in past Yom Kippurs. A handsome man approached, put his hand on my shoulder,

"Have you lost a loved one, too?" he asked. Not sure how to reply, I nodded. I wiped my tears as I was ushered upstairs to sit with the women.

At the break, the congregation gathered outside on the steps. Strangers introduced themselves, inviting me to their homes for dinner that evening. I felt connected even though I was a foreigner. At the time, the import of these synchronistic events was not clear to me, but in retrospect, I recognized that they connected me through the collective unconscious of our Jewish heritage.

A reunion with cherished Antioch classmates
Left to right: Christie, Sara, me, Ailish

Late Bloomer

1978–1984

I am a great believer in late bloomers because, like my mother, I too was one. With my children grown and living outside the home, I was seeking new avenues of growth, exploring the Human Potential Movement through study and seminars. My roommate at one weekend workshop at the Esalen Institute enthusiastically described the Holistic Studies Program at Antioch University West in San Francisco, where she had just enrolled. Her description of this new three-year experiential master's degree program seemed to be exactly what I was looking for.

Will Schutz, who founded and created the Holistic Studies Program at Antioch University West in San Francisco, happened to be teaching at Esalen the weekend I was there. Schutz, a doctor of psychology and scholar from Harvard, had left academia to help found the Human Potential Movement with headquarters at Esalen, in California's Big Sur region. Having been away from school for forty years, I wasn't sure if I would be admitted into his graduate program in psychology. I was also hesitant about attending the required evening classes because I considered myself a "day person." Dr. Schutz encouraged me to apply, saying, "You can choose to be a day or a night person." His belief system was that everything is your own choice, whatever you do. You can choose to discover and live your full potential. You are responsible for all your actions. The concept that I was responsible for my own choices gave me a great sense of empowerment.

Those powerful words struck a chord at the center of my being and so, at the age of fifty-nine, I returned to school, but not without some trepidation. Could I keep up with the coursework? Would the younger students accept me? I put my doubts aside and jumped right in. I deliberately changed my day-person thinking and, surprisingly, adjusted to night classes.

Antioch University West was an unusual place and proved to be a unique and incredibly rich experience. The graduate students came from all over the United States, Holland, England, Spain, Korea, and Israel. Many were professionals— lawyers, nurses, artists, social workers, dental hygienists, and massage therapists.

I was older than the other students, most of whom were in their twenties and thirties, and I appeared to them to be traditional and established because of the fashionable way I dressed. I thought a few of them were crazy pot smokers, although all I knew about pot was from Rob and Lyn, who at one time or another smoked. At first my fellow students didn't take me seriously, but I was so engaged and participated so fully that they came to appreciate me. In turn, I began to see that they were intelligent and out of the ordinary people who were open to new ideas.

A whole new world opened up before me. We were introduced to Rolfing, acupuncture, meditation, Feldenkrais, the Aston technique, running as therapy, psychodrama, sensitivity training, group process, and other modalities of the Human Potential Movement, which were designed to teach us about the mind, body, and spirit. During a weekend program at Esalen I signed up for a Rolfing session (a form of massage to release and realign the body). In those days I was running regularly, and after my first Rolfing, my hips moved more freely, making my running stride longer and easier. I also received instruction in Feldenkrais, a system for alignment and movement through self-awareness. It was Dr. Schutz who first brought Moshe Feldenkrais to the United States to teach his innovative methods of healing the body.

We were introduced to Chinese medicine by Jack Worsley, who responded to Dr. Schutz's invitation to teach our class, the first graduate program in holistic studies in the United States. Jack, the leading authority on Chinese medicine, had studied acupuncture in China for many years and it was he who introduced it to the Western world. At his London school, he trained acupuncture students who came from all over the world, to become some of the best in their field. To this day, I continue to use this powerful treatment for aches and pains.

Will Schutz was well known to be a master at leading encounter groups. We sat in a circle to talk about whatever was weighing on our minds. There were two important guidelines: that you tell the truth and that you be responsible for your own actions. Will had a knack for looking around the room and spotting those people whom he felt had "energy and were ready to speak." The rest of us were encouraged to respond honestly to what was being said, often saying things like, "That's a bunch of crap," or "What a cop-out," or "You're boring."

For some students it was easy to speak up, perhaps because of their age or prior experience, but for me it was most difficult. I didn't feel comfortable airing my inner feelings to a group, nor did I trust their reactions. Whether because of my age or my upbringing, this blunt and often harsh method of responding to another's vulnerability was a completely new way of relating. Will's philosophy was to sit back, listen attentively, and at appropriate times direct the discussion in such a way that we felt comfortable in revealing ourselves. I took a long while to open up, but as the group grew closer, more and more I began to trust those in the group.

In one challenging exercise called "High School Dance," Will asked us to form two lines, women on one side and men on the other. The men would choose a woman partner they desired. Imagine my anxiety as I waited to be chosen, knowing I was the oldest in the group. We would then discuss our feelings about being chosen, left out, feeling undesirable or unloved. Then we reversed it with women asking men to be their partners. Often the discussion that followed these exercises brought up deep issues of inclusion or rejection in our lives.

Late Bloomer

One day Will announced that we would have our next encounter without clothes! One woman kept covering a scar on her stomach, claiming it made her ugly. Even though she was the most beautiful woman, she saw herself as ugly because of this scar. I was focusing on the other women's tight, firm bodies, while feeling mine was sagging here and there. But to my surprise, the students in the group didn't see me that way. They told me I was beautiful as I was, which came as a revelation to me.

Angelina, a student from Madrid, raised her hand one day in an encounter group. In tears, she said, "I have herpes and what will I do when I return to my fiancé in Spain?" There was silence, and then another woman said she too had herpes. But, she said, she had learned how to treat it when it was about to break out. A few others offered their experiences and advice. Will Schutz said, "Will those people with herpes please raise their hands?" Gradually, one by one, almost everyone raised a hand. Angelina slowly wiped the tears from her eyes, realizing she was not alone. That's one of the most important things we can learn—that you are not alone; that there are many people out there like you. Realizing that our individual vulnerabilities might be shared by others, that we were not alone, was a huge benefit that came out of this group process.

Special Friends from Graduate School

Some of my closest lifetime friendships were formed during this three-year M.A. program at Antioch. While I was working on my master's thesis, I met with Marilyn Kriegel every week at her home office in Muir Beach. She was the instructor at Antioch who instantly confirmed the value of studying positive models of women in their seventies and eighties, which I had chosen as my research subject. She was supportive and encouraging throughout the long process of interviewing and writing. We established a close relationship that after our Antioch days became a friendship that included a kayak trip with Marilyn to the Sea of Cortez to see whales mating and a weeklong Salmon River trip with her husband, Bob, and Don and me. When we were assigned to give a talk in Marilyn's class on thinking, I appeared in hiking clothes and boots, wearing my backpack. When asked why I was in this get-up, I replied, "I'm dressed as if I am in the mountains on a backpack trip, where I feel completely at home and confident." In my hiking clothes, my level of comfort and confidence carried over into my talk.

For me Christie, Sara, and Ailish were the most interesting of all the students at Antioch. Christie was blonde, blue-eyed, and came from an upper-class family in Chicago. It was evident as soon as she spoke that she was well educated, bright, and had a great sense of humor. She began a friendship with Paul, an articulate, athletic, and spiritual man in our program. Christie and Paul became the center of the in-group, inviting other students over for dinners and parties. I suspected that I was not invited to those parties because of my age.

In our second year at Antioch, Christie and I discovered we had both been to India and were interested in Vipassana meditation. We drove off for a week of silent meditation with Ruth Dennison, a master Zen monk and respected teacher of Vipassana, to the southern California desert near Joshua Tree. Heading over the Carson Pass, we encountered treacherous ice on the road and stopped to spend the night at a bed and breakfast. Christie and I talked long into the night about everything—our mothers, family, hopes, and dreams—and became close friends by opening up to each other. In the morning, with the sun out, we headed south on Route 395 to the retreat.

Our retreat schedule included early morning meditation and an organic, healthy breakfast, then more meditation, lunch, and a break until afternoon meditation. Reading, writing, and speaking were prohibited at this retreat. I found a trail that I ran on during the break, though running was also a no-no. I couldn't have made it through that all-day sitting without the exercise. Ruth Dennison offered about forty minutes instruction per day on "sensing" meditation, moving our attention to different parts of our body. At one point when my back was beginning to hurt from sitting in the lotus position for hours on the floor, I directed my thoughts to that painful place in my back and, astonishingly, the discomfort disappeared. Later, I asked Ruth if this was a way of pain management, and she replied that it was a reliably effective way. Vipassana meditation taught me a valuable tool, how to watch my breath, focus, clear my mind, and deal with pain.

This week at Joshua Tree cemented my friendship with Christie for the rest of our lives. We came away from the silent retreat clear-headed, high, and happy to have shared this deep experience. Since Christie lived in Berkeley, I introduced her to my younger daughter, Lyn, who was also living in Berkeley attending Boalt Law School. About the same age and with similar interests, the two young women became friends. Their friendship continued later when they both lived in Washington, D.C.

Christie met Roger in San Francisco in 1983 in the waiting room of a therapist. Christie would come out tearful and Roger, next in line for the therapist, would be there to hand her a Kleenex and comfort her. After a few such encounters, they had coffee together which was the start of a happy relationship. Christie and Roger married, then had their first child, Ben, right after she finished coursework for her Ph.D. in 1987. Their second child, Hillary, was born on Valentine's Day 1990. Christie finished her dissertation and graduated in 1992, working in her field throughout her children's youth. She and Roger moved to Washington, D.C., where Roger started a career that eventually led him to the U.S. Green Building Council.

Between 1997 and 2002 Christie finished training as a psychoanalyst at the Baltimore Washington Institute. In order to remain fit through it all, she exercised daily, driving to her gym at 5 a.m., racing back home to feed the children when they awoke, then rushing to the office for her first appointment with a patient at 8 a.m., working until she left to pick up the kids from school at 3 p.m. I have always been so proud and inspired by Christie's ability to manage marriage, children, and career while remaining current and beautiful.

Sara, an artist who had lived in France and spoke French fluently, was assigned to be my partner in the sensitivity training course. Sara talked and cried a lot; the world was so sad for her at this time in her life. I couldn't figure it out. She was young, bright, attractive, talented, and articulate. I thought she could do whatever she wanted with her life, that she possessed great presence and charisma, and I told her so. Sara was a storyteller who could take a simple incident and make it into a wonderfully funny story. She was also an excellent writer. Despite all these attributes, she lacked self-esteem and did not feel good about herself or lovable.

Sara wanted to meet men. Since I was hiking with the Sierra Club, meeting all kinds of interesting men, at my urging she joined the hiking section of the Sierra Club. She found that she loved hiking and it also gave her the opportunity to meet new friends, and eventually a handsome boyfriend. She became such a passionate hiker that she took the Sierra Club's leadership training and led trips around Mount Tam and the Bay Area. After Sara graduated from Antioch, she became a sought-after therapist and could afford to travel on hiking trips in Europe. Wanting to meet some Jewish men, she joined the Jewish hiking club. Alas, Sara claimed, there were no men who interested her in the Jewish hiking club, but she did meet great Jewish women.

At Antioch I also met Ailish, a massage therapist in her twenties from New Mexico. We instantly became friends. She was voluptuous—full-figured, with big breasts, and when she embraced me I felt her warmth and affection. Ailish supported herself through practicing massage at a clinic in Oakland, generously offering reduced rates to fellow students.

While we were students at Antioch, Ailish joined our family one Thanksgiving dinner, sitting next to my mother. The two found they shared mutual interests in travel and China, where Mother had lived and Ailish hoped to study. It felt good to have Mother and my new friend meet and know each other. Ailish often stopped by our house on Hillegass Avenue for talk and a cup of tea. I admired her easygoing, positive attitude and she in turn admired my adventurous spirit. We found that we both loved the mountains and shared a spiritual view of nature. Remaining good friends after our Antioch days, Ailish and I arranged physically challenging hiking trips well into my seventies and eighties in the Sierras and Yosemite, savoring our love for nature and the spiritual qualities of the mountains.

When Ailish and her partner Harry (another student at Antioch) became a couple, they moved into a small house in Berkeley. Neither of them owned a typewriter, so they borrowed mine to write term papers. Coming and going from my house, we'd end up having long, intimate talks. Harry was into wheeling and dealing with hedge funds. He paid his way through Antioch with money he made on the stock market. They spoke with high hopes for their budding future careers in holistic psychology. Their openness in airing their problems astonished me, for I was yet to learn to talk about personal problems with friends.

Ailish studied and knew much about health, nutrition, and

alternative healing. She and Harry fasted regularly for cleansing and health. Ailish fasted sensibly, but Harry took fasting to the extreme. After one thirty-day fast, he was so thin he looked emaciated, yet claimed he felt great.

All of us in the program noticed that Ailish and Will Schutz, though twenty-five years apart in age, were spending time together and becoming interested in each other. We lived through Ailish and Will's protracted courtship and were delighted to eventually receive their wedding invitation. It read:

Come! a Vedink!

Her first, His last

Plump Spinster, Aging Geezer

Because of their age difference (she thirty-five and he nearly sixty), I silently wondered how it would be for Ailish when Will died. Their relationship seemed so rich and full that I wished a long happiness for them.

After their wedding, I gave Ailish decorating ideas for their home in Muir Beach. Ailish admired my use of color at Hillegass and wanted to bring more color into their environment. I took great pleasure in our meetings at her home in Muir Beach, which usually included lunch and a heavenly walk along the ocean. We were always able to talk openly and honestly about any subject including ourselves, the men in our lives, our careers, and our hopes and fears.

Theirs was an incredible marriage. Will was inspiring and creative but had not a speck of business sense; Ailish, on the other hand, was a business whiz. After Antioch, she had returned to school for a special program to study finance, which we all thought was a crazy idea. The school was very expensive but she borrowed $5,000, a huge sum then, to take a high-level six-week crash course on finance.

I was fascinated by her desire and motivation to learn about economics and business, subjects that I had avoided in college. Later I regretted that choice, for learning to handle my portfolio had been a challenge after divorcing Rudy. I studied, joined a women's investment group, read books on personal finance, the business reports in the newspaper, and eventually learned the ins and outs of investments. Ailish, on the other hand, found business stimulating and fun, and this learning experience changed her life. She came out of the course with business expertise, understanding investment strategies, venture capital, and how to run a company. Combining her psychology background with business, she grew to become a brilliant and successful businesswoman.

Will and Ailish founded a company together, Will Schutz Associates, teaching managers and lower-level employees how to work harmoniously with each other. The program was sound, marketable, and desirable for big companies. With Ailish's amazing business acumen and Will's skills in psychology, they put together a competent staff and began selling the program to government agencies such as NASA and businesses such as Proctor and Gamble. Many big companies in the United States used the program, and as a result their business flourished. Word of the program's success soon reached Japan and Europe. Will, Ailish, and a group of highly trained facilitators traveled all over the world to present the course.

Will Schutz Associates had two successful decades in business. Will and Ailish enjoyed a happy blending of working together in business and marriage. When Will was diagnosed with Parkinson's disease in his early eighties, they decided to sell their successful company to a Japanese group for a good price. Following Will's death, Ailish stayed on as an advisor under the new Japanese owners.

After earning a generous salary for five years, Ailish left the company to explore other interests. That's when she entered what we all referred to as Ailish's "Peruvian period." She had heard a Peruvian musician, Tito La Rosa, whose music she thought was out of this world. Ailish even invited Tito La Rosa to give a concert for friends at her house. In Peru, Tito was considered a living treasure and had built a devoted following around his music and shamanic abilities. When Ailish first visited Tito's village in the Andean mountains, she saw a remote and beautiful village with neither school nor medical facility. She worked hard to lay the groundwork and establish a school and a clinic there in the mountain village, which continues to this day.

She spent the next five years working to improve the projects she had established, spending part of each year in Peru and the rest at Muir Beach. One day many years after Will had died, she met a Peruvian sociologist, Rafe, and the two fell in love. She and Rafe are now working together to set up a home and day treatment center for poor old homeless women in this Peruvian village. My friendship with Ailish over the years has given me love, caring, and wonderful happy times together.

Mother, My Role Model

By my second year at Antioch University West it was time to begin focusing on writing my master's thesis. In an effort to help me narrow in on what I wanted to research, Will asked, "What do you have energy for?" I had been floating around the idea of studying older women. Not only had my mother been an inspiration because of her zest for living, but now, in my early sixties, I was beginning to think about my own old age. I was definitely beginning to notice little things about growing older, becoming aware that I couldn't do everything I used to. I exercised, hiked, backpacked, skied and watched my weight, yet I worried about how I would feel if I could no longer pursue these activities.

I knew what I wanted to study—women and aging, but not just women in general. I wanted to study women who aged well, who were inspirational and admired. I didn't want to study the downhill syndrome. Past research on aging focused on boredom, retreat from life, stasis, and decline. I wanted to study a new model for vital aging focused on growth, change, and aliveness. Fortunately, I had the perfect role model in my mother, who always said that the last years of her life were the best—by far her most exciting, productive, and creative. She showed me how to live and how to age in an inspired and inspiring way.

After working for ten years to keep us afloat during the Depression, Mother had happily remarried and settled into a contented homemaker and helpmate for my stepfather. When Walter died suddenly of a heart attack in 1956, she was on her own again, looking for work at age fifty-six. Walter had not left Mother money to live on comfortably.

Mother took classes in adult school to brush up on her secretarial skills—shorthand, typing, and accounting—and set out to search for a job. She had many interviews but no luck until the day she lied and said she was forty-six, ten years younger than her real age. The job she found, running a private contractor's office, was an enormous amount of pressure, and eventually she decided to look for something different. She needed a job that offered a secure retirement so she took a civil service exam. She got a high score, qualifying her for a position as a payroll clerk in the personnel department for the Bay Bridge Authority. Fifteen years later, she ended up in charge of the entire personnel department, with 200 people under her supervision.

Mother loved her work and made a host of friends. She learned how to drive in her late fifties so she could get to work on her own. She took up bowling with co-workers, and joined a book club in addition to studying French. At seventy she was forced to retire, but comfortably, with an adequate government pension.

Mother was full of energy and intellectual curiosity. After retiring, she continued with the book group, studied French, traveled widely, and still bowled weekly. Active in politics, she became a precinct captain for the Democrats, ringing doorbells to discuss candidates and vital issues. She was also a big letter-writer. Whenever something bothered her, she wrote a letter. "It makes me feel better," she claimed.

Throughout the years, Mother developed special relationships with each of her grandchildren, encouraging their interests and finding things she could do with them individually.
By the time they reached their late teens, BJ, Robbie, and Lyn
still found her fun and easy to be with, always ready to take
them to interesting events or activities of their choice. They
would worry if they didn't hear from Grandma for even a
week, and would eagerly call her to see if she was OK.

Mother was still physically active when she retired. She
became a regular exerciser at The Best Me, a Health Club I
belonged to on Lake Merritt in Oakland where all the members ended up adoring her. Her apartment in Oakland was in
a nice building right on Lake Merritt and every day she took
a brisk walk around the lake. She felt she had a good life and
clearly loved being alive.

A New Model for Aging

The master's degree program became a priority and a passion that transformed my life. Because the Holistic Studies
Program was so innovative, it offered a vehicle through which
I could study this new field of women and aging. I eagerly
embarked upon a personal quest, seeking deeper understanding of the psychological aspects of the aging process and more
thoughtful answers to the underlying questions of women and
aging in our society. Why do some women age well and others do not? What are the societal, psychological, and personal
factors that influence whether one continues to reap growth,

vitality, and well-being into old age while others decline?

Along with highly visible women of my generation such as Georgia O'Keeffe, Imogen Cunningham, Katharine Hepburn, Margaret Mead, and Eleanor Roosevelt, there were many women out there who were vital and engaged in their old age. Although not as well known, in their professional and personal communities they were recognized as rich repositories of wisdom and personal experience. I was convinced that there was much I could learn from such older women.

Eager to talk to older women who were living with zest as they aged, I selected women who were the best examples of positive aging for my study. Vitality was a common denominator. Between 1979 and 1980 I interviewed twenty-two women in the San Francisco Bay Area over seventy years of age. Each had been recommended to me as an outstanding role model in her community.

The new model on which I based my research focused on growth, change, and aliveness. The background for this model was based on the work of researchers Erik Erikson, Abraham Maslow, Bernice Neugarten, and Carl Jung, who shared a growth-oriented model of behavior. These psychologists were concerned with what a person can become, and they held an optimistic view of humankind. They believed in an individual's capacity for expanding, enriching, developing, and fulfilling their potential.

The women in my study found pleasure and meaning in the world around them and reported old age to be the best time of their lives. Not only did this study end up shattering any negative stereotypes about aging women being depressed, filled with despair, and declining physically, but the conclusions struck home when I recognized that I too, had it in me to become a vital older woman. No longer need I fear growing older. My life took on even deeper meaning when I realized that in spreading the word that old age could be rewarding, I could help other women looking for guidance in aging. What a wonderful gift I offered.

The Spirit of Kilimanjaro

As in the Chinese proverb, "When the pupil is ready, the teacher will come," I felt it was time to seek higher mountains again. I had been working diligently on my thesis for two years and was ready for an adventure. Since my first trip to the Himalayas in 1970, it had long been in my dreams to climb Mt. Kilimanjaro in Tanzania, known as the "Mountain of God." Rising 19,340 feet from sea level, lying only three degrees south of the equator, but crowned with a permanent ice cap, it beckoned me on a spiritual quest. In the mountains I feel a greater Self, something bigger than me. Lying in my sleeping bag under the stars, I feel the vastness of the universe touch and overcome me. It is addictive, and I crave that exhilaration.

My close companion of the past few years, Jack, and I decided that Mountain Travel, the company we trusted because of previous treks to the Himalayas, would be our choice for Kilimanjaro. Any person in good physical condition can climb the mountain, and at sixty, having worked out and run for years, I believed I was ready for this rigorous challenge.

Our six-day Machame Route was regarded as more difficult than the others. We started out from the Kibo hotel at 5,000 feet, where we met the very helpful Masai porters who would accompany us. For the first two days we hiked in tropical weather wearing shorts, passing through plantations of coffee, maize, and bananas, then a forest belt and grasslands. On our third day we bathed in an icy stream, then changed to long pants and jackets before arriving at 9,000 feet. The climb became more arduous around 12,000 feet, the start of moorlands, glaciers, and snow. At 18,000 feet I was wearing subzero-down jacket, hat, and insulated gloves to avoid the freezing temperatures.

En route to the summit of Kilimanjaro

The night before our big climb, we made camp 3,000 feet below the summit and turned in early to rest for starting up to the summit at 3 a.m. Our campsite was rocky terrain, where we were obliged to find crevices within the rocks to put our Therm-a-Rests and pitch our tents. The climb to the summit was long and grueling, yet I felt carried upward by a force greater than myself, as if I were one with the mountain. When I finally reached the summit, past icicles and through snow, the sun was glistening on snow-clad Kilimanjaro. I was greeted by loud cheers from Bill, our British guide, and another hiker, as the third climber in our group to make it to the top. This transcendental experience on Kilimanjaro lives on with me to this day.

Losing Mother

Mother was healthy, vigorous, and living contentedly alone when she died in a fire in her apartment building at age eighty-one. If not for the fire, I believe she would have lived to a much older age. Losing her so suddenly in this tragic way was the lowest period in my life.

It was a Friday night in 1981 during my last year at Antioch. On Friday evenings Mother often came over for dinner, but on this particular night I was at an event in San Francisco. I called her to check in and she didn't answer the phone. A short time later I called Mother's younger brother, my Uncle Myron, who lived in the same building on another floor and he told me that Mother had just called to tell him there was a fire in the building and that they should get out. I tried to call Mother again and again, but she did not answer. I became frantic.

About midnight Robbie called and said, "Mom, I just saw on the news that there's a fire in Grandma's apartment building and they're wheeling an older woman out on a stretcher. I'm going to the morgue to see if it's Grandma." I was hoping against hope that it wasn't her but when he called me to tell me it was Mother, I was in complete shock. My mother was nearly deaf and whether she had her hearing aid in or not I don't know, but the firemen were out in the street with bullhorns yelling that everyone on her twelfth floor should go into their apartments, close their doors tight, and not go into the halls. I think she didn't hear the firemen and instead went into the hallway to escape. She was overcome by smoke inhalation. On the elevator door, which was stained with smoke, she wrote, "HELP." When I visualize her last moments, which I do often, I am consumed by agony. Yet to live past her tragic death, I clearly remember her alive and smiling.

Robbie, BJ, and I gathered at my house. Lyn was in Washington, D.C., but jumped on a plane as soon as she could. Mother's death was a devastating blow. She had been a strong and loving presence my whole life and suddenly she was gone. It was especially crushing that she died in that awful way, so unexpectedly. We bolstered each other as best we could, remembering Mother and talking about her strengths, her loving nature, and vitality. The wonderful friends I made at Antioch, who had all known her, were helpful and supportive. To deal with the grief, my research took on an additional dimension of tribute to my mother. I was determined to give to other women the option of aging joyously as my gallant mother had done.

With Mother at my cousin Gay's engagement shower

Stage Fright

In 1981, after three stimulating years at Antioch University West, I had completed my research and my master's thesis. It was an honor to be invited to speak at our graduation ceremony. I thought long and hard about what I would say, yet when I rose to speak, I spontaneously burst out: "This is one of the best days of my life. I have a new career that I love. And I am not afraid of growing older!" Following that introduction, I described my trepidation about returning to graduate school, my challenges of taking night classes, the extensive reading, and the joys of meeting and becoming close friends with younger participants in the Holistic Studies Program. After the talk, people in the audience approached me and asked, "Will you speak to our group?"

Public speaking presented challenges. It was frightening to get up before an audience of peers to talk, and inevitably before speaking I felt nauseous and as if my legs would collapse beneath me. I went back into therapy with Kay Bradway, a Jungian, who had also had a fear of public speaking and had been able to overcome it.

During our sessions, an early childhood memory surfaced about special Saturdays with Father when I was about seven. One particular day I had expected our day to be just Father and me but he told me he wanted to introduce me to a special friend of his. My father and his friend, a beautiful woman with black, wavy hair, sat next to each other on a love seat and I sat opposite them. She spoke with animation, and each time she turned her head to look admiringly at Father, her long dangling earrings swayed. They were clearly having a good time talking and although he urged me to participate in the discussion, all I could do was feel sad and awful. Finally my father said to me, "Cecelia, has the cat got your tongue?" I wanted to go through the floor and disappear; seeing my father's face oozing with pleasure and adoration for this woman left me feeling insignificant in his life. After recalling this childhood story, I was able to get on with learning to speak publicly.

It was still a difficult process. Dawn, an encouraging and knowledgeable communications coach, helped me before each presentation through careful and exacting rehearsals and critiques in front of a mirror and before a video camera.

Every time I stumbled with a hesitant "er" or "um" she'd drop a coin to make a loud sound in a can. It took me weeks of practice to overcome my stage fright.

Feeling more confident, I began speaking and giving workshops at Esalen on late life potential and creative aging, incorporating my research findings. I presented lectures at the American Society of Aging and the Gerontology Society of America. Often I was invited to give workshops on vitality in aging at health and fitness resorts, where I was paid generously for each engagement.

Reuniting with Don

One day in 1984, Don invited me out to dinner rather than to lunch. He had told me that his marriage with Shirley wasn't satisfying and that, after fifteen years, he was planning to divorce. Not surprised, I asked, "What's going on?" He reminded me that the reason he married was because he was tired of being single for six years and waiting around for me. Shirley was eager to hook a man like Don who had two houses and a nice car, offered stability, and was handsome. What Don liked about her was that she was a great cook. However, after marriage, Don found out their values were very different. Shirley was a conservative Republican from Texas, opposed to the California teacher's union. And although Don felt the relationship was dull, he stayed in it because he felt insecure about living on his own. In the back of his mind, he dreamed of the time when we two could get together.

Since I was scheduled to speak at a gerontology conference in Australia, the news of Don's impending divorce provided a unique opportunity for me to invite him to join me on this trip. I knew if we spent some intimate time away together, we could review our years apart, renew our friendship and love, and discuss what we hoped for in the years ahead. We had four glorious weeks traveling about Australia and New Zealand, discussing our possible future. We were well aware that living together at our ages, I at sixty-four and Don at fifty-eight, was a decision that would affect the rest of our lives. To my dismay, upon returning home Don felt he needed to give his marriage one last chance before going ahead with the divorce. He decided he would move back into his home for six weeks with Shirley. After our loving, intimate month together, Don's return to Shirley was a miserable time for me. I questioned whether he would choose the safe path and stay in the marriage or have the courage to make the break and divorce.

Within a few weeks, Don realized that his reasons for ending the marriage were valid. He moved out, found his own apartment, and initiated divorce proceedings. A few months after he received his divorce, we were living together in my home on Hillegass Avenue.

Our transition wasn't totally smooth. I had planned my time as a single woman living alone for so long that on some occasions I didn't consider Don. When we began living together, I'd breeze into the room to announce that I was off to hike with friends. It didn't occur to me to ask if he'd like to go along, or how he felt about my plans. Understandably, Don was hurt when I made arrangements without consulting him. After a couple of months Don said, "You know, there are two of us here; I might like to join you." From then on I'd invite him to accompany me in my activities, and Don could decide whether he'd like to or not. Don and I were very different— I am outgoing, energetic and busy, and Don, is more quiet, relaxed, and a homebody by nature, yet for the most part we found that our differences complemented each other. I felt thrilled and deeply satisfied to finally share our lives together.

Don's early years were quite different from mine as well. He grew up on a ranch in Turlock, a small town in the San Joaquin Valley, with his parents and two brothers. His father was away working at his own electrical contracting business a lot, and then he went off to war. Don took on a lot of responsibility helping his mother run the ranch. By the time Don was sixteen, he was running the ranch himself.

Don's early experiences in nature were unique. Most summers, starting when he was ten years old, his mother would take Don and his brother Hugh, who was two years older, to Yosemite, give them some food, and leave them there to camp for a month. She would return once a week to restock their supplies and check in with them. Don doesn't know whether this was meant as a coming-of-age experience or if his mom just wanted the two boys out of the house, but he learned a lot and found it to be a very exciting and rewarding time. The mountains were very safe in those days, and no one worried about the two young boys being harmed by other people. The boys did get all their food stolen by bears one night, however, and they had to ask some other campers to help them out.

After high school, Don attended San Jose State College, where he graduated with a degree in industrial engineering. He became a high school teacher and just loved it. Always excellent with his hands, Don taught drafting, woodworking, and furniture making. He eventually started a summer job at Pinecrest Lake, near Yosemite, renting out a fleet of small sailboats. He also captained a tour boat and gave rides around the lake several times a day. When his two sons became old enough, they helped him at the lake, becoming very good sailors themselves in the process.

When Don and I decided to live together I was so full of my expanding experience at Antioch, that I felt he needed to speak the language I had learned at Antioch—he needed to understand the philosophy of mind, body, and spirit. I convinced him to go back to school and get his master's at Antioch in order for us to live together. Antioch's initial orientation took place at Harbin Hot Springs outside of Calistoga. In the orientation students in the program were required to be nude in order to break down barriers. Don was uncomfortable at Harbin Hot Springs, and the group nudity completely turned him off. After a few hours of orientation he drove home and announced: "Cec, that's not me. I draw the line there." I earnestly thought about it and decided I wanted to live with Don even without the Antioch orientation! Over the years, I have introduced a mind-body-spirit way of thinking and behavior into our lives.

Celebrating cousin Robin and Jim's wedding with Don

Vitality in Aging, the Research that Changed My Life

1980–1990

In 1980, at age sixty-one, I was finishing my master's thesis and putting to rest my earlier concerns about growing older. In my journal I wrote:

Here I am taking valuable time from my thesis to write this. When I entered the program at Antioch three years ago, thoughts crashed through my mind: Will these young people accept me? Will my age be a problem? Will I be able to do the work? What about the generation gap—how will that affect my relationships with classmates? These thoughts were magnified because I hadn't been to college in nearly forty years.

Right from the beginning, the program felt good. I recall my excitement that first week of school. What amazed me most was that when I told the other students about some of my experiences in life, they were interested! I felt their warmth and began to feel affection for them, particularly the women in the program. Never in my life had I felt such trust in women and received it in return. I looked forward to classes and felt that I belonged. Often, most often, I forgot my age.

A few incidents helped. One day at our first retreat, one of the young men told me he thought I was attractive. Pleased and also attracted to him, I quickly replied, "You could be my son." We talked about our feelings and, astonished, I learned that he had never really thought much about my age. It was a wonderful learning experience for me.

I feel better about my age now than I did three years ago. Writing this thesis has helped me plan my future with confidence. I have widened my involvement in life through all the new ideas encouraged by the program, and my fellow students have made me feel I am special. And you know what, I feel I may be!

For my master's thesis at Antioch University West—studying vital women as they age—I had chosen ten women in their seventies and eighties who were recommended to me as exemplars of aging, women who were enjoying their life and finding it meaningful. Eight years later, for my Ph.D. dissertation from the Center for Psychological Studies at Berkeley, I interviewed the surviving six women.

This research changed my life. I wanted to learn from women who were positive models of aging, a passion fueled by my mother, who was a wonderful role model. How could I become a vital woman? A key message I want to pass on to women who live in dread of aging is that growing old can be a period of inner richness and vitality, free from the insecurities and confusion of youth and the responsibilities of adulthood. Beauty and meaning do not necessarily diminish. Relationships can be richer than before. The present can be a more intense experience, special and cherished. Age has helped me sift through what is important. My children, friends, nature, colors, flowers, shapes, and physical touch have all taken on more significance. Old age can be a time of heightened sensory and emotional awareness and enjoyment.

To select subjects for my studies, I had contacted organizations that I knew in the San Francisco Bay Area, including the Sierra Club, the C. G. Jung Institute, the University of California Alumni Association, and Antioch University West. I had requested the names of women past seventy who had a zest for living, were enjoying their lives, and were admired by their friends and community. If a person was recommended more than once, that woman became a candidate for the study. A letter to each candidate explained the purpose of the master's thesis, to find out what gave women like them a zest for life, and whether there were common factors among women who enjoyed life into advanced age. Twenty-two women were enthusiastic and excitedly agreed to be interviewed.

The ten women I finally chose for the study were not random or representative; I chose them because they were positive models of aging and located in the San Francisco Bay Area. The ten women I chose were all white, middle-class, and college-educated. All had been married. Three were still married to their husbands of at least fifty years, four were widowed, and three were divorced.

I conducted in-depth life-history interviews with open-ended questions. I isolated common characteristics that seemed to explain their zest for life and contribute to their vitality and well-being. Following these same women for the next ten years for my Ph.D. research, I found there were five key characteristics that "vital women" had in common:

Experience life as meaningful

Optimistic

Friendships of all ages

Continue to grow

Physically active

These women lived very much in the present but had plans for the future. They realized it was important to have friends of all ages because it is in the nature of things that one's contemporaries will begin to die. They were initiators and they were optimistic. They all had a feeling of self-worth. They were self-educators, continuing to learn new things. They were their own advocates in dealing with health problems.

Contrary to my expectations, not all my informants were in the best physical condition. They had the diseases of age—arthritis, hearing problems, loss of vision—but they didn't let that stop them. They focused on what they could do rather than on what they had lost. They were no strangers to grief, having lived through two world wars and the loss of loved ones, but in spite of the upheavals and tragedies, they'd say, "After my husband's death, I learned to … " Hardships were a source of growth into richer territory, not a defeat. It was so encouraging to hear them.

Continuing involvement in the community is crucial to vital old age. So is increased inward reflection. These women were concerned about the world and the environment, and as they grew older they found themselves becoming more spiritual, shifting the emphasis from the ego to the soul.

During my background research, I had found that the literature on aging focused on men. Men researched men. Up to the 1970s, aging research accepted the view that more can be learned from studying the negative than the positive aspects of aging. Aging was defined through its diseases, declining abilities, declining health, loss, loneliness, depression, and decay. Academic research on aging excluded the perspective of women over eighty and certainly didn't study women who found their eighties and nineties fulfilling. It was almost as if old women who enjoyed life and found it meaningful didn't exist.

Everyone wants to know about creative aging and late-life potential—not just older women, because the research findings are almost the same for men. It is just that we women live much longer. It is too bad the guys don't. But now that women are out more in the world, they are likely to face reduced lifespans, as well.

Just beginning to emerge was the exciting idea that late life can be a period of rich growth, development, and creative potential, and that old age can bring untold rewards and advantages. Informing my research were the writings of Erikson, Jung, Maslow, and Neugarten, who shared this growth-oriented model of human behavior. They were concerned with what a human being could become, and they held an essentially optimistic view of aging. People's capacity for expanding, enriching, developing, and fulfilling themselves into late life was an integral part of their theories.

All four thinkers approached aging as potentially enlivening, offering a crucial theoretical background for anyone interested in vital aging. They reasoned that the extent to which one has met the earlier challenges of life determines how she or he is able to cope with the changes that accompany old age.

Wisdom comes from life experience, well digested.
—Erik Erikson

Psychoanalyst Erik Erikson said that every life forms a link in a chain of generations, and each life has continuity. He used the term "life cycle" to mean the whole of a person's life and was particularly interested in the final two stages in the life cycle, adulthood and old age. The task in old age becomes to consolidate a sense of wisdom with which to live out the future, and to accept our place in an infinite historical progression. The challenge is to convert old age from a negative experience to a positive one that offers the opportunity for new growth.

No one can make history who is not willing to risk everything for it, to carry the experiment with his own life through to the bitter end, and to declare that his life is not a continuation of the past, but a new beginning.—Carl Jung

One of the first psychologists to theorize about personality development over the lifespan, Jung wrote that in the second half of life one grows to know, accept, and integrate the qualities that make up the self. He claimed that in the latter half of life, the individuation process enables a person to give new meaning to life and at the same time begin preparing for accepting death.

The "individuation process" means becoming a single being distinguished from others. It is the conscious realization and integration of all the possibilities available to an individual. The women I studied did not accept traditional role prescriptions for women of their time, choosing instead to pursue individuation through such endeavors as psychotherapy, creative expression, spirituality, education, and a connection with nature.

The path of growth and development that Jung described involved taking risks and struggling with life's conflicts in order to become well-rounded and whole, and finally to face death without fear.

Growth is a continuous, lifelong process rather than a static step-by-step progression.—Abraham Maslow

Maslow believed that self-realization is not solely a rational or intellectual process but depends on the individual's life experience. He identified two kinds of needs: basic requirements and growth requirements. He felt that healthy individuals who have had their basic needs satisfied are able to address themselves to the second category, growth. Self-actualized people are oriented toward personal growth without being self-centered. They learn to know themselves well and seek to discover other people's capabilities. The self-actualized have a pronounced sense of purpose directed toward problem-solving rather than toward serving only their interests. Because they can see the "big picture" and experience the unity of humankind, they are inclined to work on some of life's larger problems. They tend to cultivate lasting friendships, making conscious contributions to relationships.

Maslow's work suggested that the extent to which an individual has developed into a self-actualized person predicts successful aging. The self-actualized person would be expected to have fewer problems, both psychological and physical, than the person who is not. The characteristics of Maslow's psychologically healthy, self-actualized individuals were analogous to the common characteristics I found among the vital older women I studied.

With the passage of time, life becomes more, not less, complex; it becomes enriched, not impoverished.—Bernice Neugarten

One of the first women to research aging in women, Neugarten considered old age a developmental phase in which the psychic energy women previously used to cope with the fluctuations of the menstrual cycle and reproduction could be released for new forms of psychological and social expansion. Neugarten believed that women in their later years were more able to enter a realm of unimagined possibilities. She reported that women became more accepting of, and less guilty about, their own aggressive and egocentric impulses as they moved into later life. An initial sense of danger and timidity might give way to excitement as women realized that there were still many "firsts" to achieve.

Neugarten defined successful aging from the perspective of the individual and regarded people who are in their later years as being on the positive end of the continuum of psychological well-being to the extent that they take pleasure from daily activities, regard life as meaningful, and accept what life has been, feel they have succeeded in achieving major goals, hold a positive image of self, and maintain a happy and optimistic attitude and mood.

From a psychological perspective, aging is better viewed not as a process of engagement or disengagement, Neugarten believed, but as one in which the aging person not only plays an active role in adapting to changes but creates patterns of life that provide the greatest involvement and satisfaction.

Neugarten's studies led to the hypothesis that personality type is pivotal in predicting which individuals will age successfully. While prior studies demonstrated that health, financial resources, and marital status are significant in influencing adaptation in older people, Neugarten regarded personality as the mediating factor in determining whether aging would be successful. She believed it was important to study a person's perception of life changes.

I was so sparked by Neugarten's theories and views of aging that in 1980, still interviewing women for my master's thesis, I spontaneously wrote to her explaining my personal reasons for returning to graduate school to study women and positive aging. She replied that little research was being done about women past the age of seventy and encouraged me to continue mine, offering to advise me as I progressed. She gave me excellent advice on how to analyze my data and clarification on the kind of qualitative research to undertake. We corresponded until my master's thesis, "Vital Women in Their Seventies and Eighties," was completed and continued our relationship after that. Dr. Neugarten urged me to continue working toward my Ph.D. in adult development, which was her specialty.

Two years later, in 1985, I embarked on my Ph.D. in late life development, a focus not offered by my graduate school but one I was allowed to pursue by taking special coursework at UC Berkeley's School of Psychology and School of Education. I corresponded with Neugarten throughout my dissertation. Caring about the work, she kindly mentored and advised me without ever asking for remuneration. When she received a copy of my Ph.D. dissertation in 1990, she congratulated me and said that I was one of the oldest of the one hundred fifty women she had influenced to receive a Ph.D.

The following vignettes give a flavor of each vital woman I studied for my Ph.D., based on interviews conducted between 1987 and 1990 as follow-ups to my master's research earlier in the decade.

Ann W., the oldest member of the group at ninety-two, had lost her hearing at seventeen following a bout with influenza.

"Well, the worst thing that ever happened to me was when I was seventeen and lost my hearing," Ann told me. "Somehow or other, I overcame it. So now I can overcome anything." Soon after she enrolled in college, a professor convinced her to not be ashamed that she was deaf and instead announce it to her colleagues. Ann was able to turn her disability into expertise.

She went on to write two books on lip reading and made a career as an advocate for people with disabilities. She became known as the mother of the first programs to place disabled people in industry. As an active member of the President's Commission for the Employment of the Handicapped during the Roosevelt administration, Ann gave presentations around the country about how to integrate the disabled into schools and a regular life. Miraculously, a new form of surgery restored some of Ann's hearing when she was in her late sixties.

Her Berkeley home of many years was a comfortable and lived-in haven for her diverse activities and many friends. Her telephone rang frequently with calls from people of all ages. When I visited, a typewriter and papers sat on her dining room table, as she was completing her autobiography. She had recently taken a class in journal writing to help her with the book.

Accompanied by her hearing-assistance dog, we went outdoors for the interview to a favorite spot in her garden, a shaded redwood table and benches amid colorful flowers and bushes. Ann cut fresh flowers daily for her home and still took pleasure in gardening, although a gardener did most of the heavy work now. She told me that the garden gave her a sense of well-being and was a great place to read, entertain friends, eat meals, and relax.

Ann no longer drove because of her failing eyesight and walked shorter distances more carefully and slowly, but otherwise there was little outward evidence of change in her appearance. She still walked her dog daily, swam weekly, and attended a gentle exercise class. When I first met her she lived independently, but by our second interview she needed a live-in companion who helped with cooking, driving, and shopping.

Her life was refreshing evidence that a ninety-two-year-old woman need not fit the stereotype of declining sociability and spirit in old age.

Katherine's house was perched on top of a hill in San Francisco. When I first met her, she greeted me at the door in leotards, having just finished her regular dance movement session. When I returned eight years later, a young woman whom Katherine introduced as "my staunch helper" answered the front door. Katherine, age ninety-one, had remained slim. She told me that she regularly walked outdoors with her helper and occasionally had a morning session of music and dancing. But she appeared fragile and no longer possessed the ageless quality that had impressed me eight years earlier.

Katherine's charm and southern manners were evident as she offered me tea and cookies. I followed her as she carefully climbed a flight of stairs to her penthouse studio. There, overlooking San Francisco, we began our next series of interviews. She had built this studio addition in her eighties, when she decided that she didn't want to commute to Berkeley any longer to teach. Yet this past decade of her life had been full. The university allowed her to continue conducting her well-attended classes in human development out of her home.

Professor, author, and Jungian therapist, Katherine achieved prominence early in her career in the field of nursery school education and had published books on child development, adolescence, and parents and children. Her intellectual pursuits had always paralleled her family life. "Having my children," she said, "has been and continues to be one of the greatest fulfillments I have known."

Katherine had entered a doctoral program at Columbia University in her mid-thirties. With three children, two part-time jobs, a half-hour daily commute to school, and analysis five times a week, she managed not only to get her doctorate but, out of necessity, founded the first cooperative nursery school in the United States. She told me that her life was "so much more interesting" after she retired at age sixty-five, and that she had "really just loved" what she had done.

The year after her official retirement as a professor at the University of North Carolina at Pembroke, she received a Fulbright scholarship to teach in New Zealand. The next year she traveled to Zurich, where she studied Jungian psychology. At age sixty-eight she spent a year at a Quaker retreat, writing a book on active imagination. She then moved back to California to live near her son. He had bought a house for her and she moved in without having seen it beforehand, trusting his judgment. I found trust to be one of the most important characteristics in the women I interviewed.

Katherine spoke articulately of moving into the next world. She had lost interest in many pursuits that had once been a part of her life—traveling, entertaining, going out. It was as if she were standing back and looking at a world of which she was no longer a part. She had always been a spiritual person and believed that the spirit goes on, that death "is another great adventure, which we don't know very much about, but certainly it isn't the end of things. The biggest adventure lies ahead." Nine months after our interview, she died of pneumonia in her home at the age of ninety-one.

When Frances, then eighty-six, greeted me with a smile at the door of her garden cottage in the Berkeley hills, where she had lived for more than thirty years, she looked thinner and frailer than before. She was wearing a long, neat wraparound shirt, which she explained was easier to put on than pants. She told me that she weighed 110 pounds instead of her former regular weight of 135 pounds, and she walked with a cane. But her conversations remained infused with wit and wisdom, and it was clear that this author of numerous books and articles on nuclear energy continued to be a reflective thinker and articulate observer of the world scene.

I noticed a thick thesaurus, opened at the letter E, beside her reading chair. I asked, "Are you writing a new book or an article?" "No," she replied, "I am studying the thesaurus, and have gone through letter E, so that when I forget a word, a new word I have learned will come to me." I noted the name of her thesaurus, *The Synonym Finder* by J.I. Rodale, and promptly bought one for myself.

Frances had returned to university studies when her son was a teenager, earning her Ph.D. in philosophy at age fifty. She taught courses in ethics and social justice and had been involved in research and writing at the university level. Since retiring as a professor at age sixty-five, she had devoted her considerable intelligence and energy toward causes for peace, giving talks on the subject around the world.

Not long after Frances retired, she decided to take a degree in engineering and physics at Berkeley because she wanted to understand the implications of atomic energy. She became an expert on the subject, wrote an influential paper titled "Split Atom, Split World," and founded the International League for Peace and Freedom. During the Vietnam War she was an activist and at nearly ninety had amassed a huge peace library, providing information for peace groups around the country.

It gave her great pleasure to view the outdoors from her desk, which faced her garden. The papers and journal articles covering her desk were evidence of the three hours she spent reading or writing each day. At the time she was reading Mikhail Gorbachev's just-published *Perestroika,* spoke of the upcoming U.S. presidential elections, glasnost, Nicaragua, and her continued passion for world peace. She wrote or received six or seven family letters a week.

As we talked, Frances brewed herbal tea. Also in the room were bookshelves, a file cabinet, a comfortable easy chair, a bed, and a stationary exerciser a friend had designed so Frances could sit in her easy chair and bicycle with her feet in front of her. She used it when bad weather kept her from walking.

Frances felt fortunate to receive calls and visits from friends of all ages who kept in touch. She particularly enjoyed her friendships with older women whose continuing ability to function well inspired her. Often these friendships had to be maintained through letters and telephone conversations, for the women were no longer able to travel to see each other. Every Sunday morning, Frances's fifty-two-year old son came to her house for breakfast. He took care of her car and assumed responsibility for the maintenance of her home.

Since receiving radiation treatment for cancer ten years earlier, Frances had experienced diminished mobility in her legs, shoulders, and upper arms. Consequently she could no longer drive, but she kept her car so that the student who helped her three times a week could use it to take her shopping and to medical appointments. She said she seldom left home to attend meetings and cultural events, as she had in the past. "But I really enjoy my life at this stage," she told me, "now that I've adjusted to its limitations."

Jane's house was filled with arts and crafts from her travels around the world. Letters, paintings, photos, maps, and programs of events and concerts—evidence of her children, grandchildren, and friends—occupied places of honor on the walls and tabletops.

Jane was erect and seemed hardy at age eighty-four, although she moved more slowly and had gained some weight in the eight years since our first interview. She had had a hip replaced, and though she still drove, would possibly need cataract surgery to keep driving in the future. She admitted that her energy was down and she had to rest more; she had consciously cut down on her contact with people to preserve her energy. "If you get too tired," she said, "it takes some days to recover."

Jane and her husband had met C.G. Jung early in their marriage, and it was a turning point for them both. Upon Jung's advice, her husband received his medical degree, and they both completed their study of analytical psychology in Zurich before World War II began. The individuation process had been a theme for Jane throughout most of her adult life, and through her contact with nature it continued to be significant to her experience of old age. She considered the wilderness important to her psyche and her creative self. She and her husband of sixty years spent half of each year on a remote ranch, where she felt nourished and was able to write.

Jane believed that an important task of old age was to let go of the ego. She sought and appreciated solitude, claiming that old age was an introverted process even for extroverts. "The exit is alone, and therefore solitude is not only a preparation but is the real stuff of old age," she wrote in one of her books. "One will no longer fear death, but rather see death as a part of life."

Jane was still taking risks in the realm of ideas. She had become a prolific writer on aging, death, and Jungian perspectives of the women's movement. She and her fifty-seven-year-old daughter, also a Jungian analyst, collaborated on books and occasionally presented lectures on mother-daughter relationships.

Kay at eighty-one said, "I feel wonderful. It's good to be here." And I felt happy to be seeing her again. She had moved to her own apartment in her son's home in Madison, Wisconsin, where I flew to interview her. She had three rooms of her own, including an office area and a comfortable living-reading-music room filled with books, a stereo, and video and music tapes. Each of her three rooms overlooked a garden with maple and hemlock trees. Dressed in pants and a printed scarf, with her gray hair up in a short, curly, style, she appeared radiant and energetic, exuding a contagious *joie de vivre*.

Kay had had two knee replacements and was thrilled that after ten years of living with aching knees, she was completely pain-free. She was delighted to use the stairs at this new home, which was purchased with an elevator because she thought her mobility might be impaired after the knee surgeries. She could walk again, quite quickly, and traveled all over the United States presenting workshops and public celebrations of life. She was internationally known as a healer whose media were music, movement, color, and massage. She invariably won the trust and commanded the respect of everyone around her.

During our first interview, I was able to take part in one of her holistic sessions in music and relaxation. It was a chance to experience a real artist at work. The long day spent driving to her home in the Santa Cruz mountains and interviewing her had left me tired, so at the end of our interview, Kay suggested that I do her relax-and-rebound exercises with her accompaniment at the piano. After ten minutes I felt energized and ready for the drive home.

Kay had run a residential center in California and took her nonprofit organization to Wisconsin. There she presented weeklong workshops, which by the time of our follow-up interview were mostly given by her trained and certified facilitators in various cities around the country. She reported that after many years of shouldering the responsibility and work of running the center, it was a tremendous relief to let it go. Her growing ability to let go and accept things as they were had left her feeling more comfortable with herself than she had during our initial interview.

Kay had a few close friends and grandchildren who were her delights. She still enjoyed writing, traveling, and training others in her work, as well as consulting at workshops. She felt that she was fulfilling her destiny. Her creative lifestyle seemed to keep her vital and ageless.

Ann O., the youngest of the group at a spry eighty, told me that "I get up and look out and see an absolutely glorious world. It's always beautiful." A painter all her life, she lived on several wooded acres in Marin County. Her home was filled with textiles, books, music, sculptures by her late husband, and vivid paintings of her own. Her painting studio sat a few steps up a path from the main house.

Ann appeared to be in the same health as when I first met her. She continued to drive, still walked with a relaxed, easy gait, and considered herself to be in pretty good shape. She believed that her greatest challenge was to keep up with people who were younger and who expected her to bow out of the scene.

Ann took me out to a neighborhood cafe for lunch. She ordered wine, which she enjoyed and considered a necessity with good food. Afterward we returned to her home to continue the interview, which was frequently interrupted by telephone calls and visits from students and friends.

As usual, Ann spoke with great ease, hardly pausing between ideas and building those ideas with the same dexterity that made her teaching so communicative to her scores of students and admirers. We talked through the afternoon, and I lost track of the time until it was almost dark.

Ann taught expression through painting, sculpture, a variety of visual media, and in unique workshops on the "yoga of seeing." These workshops developed visual perception, challenging one to think about the visual world in new ways. She had met her husband at the Art Institute in San Francisco when both were poor art students, and they had decided to devote themselves to artistic creativity rather than have children. They were married for fifty-two years.

Their vision had been to create a center for the study of art and nature, where all kinds of people could come to learn the visual arts and grow. They worked hard to make their dream a reality, and the art center is now thriving. Ann intended to continue to work, expand her perceptions of art, and live on the land that she and her husband had bought many years earlier.

The common characteristics I identified in my research have been a guide to my own successful aging. When my painful, worn-out knees limited physical activities such as running and aerobics, I consciously chose to focus on what I could still do. I could walk in the neighborhood and on the easy trails in the Berkeley Hills. I did my errands by walking to the bank or the cleaner. Strolling three blocks to College Avenue for coffee, or taking mail to the nearby and bustling College Avenue post office –– these have become the exercises that bring me joy and meaning, even though they reflect my new limits. I have learned more about growth and perseverance as I have encountered setbacks.

Each woman I interviewed was an amazing example of positivity and optimism. It was not what happened to these women, but how they perceived what happened to them that determined their sense of well-being. Frances, for example, had walked 200 miles on her honeymoon, in her twenties; at eighty-eight she had to use a walker but still walked up and down her block, albeit slowly. She cheerily told me that she was "so happy that I have my good friend, the walker."

That these women maintained friendships across the generations was also important. When I give talks, most people in the audience are in their forties and fifties. I ask, "How many of you have friends in their seventies and eighties?" It is important that younger people have older role models in their life, just as it is crucial for older people to have younger friends. Ann W., who was in her early nineties, told me, "Every time one of my friends dies, I make sure to make a younger friend." Since going back to school in my fifties, I have been blessed to have made a whole circle of younger friends.

Recalling these women's inspirational stories, I have made a point of reframing my thoughts more positively. In 2011, when I unexpectedly developed congestive heart failure, I couldn't breathe or catch my breath when exerting myself. Consciously, I reframed: "This limitation will not be the end of my life, but instead a different and slower approach to living and moving." Instead of rushing to the airport, to a play, or to a concert, I now plan an earlier departure and arrive well ahead of time. This allows me ample time to find my place, relax, and enjoy the process of arriving and being.

If I had not spent a decade learning from these extraordinary women, I would not have been able to overcome these challenges in my nineties. In my late eighties, the glaucoma I'd been living with for the last twenty years suddenly got much worse. I noticed the change when I walked into the doctor's office and asked: "What's wrong with the light in here? I can't see to read." The light was the same as before; it was my vision that had gone downhill. The ophthalmologist informed me that the glaucoma's progression would mean that eventually, if I lived long enough, I would lose my sight.

I was devastated. I came home ready to throw in the towel, saying: "Don! What's the point of living? I am going to end up blind. I don't want to live that long!" Soon I realized that I could not see well enough to drive. But I knew I had a choice. I said to myself: "There is still much I can do. My life is still meaningful. I am going to learn to live harmoniously with this."

In the years following the transformative car accident in my forties—when I told myself, "If we get out of this alive, my life is going to be different"—I went on to create a richer, more rounded identity by exploring my potential. Climbing mountains became a metaphor for taking on greater challenges. Traveling to India, going back to graduate school, working in the environmental movement, and advocating for older people have brought additional growth and meaning to my life.

As I've grown older, I've become less concerned about conforming. When people see me in gorgeous and colorful red shawls and orange outfits, some remark that I do not dress as an older woman should. And beside me is handsome Don, my loving partner and companion of thirty years, who is eight years younger than I and not my husband. An eccentric risk-taker I proudly am!

My dissertation explored women who had defied the stereotypes of what it is like to grow old. A major implication of my dissertation, published in 1990, was that vital women can continue to be actively involved in living well into their eighties and nineties. They accepted the fact they were aging but were not intimidated by it.

Old age holds enormous potential for developing hidden aspects of the self and can be as meaningful and creative a stage of life as adolescence, young adulthood, or midlife. Not only is there more time for inner exploration, but growth is facilitated by the wisdom and experience that come from a life well lived. An optimistic outlook and adaptation to the negative effects of physical changes were predominant features among these vital older women. Their optimistic outlook on life proved wrong the stereotype that all older women are passive, dependent, bored, or depressed.

As we grow older, having meaning in life is key to our well-being and sense of self—doing something we're passionate about, something outside of ourselves that makes us feel good for having contributed in some way. Other-directedness offers a balance to our tendency to focus on "me and mine."

Instead of thinking of ourselves as dependent and less proactive as we grow older, the wisdom of our years can give us the strength and capability to live active and creative lives. Change can bring growth and strengthen a sense of self and meaning. A highly developed sense of individuality does not depend on affluence or material possessions but comes from a deep acceptance of self—who you have been and are now.

Over the last twenty-two years, since finishing my dissertation, aging has become a hot topic. Baby boomers have come face-to-face with their parents' aging and are now becoming the next generation of old folks. In true boomer fashion, they are in the process of creating their own reality. They are beginning to explore aging as a transformative experience.

There are thousands of books on aging now, and compilations of interviews with elderly people who reflect on their experiences of growing old. Many books deal with healthy aging, exercise, longevity diets, anti-aging diets, diets that erase wrinkles, or the authoritative word from doctors about well-being as we age. There are books that celebrate aging and explore how to grow old gracefully, but equally as many are guides to denying, reversing, and actually ending aging. There are how-to books on staying young, fit, strong, and sexy beyond eighty. There are guides to making aging into an art. Some delve into the biology and neurology of the aging brain; many talk about how to avoid Alzheimer's disease. There are books about secret anti-aging miracles that supposedly are being hidden from us, books that discuss the gender and culture of aging, books on the positive power of the aging brain, or social gerontology. There's so much out there, it's staggering.

Yet since completing my masters and Ph.D., I have not found any books that explore the key characteristics of vital women in their seventies, eighties, and nineties. Most books look at one specific characteristic on its own; none view the uniquely relevant combination of psychosocial factors that I found in these women: experience life as meaningful, be optimistic, have friends of all ages, continue to grow, and stay physically active.

In May of 1990, when I was awarded the degree of doctor of philosophy in developmental psychology from the Center for Psychological Studies, I was seventy years old. I was elated that I was on my way to being one of the vital older women I had written about.

With Lyn on our Hunza trek

Activism, Research, Adventure

Shortly after receiving my master's degree, I had started giving talks at conferences and meetings about my research on women and vital aging and continued after I received my Ph.D. A talk in 1983 at the Western Gerontological Society of America in Albuquerque, New Mexico, had garnered a rave review in the local press ("Researcher Finds that Seventies and Eighties Are the Best Time of Life"), which was soon picked up by the Associated Press. I was inundated with letters and calls from reporters and women from all over the country, seeking interviews and more information on this unique topic.

When the Esalen Institute in Big Sur invited me to teach a weekend workshop on creating a new career in late life, I was delighted to accept. I introduced experiential exercises into the workshop to illustrate the importance of taking risks, asking each participant to describe three risks they had taken in the last year that had made a difference in their lives. In my talks on creative aging, I described the research showing the positive effects of having friends of all ages as we grow older and asked participants to name friends they saw regularly who were under twenty and over seventy. The exercises illustrated the value of incorporating these life-supporting behaviors into a healthy aging process.

I was asked to speak at workshops, conferences, and other professional meetings around the world. Creative aging was a hot topic in Australia, where retirement is typically required at age fifty-five. In 1997, I spoke to overflowing audiences at Flinders University in Adelaide and Macquarie University in Sydney. After my talk at Macquarie, an animated group gathered around me to discuss the five characteristics of vital agers and the ways their own lives might be enhanced by incorporating these characteristics. Combining my new professional life with travel, Don and I spent three glorious weeks in Australia and two weeks in New Zealand.

At the International Congress on Gerontology in Pune, India, in 1992, I met Swati Piramal, a doctor who was fascinated by my talk. We were on similar paths; she was offering a program on women and healthy aging at the Gopikrishna Memorial Hospital in Mumbai. We corresponded for a few years, but it wasn't until early 1997, after much writing back and forth, that we set a date for my return to Mumbai (formerly Bombay) to present my research to the doctors and staff at her hospital. She urged me to stay longer to talk to the Rotary Club of Bombay, inviting me to be a guest in her home and offering a generous gratuity plus a car and driver at my disposal.

The prestigious Rotary Club of Bombay was the first rotary club to be established in India, in the 1860s, and was known for its progressive views, having opened its membership to women. Dr. Piramal was among its well-placed members who met regularly for a grand lunch at the famous Taj Mahal Hotel in Mumbai. Following the club's event, I was featured on the cover of the *Times of India*, a journal similar to our *Time* or *Newsweek*, with the headline "Age of Vitality." The local Mumbai newspapers ran a photo of me leading the Rotarians in simple stretching exercises in the hotel's grand ballroom after lunch, with the caption "It's never too late to start exercising."

Article in the health section of a Bombay newspaper,
March 31, 1997

Great Old Broads

In addition to my activism around aging issues, I became more involved in environmental activism in these years, partly through my introduction to the Great Old Broads for Wilderness (or GOB). This organization, dedicated to protecting lands threatened by development, mining, off-road vehicle abuse, or grazing, and to creating new wilderness areas, has given profound meaning to my life for twenty years and has inspired thousands of older women across the country.

In 1989, the Bureau of Land Management (BLM) was about to build a new road into an unspoiled wilderness because "old people did not have access to the area otherwise." Susan Tixier, our founder and an environmental activist, replied, "Wait a minute, of course we can hike in those areas! We don't need roads!" She recognized how important it is to not stereotype older people or treat them as less than they are.

She organized a group of twenty women who were over sixty-five years old and called them Great Old Broads for Wilderness. Our first hike was through the El Dorado Wilderness Area near Boulder, Colorado. Wearing backpacks, straw hats, and knee braces, and carrying walking sticks, we Great Old Broads were quite a sight. The media loved us, providing extensive coverage of that first hike. The proposed BLM road was never built, and the Great Old Broads realized we could be an effective force for protecting the environment. Another example of the group's power was our success in persuading Conoco to drop its oil-drilling lease in Utah's Grand Staircase–Escalante National Monument.

Over 2,000 women from all over the United States are now members of Great Old Broads. Most members came to us through word of mouth or by reading about us. In addition to our grassroots advocacy, we Great Old Broads have a lot of fun hiking, camping, and exchanging ideas. When our daughters or their friends want to join us, we now offer a new membership category called Great Old Broads in Training. A few men give us their support, as well. As a former member of GOB's board of directors, I feel proud to be a member of such a group of women, working to leave the world a better place.

Mountain Biking with BJ

In 1991, my daughter BJ invited me to join her on a mountain biking expedition on the White Rim Trail in Canyonlands National Park, Utah. This trip covers difficult terrain, over slick rock and sand. I wanted to share this adventure with my daughter, but I had no experience with mountain bikes.

I called one of my best friends from college, Lou Winnett, and suggested: "How about we rent some mountain bikes? I'd like to buy one, but I want to try it out first." We tootled around the University of California on our rented bikes, having a great time looking at all the buildings we remembered from so many years ago. When we returned the bikes, we decided which ones we'd purchase the following week.

That night, after talking to her children and husband, Lou called back and said: "We can't buy mountain bikes, because you know what happens to old folks like us when we fall—

we'll break our hips! And that's the end!" She backed out of buying a bike. I almost did, too. But I put aside her negative thoughts, thinking to myself: "I'm not going to break my hip. Damn it, I'm going to do it anyway." I hastily bought myself a twenty-one-speed bike, because I so wanted to be with BJ.

My only experience riding a bike was with an old-fashioned single-speed Schwinn I had in high school. My friend and yoga teacher, Nancy Minges, showed me how to get on the bike and shift gears while I tested riding the bike on our block. Otis, the eighteen-year-old son of my friend Marilyn, offered to practice riding with me in the Berkeley hills. Many times I fell or lost my balance, but with Otis encouraging me and telling me I was doing great, I eventually learned to ride my new bike.

I did go on that seven-day trail ride in Utah with BJ! When a hill was too much, I walked the bike up, and when I became tired, the "sag wagon" picked me up. Did I take a risk? Yes. Was I challenged? Absolutely. Did I overcome my fear? Definitely. Did I grow? Indeed I did. My daughter and I had a marvelous time and grew closer. I made new friends and came away healthy and fit, with great memories.

The Road to Hunza Valley

I had been fascinated by the health and longevity of the Hunzakuts—the people of the Hunza Valley in Pakistan— ever since reading a 1965 *National Geographic* article about the region. The Hunzakuts are Ismaili Muslims—a small, moderate sect of Islam—and while the men had been investigated in depth by male researchers, the women had never been interviewed or studied because they typically do not show themselves to men other than those in their family. It was my dream to one day meet and interview these women and to explore the secrets of their purported long lives.

The pulls of fantasy and desire from that *National Geographic* article remained with me for almost thirty years. In September 1992, at the age of seventy-three, I was invited to address the International Federation of Aging Conference in Mumbai, "New Roles for Older People." Traveling to India would bring me geographically very close to Hunza, so it seemed a propitious time to fly to neighboring Pakistan following the conference and interview the older Hunzakut women to find out if they lived as long as *National Geographic* had reported the men did.

I hoped to put together a diverse group of friends who I thought would be interested in hiking in Hunza but would also want to learn about and exchange ideas with the Hunzakut people regarding their culture, and how lifestyle and diet affected their health and longevity. I also knew it would be unsafe and difficult to travel alone as a woman in a Muslim country. After sending a letter inviting twenty friends and my two daughters to join Don and me on this cultural trek, I was thrilled that six adventurous participants signed up.

My fellow travelers were an enthusiastic group. My contemporary and bon vivant friend Georgette, from Paris and Saint-Tropez, France, had eagerly joined me for outdoor adventures when I was with her in Saint-Tropez and when she visited us in the United States. My daughter Lyn and I loved to hike together, and she excitedly flew in from Washington, D.C., to join us. Lyn has known and adored Georgette since she was a young girl, and our trek would be relevant to Lyn's environmental advocacy in the nation's capital. Yvonne, a nurse from Lake County, California, was not only an interesting woman but also a strong hiker and hardy person. When I first met Yvonne on a Sierra Club hike, she was the first to volunteer to lead our troupe over a treacherous glacier—she had a lot of spunk.

Lola and her husband, Abe, recently married, were a quirky, extravagant, and wealthy couple. Lola, a born-again Christian and newcomer to hiking, was an awkward partner at first, yet she turned out to be a compatible trip member. Before Abe's marriage to Lola, he was a well-traveled *National Geographic* photographer whom I first met in Sri Lanka. He had joined Don and me for treks in India, Papua New Guinea, and the Dolomites in Italy, as well as an early-spring hike in the desert at Borrego Springs, California, and a ten-day silent Vipassana retreat in Santa Barbara. Whenever Abe came up to Berkeley from Santa Barbara, we gladly received him in our home, for he was a charismatic friend, a wonderful storyteller, and an easygoing houseguest. Stan, the final member of our group, was a gastroenterologist from Berkeley and an avid hiker, and was interested in finding out whether the rumors about Hunzakuts' health and longevity were true.

Planning for my interviews in Hunza, I knew that I would

need interpreters, but finding them was a long and difficult process. I wrote to the Aga Khan, the Ismaili spiritual leader, in Geneva, and to Muslim friends in Mumbai, noting that I had received permission to interview the women in Hunza but that now I must locate women interpreters who could speak Barakshi (the local language), Urdu, and English. Through extensive networking with my Indian friends, I finally found two interpreters, both teachers in the local school—one who could translate from Barakshi to Urdu, the other from Urdu to English.

Our group of eight, flying from various locations, met in Islamabad only to find that Pakistan had been ravaged by unusual floods. The Karakoram Highway, our only route into the Hunza Mountains, was completely washed out in sections, with huge ruts and boulders on the parts of the road that remained. Not wanting to take an American group over this hazardous route, our trek leader, Rahmatullah Baig—known as Beek—a thirty-six-year-old Hunza native and qualified mountain guide who had made three ascents of K2 and had a super twinkle in his eyes, suggested we change our plans. Rather than hiking in Hunza, wouldn't we perhaps like to spend our three weeks doing a comfortable Jeep tour of the world-famous cultural and anthropological sites of Pakistan, taking mini-safaris by elephant and camel, staying in four-star hotels, and shopping in numerous handicraft centers along the way?

Unanimously, we rejected his plan. We were of one mind, intent on hiking in the region of Ultar, a peak at 21,300 feet in the mountains of Hunza. We resigned ourselves to hiring an expensive private helicopter to drop us in Hunza. We lost a day waiting, only to learn that all aircraft were engaged in emergency evacuations. Then, miraculously, we heard that the Karakoram Highway had been cleared far enough to get us to our destination, but only if we were willing to scramble over the remaining rock slides on foot. We were all game, enthusiastic, but little did we know what lay before us.

Lola, Cec, and Georgette clearing the Karakoram highway

The Karakoram Highway is a Himalayan segment of Marco Polo's legendary silk route from Europe to China, a narrow, serpentine road hand-carved into sheer cliffs along the roaring Indus River, through a deep gorge gouged out over millions of years. It was built by the Chinese as a route from Pakistan to Kashgar, China. Our intrepid group jammed onto an old bus, and when we hit a section of road that was totally blocked by rocks, we pulled on our hiking boots, grabbed our daypacks, and scrambled over the debris. It was frightening, ducking the rocks falling from above with the Indus River roaring ominously below us. Once past the obstructions and back on the road, we would hop onto another stranded vehicle that would take us to the next impasse. After a couple hours of jolting along in a cramped vehicle, it was a respite to get out and climb over rocks and boulders in the fresh air.

For Abe, who had an extreme case of acrophobia— fear of heights—the challenge was to not look down at the raging Indus below; he kept repeating to himself, "We're going to make it." Climbing the rockfalls was terrifying, and we raced to get beyond them as quickly as possible. When we did take a moment to look down at the loose gravel surrounding the fallen boulders, we discovered we were in the middle of a field of garnets, newly exposed by the landslide. The Hunza Mountains are famous for their gems. Excitedly we filled our pockets with hundreds of the beautiful jewels, calling the area Garnet Heaven. Throughout the rest of our trip, we gave these precious garnets as gifts or in exchange for help or services, though we still came home with many of them.

After three days of traveling this tortuous route, we reached the scenic and busy town of Gilgit, the hub of the Karakoram Highway at 4,500 feet in elevation, where we spent the night in a hotel, acclimating. It took another two days for our bus to climb the narrow, rough road to our destination, the village of Karimabad in Hunza.

From there we started out on a two-week hike near the Ultar Mountains, in snowy territory on the side of a glacier in the high mountains above Karimabad. We had read in *Time* magazine about a Japanese climber who had died attempting to summit the mountain, swept away by an avalanche. We established our tents not far from a memorial to him. The porters had no more than set up camp overlooking the glacier when we heard a massive boom—an avalanche!—and Beek yelled, "Everyone into their tents, quick!"

Don, Lyn, and I got into the tent and held hands, praying, "I sure hope we get out of this alive." The snow fell on our tents for three or four minutes, every one of which was terrifying for us, holding on to each other and repeating how much we loved each other. We thought we were going to die, buried alive in the mountains. Luckily, by the time the billowing cloud reached us it had been reduced to a light snow.

It was at this camp that half of our number made the difficult decision to return and not cross over the pass. Don had altitude sickness and Abe and Stan were both afraid of heights, so I accompanied them downhill over a treacherous route back to Karimabad. Georgette, Yvonne, Lyn, and Lola continued the arduous three-day hike over the high-altitude pass. One day the porters arrived at our hotel in Karimabad quite out of breath to announce that the women trekkers had returned. We rushed out to a scene that I shall never forget! The four women marched triumphantly abreast down the middle of the main street in their colorful costumes and heavy hiking boots, with the biggest smiles on their faces. We all applauded. Their success had been announced to the whole village, and all four were decorated lavishly with flowers and apricots by the proud Hunzakut women. The four said that crossing the pass was the most empowering personal experience of their lives.

Hunza, the fabled and remote place "where four worlds meet," is a land of cultural and ethnic diversity. From the cities of Gilgit and Karimabad I saw people with Chinese features, some who looked Indian or Pakistani, and even some with lighter skin and red hair. For hundreds of years the Silk Road caravan route traveled through this region, exposing the people to a range of cultures from Europe to China.

We found the Hunzakuts quite open and accepting of people of different ethnicities. Stan Goldberg had a particularly touching experience. The Pakistani government officially disliked Jews, and Israelis were not allowed in the country. One day Stan was chatting with a villager who asked him if he was "Hebrew." Stan said he was, and the man replied that we all had one God but different ways to worship, and that was fine. Stan recalls it as a profound moment when he "could have been in Berkeley" for the open acceptance he felt.

Pakistan is officially an Islamic state, and Abe, for one, found it a real eye-opener to observe a society absolutely free of alcohol (even though hashish was legal), with nary a pig to stink up the villages.

When our bus first entered the Hunza Valley, I gasped upon viewing what must be some of the most spectacular scenery in the world. This area of northern Pakistan, bordered by China, India, Afghanistan, and the former Soviet Union, remains vivid in my memory, with its villages nestled in high mountains, clifftop orchards, waterfalls cascading down to vineyards below, and romantic castles perched on crags high above gorges. Orchards were laden with luscious apples, apricots, and peaches, and the fields were abundant with vegetables during our September visit. The apricot is so important in Hunza's economy that apricot trees can be willed separately from the land on which they stand. During the winter, heavy snows isolate Hunza and its valleys from the rest of the world for six or seven months.

Hunzakuts are friendly, hardy, and protective of their unique traditions. They take pride in their land and live in close harmony with the environment. The bulk of the population, then 40,000, lived in small mountain villages along the rivers. Each village is the focus of an intricate network of irrigation canals meticulously carved into the hills and cliffs. The villagers are ingenious farmers and pastoralists. Every village is an oasis, with terraces, walls, and waterways nestled among lush farms, orchards, and vineyards. The Hunzakuts produce apricots, peaches, walnuts, apples, cherries, grapes, mulberries, melons, potatoes, corn, wheat, onions, and turnips. Fruit, especially the apricot, is the staple food. Even the apricot stone is used for fuel, and the kernel is ground into flour, pounded for its oil, or eaten as a nut.

I observed that theirs was a subsistence economy, with neither poverty nor great wealth (with the exception of the governor). When a father died, his oldest son inherited the land and the other sons were given land from a community reserve. All the sons were also given the basic necessities to begin their own households.

Hunzakuts produce essentially everything they need, and their society is not consumer-oriented or materialistic. Much business is done by barter. Their main concerns are to be able to grow enough to feed their families and to have enough fuel and food to last the winter. Food is cooked atop an open hearth in the floor. There is no chimney, so smoke escapes through a hole in the roof, which uses passive ventilation to pull out the exhaust. During winter this vent must be closed, and the low-ceilinged houses are often heavy with fumes.

In 1992, Hunza households did not have refrigerators and other electrical appliances, except for transistor radios. The men and boys of Karimabad did gather in the evenings at the local restaurant to watch tapes on the only TV/VCR in the village. With the recent electrification of the region, however, much of this may be changing.

Before our trip, as I mentioned, I had written numerous letters to well-connected friends in Mumbai and Delhi, asking if they had any leads or connections who could inform the Aga Khan, the Ismailis' spiritual leader, about my planned research on the health and longevity of the women of Hunza. As a result, our trekking group was invited to stay at the legendary Mir of Hunza's palace in Karimabad, the old capital of the former Kingdom of Hunza.

The Mirs of Hunza had ruled the region for 1,100 years, until 1974, when Hunza became part of Pakistan. Although the old government was abolished, the now-honorary Mir remained in his palace. Educated abroad, the current Mir had traveled back and forth from Hunza to Europe.

Upon our arrival, the Mir was at the palace to welcome us. The palace was huge with beautiful, well-kept grounds, but inside most of the rooms were neglected and in disrepair. Our large rooms were cold and sparsely furnished. The bathrooms' old-fashioned fixtures dated to before World War II. Hot water was nonexistent; when Don and I wanted to bathe, we were given two pails of water heated on the stoves by the small remaining staff. We learned to bathe completely on one bucket of water! We spent our two days at the Mir's palace acclimating to the altitude.

When our group of travelers first viewed Karimabad, we saw a compact village with a post office, bank, small food store, bookshop, separate girls' and boys' high schools, a few small hotels, and the Aga Khan Women's Health Center. Although the Aga Khan lived in luxury in Europe, he contributed to his followers' education and welfare. He was dedicated to building schools and supporting education for women, a revolutionary idea at the time.

In Karimabad, artisans sold local crafts in tiny shops—embroidery, semiprecious minerals from the nearby mountains, handwoven jackets and hats, and some household items that had been brought over the Kashgar Pass from China. Our group enjoyed wandering in and out of these shops, talking with the local people, and purchasing unique handicrafts to bring home.

In order to be appropriately dressed in Pakistan, upon our arrival in the country, we five women had adopted the Muslim traditional national dress: the *shalwar kameez,* a loose, long top and baggy trousers, and a *dupatta,* a lightweight scarf draped around the shoulders and head. I found the *shalwar kameez* extremely comfortable and cool, especially while we were clambering over the rocky landslides along the Karakoram Highway.

I happily wore this local dress throughout our trip and was met with many appreciative smiles from Hunzakut and Pakistani women. Loving color, I found the Hunza women aesthetically exciting in their brightly colored *shalwar kameez* and *dupattas.* They did not wear the *purdah* (the veil), as in the rest of Pakistan. Mature women painstakingly embroidered small skullcaps, wearing them proudly and taking great pleasure in their own creativity. Counting each silk thread, these women blended rich reds, blues, greens, oranges, yellows, and purples into the colorful headwear.

Our guide Beek was born in Karimabad and had lived there all his life. Beek had told the local women about my research on women and aging and had arranged home visits with older women so I could interview them. On an initial visit with the women in the village, I invited my daughter Lyn and two other women in our group, Lola and Yvonne, to accompany me. The purpose of this visit was to give the women some background on the reasons for my research and tell them a little about myself, so they would feel comfortable and at ease during our interviews.

Dressed in traditional Pakistani garb, the four of us were welcomed into our hostess's home. As we entered, I could smell the delicious fragrances of baked cakes and appreciated the table set with apricots and nuts for snacks. Gathered around the main living area were many women—grandmothers, mothers, daughters, daughters-in-law, granddaughters, great-granddaughters—all interested in us and thrilled that my daughter Lyn was traveling with me. We were able to communicate nonverbally through smiles and gestures as they proudly showed us around their home. I showed them photographs of my family, explaining that they lived in the United States, and passed around photographs of our home. We promised we would return the day after next.

Two days later, tape recorder in hand and with the help of the two young Muslim women interpreters, I was able to navigate the complex language issues. I was pleased with their sensitive translation and felt very fortunate to have their help. I interviewed twelve women in Karimabad and the nearby village of Dueker. Eight of the women were between sixty and ninety-one years of age. Some suspected they were in their late seventies or eighties but weren't sure of their exact birthdates.

These women were friendly and hospitable, asking me to return and to bring my friends and family. Wherever I visited with the interpreters, we were offered walnuts and dried fruits as presents. Without exception, each woman I interviewed offered freshly baked unleavened bread, which had been prepared on a stone hearth. Apricot jam was drizzled on the hot bread and served with tea.

Meeting with local women in Karimabad, Hunza, 1992

In that first interview, Beek had arranged for me to meet
with women from various families in one home. On subsequent interviews I traveled to each woman's house to interview her individually. I asked each about her life, early marriage, children, and relations with her husband. I had asked
the interviewees to invite other female family members, for I
had been advised that their presence would stimulate more ac-
curate accounts. These other female family members, clearly
intrigued by me and the two translators, sat transfixed during
the interviews, responding by nodding their heads and speaking among themselves, at times corroborating or correcting
the claims of the woman being interviewed.

In the course of these interviews, while walking about to various homes in Karimabad, I observed how similar they were in size and layout, none particularly more affluent than the others. It felt to me that there were few class distinctions, although an occasional home had the amenity of running water from cisterns and flush toilets.

I learned that marriages were arranged at an early age. Often the bride and groom did not see each other before marriage. When the girl reached puberty, she moved into her husband's family's home and the marriage was consecrated. Both families put much time and thought into the selection process, and surprisingly, these arranged marriages worked for the Hunzakuts. My teacher-interpreters, both in their early twenties, wanted me to know that their contemporaries were no longer bound to accept their parents' first choice in an arranged marriage. One interpreter related that she was able to meet other prospective partners recommended by her parents before she chose the man she would marry.

Toward the end of the second interview, I gathered courage and inquired about the role of sexuality in the women's lives. In Ismaili Muslim society, the sexual drives of both men and women are recognized as a natural instinct. Procreation does not need to be the reason for the enjoyment of sex between a husband and wife.

One woman I interviewed, who was sixty-three and whose husband was eighty-one, took me by the hand and led me away from the interpreters and the rest of her family to a separate room she shared with her husband. She sensually patted the hand-sewn quilts on the single bed to indicate in body language and gesture that this was the conjugal bed. She took me into the bathroom, which in this household, better off than most, had running water and a flush toilet. She demonstrated how she carefully washed her face, underarms, and body. Looking at her image in a small mirror, she smiled and simulated putting lotions on her body and in her hair. As she combed her long hair slowly and sensually, it was evident that she was preparing for sex with her husband. Her final nonverbal act was to lie on the bed and move her body in a fluid and sexy manner. There was no doubt what she was telling me.

From my interviews I learned that husbands were, on average, ten to twenty years older than their wives. In my interviews I did not hear any woman claim she was unhappy with her husband. It may have been that some of the women did not want to divulge complaints about their husbands to an American researcher. But in my observation, these women seemed satisfied with their lives and devoted to their families.

In one interview, when I asked, "Who makes the important decisions in the family?" the woman pointed to herself, nodding and saying, "I do." Immediately there was a hum and chatter as the other women shook their heads no and made her correct herself. "I take care of everything in the home," she amended. "My husband takes care of the financial matters."

Talking about division of labor in the home, one elder woman told me: "My daughters-in-law obey me. But we work together." I was repeatedly told, "We combine, meet together, work together, and solve any difficulty." During this interview one woman told me: "We women worked not only in our home but also in the fields during most of our lives. Our household is self-sufficient." She pointed to the stacks of fruits and vegetables drying on the roof and the big bags of dried apricots.

It is the Hunzakut women who, in addition to caring for the home, work laboriously in the short summer months to provide enough food to last the family through the long winters. Families with abundant crops share their food with those who have less. Women of all ages toil in the fields, harvesting the fruits and vegetables and drying them on their roofs in the sun before the first snows. In the fall, it is the women who gather twigs and shrubs to use as fuel for the winter. They walk throughout their lives, and though some villagers may have been housebound, I did not see anyone walking with a cane.

While the women work in the fields or homes, the men's role is to father children and gather together in groups during the day to smoke and talk. Collectively they help build each other's homes and perform the hard manual labor, such as carving the terraces and maintaining the irrigation systems.

I asked each woman through the interpreters: "What happens when you grow really old? Where do you live? Who takes care of you?" I was told that as they grew older, their daughters-in-law and unmarried daughters would take over the household duties. If desired, they could continue working in the fields, albeit for shorter hours and closer to home. I noticed that grandmothers cared for the small children part of the day, when the younger women were working the fields.

One of the most dramatic differences I noted between Western society and that of the Hunza people is that the Hunzakuts considered old age a most important part of the life cycle, as evidenced by the manner in which older people are esteemed. It is customary for grandchildren to bow their heads to the elders' feet and kiss their hands.

As a woman aged, she had absolute faith that she would not have to worry about where she would live or who would take care of her. Her sons, daughters-in-law, and grandchildren would always care for and revere her. Even if a woman remained unmarried or was a widow without children, a male relative would voluntarily take on this responsibility without rancor. If this were not the case, the woman had the right to make a claim against her male relative.

Muslim women are at times portrayed as submissive and without freedom, burying themselves in the home and going out into the world timidly, veiled and escorted. This stereotype is false for many Muslim women and was not the case for the Ismaili Muslim women I met in Hunza. There, older women walked down the main street of their villages openly and unveiled, though usually accompanied by another older woman or family member.

When walking in the villages, the women looked directly at me and smiled, and I smiled back. Our smiles were a connection to open conversation; even though we didn't speak the same language, we easily communicated nonverbally.

From my interviews, I came away with the feeling that Hunza women were confident, respected members of society, skilled in growing crops, and expert in crafts and homemaking. They valued their domestic skills—cooking, raising their children, caring for their family and husbands, and doing their creative handiwork. Women worked together within the family harmoniously. Though most of the older women I interviewed had neither attended school nor learned to read or write, their outside interests, their work in the fields, their friendships with other women, and Tanzin, the important women's organization they belonged to, all gave them a sense of identity outside the home.

I heard so much about Tanzin from the women, who bubbled with excitement as they described it to me. Each woman I interviewed proudly told me that it was a social space for women to be with each other as friends and to work together, whether on handicrafts, combining crops from the fields for sale, or collecting money to put in a bank for collective savings used to help one another. Each village Tanzin group is run cooperatively, giving these women a zone of empowerment, much like the women's movement in the United States.

Social services as we know them (nurses, social workers, clergy, hired caregivers, psychologists, babysitters) are all handled within the Hunza family, so that each extended family is self-sufficient. Women in the family act as midwives.

In the past, when a wife was unable to have children or had only daughters, the husband had the right to take a second wife, while the first wife continued to live in the household. None of the new generation considered polygamy a desirable lifestyle. I asked one woman, if she had had girls instead of two boys, would her husband have considered taking a second wife? She did not believe so at all. "What if he did?" I asked. "I would kill him," she responded, which gives a flavor of the strength that some women feel in this society. Each of the twelve women I interviewed was her husband's only wife.

Family planning was not practiced among the older generation, although it was among the younger people. Infant and child mortality rates were high, so women purposely got pregnant many times because they knew chances were high that their children would not survive. A major factor in the child mortality rates was untreated water piped in from the mountain snowmelt, although before we got to Hunza the Aga Khan had installed a huge water purification system.

Researchers have postulated that the Hunzakuts may live so long in part because only the hardy survive childhood. Additionally, because the high mountains are not conducive to raising animals, the people consume very little fat except from chicken, goat, or yak on festive occasions. My own conclusion is that their longevity has to do mostly with their lifestyle—healthy food, constant exercise (and time to rest during the six-month winter), as well as incredible social support.

Stan, the physician in our group, and Yvonne, a nurse, visited the local medical clinic and found that, despite very few drugs and the lack of modern facilities, the staff took great pride in caring for their community. A nurse ran the clinic, but a physician from Gilgit visited periodically. They had just received a new delivery table, outdated by Western standards, which they displayed with great pride. When people were hospitalized, the family camped out in the clinic right by the patient's bed and provided food for the patient.

When I interviewed the two young women translators, I found that they had received eight to twelve years of education and were proud of their reading and writing skills. Women in Hunza are realizing the value of education for girls and encouraging them to attend school. With fewer restrictions on the present generation, they told me, more women were being educated.

Engaged with the land and the seasons, women continued to be physically active as they grew older. In the summers they worked in the fields. In winter, during the six months of the year when the country is isolated by heavy snowfall, the women remain indoors, working on handicrafts and making the family's clothing. They shear the sheep, spin the yarn, and weave the cloth into garments. They valued the gifts I had brought, including sewing aids (needles, pins, and thread), special scissors, and Velcro.

It was with dismay that I discovered the older women were having problems seeing their handiwork. I handed my bifocals to one woman who was astonished to be able to see the small stitches of her embroidery. Through the interpreter, I found out that the only facility for glasses was in Gilgit, many miles away and a difficult trip for the villagers without transportation. Buses to Gilgit were rare and expensive, and private vehicles were a luxury, owned only by those whose business warranted it. I promised upon my return home to send reading glasses to the village doctor to distribute.

Shortly after returning home, I bought dozens of pairs of reading glasses in various strengths, packed them, and sent them off to Hunza. Later I got word that the women were thrilled that they could again see their needlework. I also called the director of the University of California's optometry department and suggested that they have doctors and nurses do pro bono work in Hunza and perhaps set up a clinic.

Without Beek's help, our trek through the Karakoram mountains and my cross-cultural research in Hunza would have lacked the intimate flavor he brought to both. Through the miracles of the computer and the Internet, this year, as I was writing this memoir, I was able to locate Beek in Karimabad, where he still lives. Hearing his voice one morning on the telephone brought back all the vivid memories of our pleasurable trip. He informed me that since an accident in the mountains he has no longer been able to guide. His daughters, who were small children in 1992, were now grown and attending college at the University of Virginia. He remembered everyone in our group and was so happy to have reconnected.

Beek informed me that the situation is Hunza had grown worse since our visit. War and environmental disasters had plagued the villagers of northern Pakistan, while governments did little to ease their plight. Gone is the peaceful paradise we experienced.

The Karakoram Highway continues to experience landslides like the one that obstructed our bus. Recently, a landslide so large that it blocked the Hunza River created a lake fourteen kilometers long, which threatens to burst and inundate scores of villages in the Hunza Valley. Water contamination has resurged as a cause of disease, and during the recurrent crises food is often scarce.

Lessons from Hunza

Inspired by the women of Hunza, who continued to walk and to work their terraced fields late into life, I returned to Berkeley with the recognition that walking is a key to health and longevity. As I looked around at my women friends in their sixties and seventies who were leading sedentary lives, I noticed they were heavier and complained that they lacked the physical energy they had in the past, tiring more easily. In their fifties, these sedentary friends still looked quite good and seemed to have the energy and ability to participate in everyday activities, but by their sixties and seventies their bodies had changed drastically. In contrast, the new friends I had made at the health club, who exercised and walked regularly, were trim and energetic.

Exercise became my renewed priority. I scheduled work, appointments, and social life around my workouts. Exercise classes went on the calendar first; other commitments were worked around them. Three days a week I walked to my health club to take classes in pilates, dance, and weight lifting. In earlier years I had been able to take dynamic, heart-pounding aerobics classes, but with the knee problems that had started in my sixties, movements that required jumping or heavy impact were not possible.

Soon after my return from Hunza I discovered Nia (Neuromuscular Integrative Action) at Rancho la Puerta, a health and fitness resort in Tecate, northern Baja California, Mexico, where I regularly presented workshops on vitality in aging. Nia is a dance technique combining movement of body, mind, and spirit without the pounding and stress on joints. I urged the director of our health club in Berkeley to offer this invigorating class. There were few qualified Nia instructors in the Bay Area at that time, but checking around, we found a certified instructor for Nia classes at our club.

What is it about movement and music that continues to evoke joy for me? I luxuriate in sensuality when my body moves freely in space to music. Dancing buoyantly and bare-foot with others about me, I feel ecstasy envelop me. Though I was thirty to forty years older than the others in my class, with worn-out knees that did not bend well and unable to wave my arms with abandon because of a torn rotator cuff, I was one of the few dancers in our Nia classes who felt the freedom to voice grunts and joyous sounds.

In my younger years I loved to dance barefoot to my fa-vorite records on the smooth, velvety floors of the living room late at night—jumping, twirling, falling to the floor, rolling, singing. Movement has always been a natural high for me, and a great source of energy and release.

After Nia sessions I returned home energetic and rejuve-nated. Following a healthy lunch of salad or homemade soup, like those of the Hunzakuts, I returned to my bright red of-fice to write and edit my book on vitality and aging. Often I spent an hour or more working on behalf of the numerous environmental, political, and other nonprofit groups that give meaning to my life.

Several times a month I joined colleagues or friends for lunch or a walk. Remembering the Hunzakuts, at least two afternoons a week I walked for an hour or longer in my beloved Berkeley hills, often with Don joining me. Walking in nature, immersed in its beauty and accompanied by birdsong, invariably infuses me with peace and tranquility.

I also enjoyed the evenings spent with my friends Sara, Ailish, and Christie, whom I had met at Antioch University. After graduation we formed a women's group that met regularly for dinner and conversation. This group meant so very much to me. I loved how after these many years I could talk to these women in a way that I was unable to with my older women friends. We shared the language of the Human Potential Movement. We not only had a history of three years in school together but had become close friends outside of academia. Our relationships were so deep that they extended to interest in each other's families. On a visit to Santa Fe, New Mexico, I had lunch with Christie's mother, where we shared some of our life stories with each other. Meeting her conservative mother at her private club, I better understood Christie's rejection of that lifestyle and her motivation for studying holistic psychology.

By this time Christie was in graduate school for her Ph.D. in psychology. Sara was living and practicing as a therapist in San Francisco and had bought her first house. Both women did further study and each now has a private therapy practice. What a gift to have these younger women in my life as friends. As busy as we were, we made special efforts to set aside these meaningful dates. We supported each other through our lows and highs and discussed our thoughts, careers, relationships, and any other topics that came up. This was our little Tanzin; another lesson from the Hunzakuts. Though scattered now (in Peru, Washington, D.C., and the Bay Area), we remain close friends.

Don's Vision Loss

Don had dealt with vision challenges since age five, when he lost the sight in one eye due to an accident. This kept him from enlisting in World War II; he was rejected from the Air Force four times because of impaired vision. In his fifties, Don developed adult-onset diabetes, with its resulting eye vulnerabilities. In his sixties he fell on the ice while skiing and suddenly couldn't see. He had to be rushed to the hospital to repair a detached retina.

The doctors were able to restore his sight, but a few years later, while we were hiking in Italy's Dolomites, he was again suddenly unable to see. Luckily we had just rendezvoused with a doctor friend from San Francisco, Gerry Levine, who promptly got on the phone, located the nearest hospital (in Milan), and made an appointment for Don to be examined. We drove frantically for three hours through a downpour to Milan, where the ophthalmologist assessed Don's eye condition as very serious but regretted that we would have to wait two weeks for surgery, since their healthcare system was overbooked. Within a day we were on a flight to San Francisco, where Don's detached retina was immediately operated on at the California Medical Center. If we had arrived a day later, it would have been too late to save his vision.

Nearly a decade later, cataracts began to cloud Don's good eye. With Don's background of detached retinas in that eye, the ophthalmologist was concerned with the danger of total blindness if cataract surgery failed. Don asked me if I would want to live with a blind man, fearing he would be a burden to me. It was a sad and scary time for us. We spoke of how our lives would change if he was blind. I did my best to reassure him of my unconditional love, telling him that I would drive, read to him, and help him with whatever he needed. He knew the house well and could use his other senses to navigate our home. We could still make love and listen to music. This impending crisis brought us even closer.

Don questioned the point in traveling when he couldn't see, but I promised that I would describe the world before us in full detail. In 1994, as his eyesight was deteriorating, we took a trip we had planned years earlier, to Prague and the Tatra Mountains in Slovakia. In Paris's crowded Charles de Gaulle airport, buzzing with foreign languages and bustling with pushing people, I held Don's hand as I guided him toward the gate for Prague. When I needed to use the bathroom, I told him I'd be back in a few minutes and to wait right there for me. He must not have heard, because when I returned, his face was pale with fear. "Where were you?" he asked in a broken voice that conveyed how lost he felt in the chaotic airport, where he could neither see nor speak the language.

Set on the banks of the Vltava River, Prague is one of Europe's most beautiful cities, and I used imaginative language to paint a portrait of it for Don. Together we savored the street music that is everywhere in Prague, Don listening as I described the swinging trio playing in front of an outdoor coffeehouse, a group singing a cappella on the next corner, and further on, a single musician playing haunting tunes on the violin. Despite his fading vision, the sounds and music of Prague captivated him and pulled us in various directions as we walked throughout the city, visiting museums and taking in concerts.

For a full day I guided Don through the baroque Prague Castle, detailing for him the opulent, highly ornamented architecture, pillars, and spires all about us. Don claims he felt the proportions and grandeur of the castle as we walked its broad expanse. With his hands he felt the intricate carvings along the heavy marble railings as we climbed the stairs to the majestic Saint Vitus Cathedral, where we listened to the rich sounds of a baroque music recital on the great organ. We stopped regularly in Old Town Square to join the bevy of people gathered to hear and watch the astounding astronomical clock chime its hourly notes. I explained to Don how a trap door opens on the hour to display a procession of the Twelve Apostles.

Yet I often felt overwhelmed as his guide. When we arrived at the station to catch our train to the High Tatras, I was obliged to interpret posted directions and decipher multiple station announcements in foreign languages as we pulled our luggage past many train cars, Don holding on to my arm. When we finally located our car, I sighed with relief.

Once in the spectacular Tatra Mountains, we used our walking sticks to navigate the trails. I pointed out the rocks and tree roots that protruded along the trail and steered him over these and other obstacles. We communicated easily with local hikers about our common love for walking in the mountains, and they would join us for part of the way, stopping with us for lunch because it pleased them to see older foreigners on their trails.

After we returned to the United States, it became impossible for Don to travel alone, and I became his regular driver. This loss of independence and freedom crushed Don, who loved driving his car and taking me about. He could no longer read even large-print books, forcing him to listen to books on tape. It was a hard time for us. Don's ophthalmologist kept putting off surgery, until the vision in his only eye was so severely impaired that he couldn't see at all.

What a blessing and relief when the doctor finally agreed to set a date for surgery. After the successful operation, Don exclaimed: "Miraculous! I can see better than I've been able to in years." He now reads books again and even drives at night. Little did I know that within a few years we would reverse roles—I would be the one losing my sight, and Don the one helping me.

1995 White House Conference on Aging

Everyone told me I could never be chosen as a delegate to the 1995 White House Conference on Aging (WHCOA). Over 20,000 applicants were vying for a few hundred spots, yet I was intent on attending. Then-Governor Pete Wilson, Senator Dianne Feinstein, Senator Barbara Boxer, and other members of Congress chose the delegates for their contributions to the field of aging and their expertise on the issues of aging Americans.

Unfortunately, I did not know the governor or senators personally, and none of my applications were accepted. Yet I remained determined to attend the WHCOA as a delegate. I asked my friend Lynn Ferrin, a journalist and editor, to look at my application and tell me why she thought I was being turned down, for I knew I was a qualified and desirable candidate. She told me my biography needed to make a visual impact, that it was too wordy and dull. I needed to rewrite it with bullets and punchy statements and keep it to one page.

Following her directions, I forwarded my zippy new résumé to George Miller, the representative from Contra Costa County. He reported back that I was the most qualified candidate of the many who had applied and chose me as a delegate. I am convinced that my continued optimism and perseverance, along with my more readable résumé, influenced my eventual selection as a delegate.

The thousands of delegates selected from all over the United States included Native Americans, veterans, older

Americans with disabilities, grandparents or spouses as caregivers, and many others. From many political backgrounds and walks of life, we came together around this issue of "aging policy" in order to provide recommendations to Congress and the president. These were policies we felt older adults in this country were entitled to.

*I advocated for older Americans at the
White House Conference on Aging, 1995*

According to our expertise and interests, we broke up into working groups on topics such as minorities and women's issues, transportation, housing, support services, maximizing quality of life, preventative health, nutrition, safety, and

Alzheimer's research. There were public debates and presentations, and after three days we assembled final resolutions that we presented to President Clinton and the members of Congress.

Most important to all of the delegates was ensuring the continuity of Social Security, which was under threat of privatization, and advocating for a better health care system, such as a universal Medicare that would recognize needs for long-term care. Regretfully, not all of the resolutions were acted upon. Some successes were immediate, however, such as the reauthorization of the Older Americans Act, which assured funding for services such as subsidized meals, transportation, legal counseling, elder abuse prevention, senior centers, assisted living, nutrition education, and health promotion.

Flash Flood: Utah, 1997

"Move it!" BJ shouted to me just as we were putting our clothes back on after a refreshing dip in the stream. Susie Gawne, a Great Old Broad, and her daughter Lynn Hughes had been resting and waiting for us so that we could all hike out to the trailhead together when BJ heard the loud roar of water, noticed a rise in the small tributary trickling into the stream, and screamed, "Move it!" again to all of us. The stream had been suddenly transformed into wide, fast-running water.

My daughters, BJ and Lyn, had come to join me for an outing with a group of GOBs in Escalante, Utah. Our day hike to the south arm of Fence Canyon had begun under brilliant blue skies, but it rained during the course of the morning. The group ducked under a ledge until the downpour passed. Around 12:30, Susie, her daughter Lynn, my daughter BJ, and I decided to have a leisurely picnic lunch and a dip in a little stream by the trail rather than attempt to keep up with the faster-walking GOBs hiking the loop route. My daughter Lyn offered to stay with me, but I assured her that the four of us would be OK.

Now, as "Flash flood!" raced through our minds, BJ and I threw our belongings into our backpacks and ran barefoot up a trail that was rapidly being inundated by the rising mass of water. Stopping for a moment to put on our boots, we realized we had little time to get to the other side of the raging river and reach high ground, where we could hike out. Susie had already rushed ahead and crossed the swelling stream alone. Struggling across, she had been swept downstream; luckily, she was able to grab a tree branch and pull herself out.

The muddy red water was moving so forcefully that we knew we needed to get across at once. BJ and Lynn put me between them, and we supported each other, holding on tightly as we forded the rapidly rising river, terror-stricken that we would not get out of this alive. If it had not been for the two strong younger women on either side of me, I might not have made it. It took teamwork to get across. Even so, BJ and I lost our footing in the swift current and had to grab vines and tree branches on the riverbank to remain standing upright. It was Lynn's and BJ's strength and level-headedness throughout this harrowing experience that saved our lives.

Hiking out, there was no trail; it had been obliterated by the rain and wind. A passing horse packer told us we were headed in the right direction. Our visibility was limited by the mist and rain, and if not for the cairns piled on the slick rock to mark the trails, we might not have found our way out. BJ and Lynn's positive attitudes kept our spirits up, and I was particularly grateful for BJ's presence and good judgment. I felt a new bond with my Great Old Broad companions and was grateful for their help.

Justine and I in our eighties

Facing the Shadow Side

2000–2010

I've always been the positive, hopeful one, while Don has been inclined to be skeptical and cynical about the state of the world. He's often told me that I'm too innocent and trusting, that I have an unrealistically sunny picture of life. But as the year 2000 approached, bringing with it a vulnerability I hadn't experienced before, we began to exchange outlooks.

In my eighties, for the first time in my life I seemed to be facing the shadow side. My life had a different quality from earlier years as I found myself unable to do as much in a day or think as quickly. I was still an active woman, but now in an older body. The idea of my mortality crept into my awareness with each new physical challenge.

My left knee joint had worn out. In pain, I struggled up the stairs to our bedroom by putting all my weight on my good knee while hanging on to the railing and dragging my stiff left leg up to the next step. I had experienced knee injuries before, but now just walking or putting any weight on the left one was excruciatingly painful. I knew I needed to take personal responsibility for recovering my ability to walk again.

Two years earlier, not yet ready for total knee replacement surgery, I had embarked on a series of injections to build cartilage and an ambitious program of physical therapy. After two years of this, and of using pain pills, I finally decided on surgery. I had just turned eighty and wondered, "Is this what I have to look forward to?" The knee replacement eliminated the pain, but my joints could no longer take squats or knee bends, nor jumping and running. I worried that my days of glorious high-energy running and aerobic dancing were over.

I had to learn to ask for a glass of water and needed help just carrying my purse. I depended on Don, friends, and hired helpers to drive me wherever I needed to go. Giving up control during recovery was agonizing.

The doctor told me to take it easy, but I was impatient to get on with my life. I brought my doctor a picture of me with a backpack and a huge smile, hiking up a mountain. "This is the kind of life I want to continue to lead," I told him. He said that I wouldn't be able to hike any longer, to which I replied, "I want you to believe that I can recover my strength to hike again, and I want your support and help." Only after I insisted did he agree to approve physical therapy.

Determined to regain my physical vigor, I pursued a rigorous physical therapy program two to three times a week for six months, supplementing it with my own exercises at home and the gym. Strongly dedicated to my recovery, after a hard six months of workouts I was joyously hiking and exercising again.

After five active years, my right knee gave out, and I had a partial replacement performed by orthopedists at Stanford University Hospital. Six weeks later I was hiking in Yosemite and fell on my new knee. Within two weeks it was swollen, and I returned to Stanford for a second surgery to remove the water in the knee. An infection set in, and I was back at the hospital for a third procedure.

My journal was an outlet for my fear and depression. I wrote: "I'm feeling so vulnerable and frightened. The cast on my right leg from ankle to hip, with steel stays to prevent bending my knee, is weighing me down. I'm on crutches with strict instructions from my surgeon not to walk except around the house, and to keep the weight off my knee. I'm frightened and visualize being an old lady in a wheelchair. I have no timeframe from the doctor for when I can remove this brace, throw away the crutches, and walk again. All summer I've been challenged by knee swelling, pain, and now the staph infection from surgery on my right knee feels ominous. Could I lose my leg?"

Recovering from these surgeries was a long, arduous process. Most of that year I was strapped into a knee brace with strict limits on walking, driving, and physical activity. It marked the beginning of a slower pace of life, walking, concentrating on pilates, tai chi, and other low-impact activities rather than the strenuous hiking, dancing, and running that I had been accustomed to. However, though it took much energy and time, my knee healed—I did recover.

After the two knee surgeries, one night I woke up nauseous, my bedroom spinning around me. I was unable to sit up or utter a word, and Don called 911, fearing a stroke. Within a few minutes the paramedics arrived and rushed me to Alta Bates's emergency room. I was diagnosed with positional vertigo, and it continued for months. It made me nauseous and so off-balance that I bumped into doorframes and furniture. When I changed my focus or moved, the room began to spin. Feeling out of control, I was unable to leave home and unable to drive.

The doctor's only remedy was prescription medicine that made me feel dopey and sleepy, and again I sought alternatives. Researching treatments for positional vertigo, I discovered vestibular therapy, a program of maneuvers and exercises that boost the central nervous system and retrain the inner ear to improve balance and coordination. Luckily, Alta Bates had a therapist, Marcela Larrondo, who specialized in this highly advanced technique. Six months of regular vestibular therapy sessions with Marcela and at-home practice finally helped me recover.

In addition to these physical challenges, I was coping with other common diseases of aging. Without two hearing aids, I was practically deaf. Glaucoma had impaired my vision, so in order to see I needed bifocals for reading and distance, special glasses for reading, and a third pair just for the computer. Such physical setbacks were devastating.

Concerned friends and family insisted that I needed to slow down, but I wasn't ready and didn't want to. As a child I had delighted in classes in ballet, tap, and acrobatics; I played kickball and climbed trees all over our neighborhood. In college I took courses in modern dance, tennis, and swimming, and at student dances I relished in the jitterbug and lindy hop. I danced in a modern dance group until the day before my first child was born, and all through the years our children were growing up, our whole family danced around the house together to jazz records. After my divorce, I took up hiking and discovered a passion for mountain climbing. These pursuits introduced me to a whole new culture of the outdoors, the spiritual value of wilderness, and the environmental movement. I needed to keep moving.

A Locker-Room Explosion

The events of September 11, 2001, left me utterly devastated and vulnerable. I dreamed of those who lost their lives and identified with their loved ones and families. As I worked out at the Claremont Health Club a few weeks after the tragedy, my mood mirrored that of many across the country—confused, anxious, sad, and low-spirited. That zeitgeist, combined with frustration over my increasing physical limitations and a mounting anger with the club's lack of care for its older members, led to a very uncharacteristic explosion on my part.

As long as I have lived in the San Francisco Bay Area, the Claremont Hotel has been a distinguished historical landmark and a favorite meeting place for University of California students and faculty. The huge, stately old hotel, reminiscent of a castle, is nestled into thirteen and a half acres in the Berkeley/Oakland hills. Whenever I fly into the Bay Area, the Claremont's all-white structure and grounds stand out clearly.

Fifty years ago, when the Claremont first opened its pool and tennis club, Rudy and I saved up and paid the $500 membership fee to join. BJ, Rob, and Lyn were delighted to have a place to swim and hang out with their friends only a short walk from our home. During the early years I was an avid tennis player, but when a right rotator cuff injury sidelined me, I began to swim instead.

Ten years later, when I was in my late sixties, the Claremont added a fitness center and health club, and I began regular weight training and exercise classes. As we original members aged into our seventies, the club became a destination for a younger crowd—UC faculty, local professionals, and affluent young married couples with children. A swimming pool for children was added, as well as a kids' club and day camp in a separate building.

In 2001, the club's locker rooms had recently been refurbished, and I felt frustrated that the needs of older members clearly had not been considered. The light was so dim that I couldn't see well enough to open my combination locker. The comfortable old benches had been replaced by low three-legged stools that toppled over as I sat to undress. There was no place to put my gym bag except the wet floor. I wrote numerous indignant letters and even called the management about the inadequate lighting and the need for benches and mirrors, but no one responded.

On the day in question, feeling low in spirits, old, ignored, and marginalized, I entered the hall leading to the pool and impulsively wrote on its pristine, newly painted white wall in big capital letters, "MIRROR PLEASE!" At that moment a young female attendant came in, and she sternly demanded my name. Taken aback by my own behavior, I gave it to her.

I went outside and sat by the pool, then, overcome with remorse, rushed back in to wash the writing off the wall. Alas, I couldn't remove the indelible black ink. Resigned, I returned to the pool to sort out my conflicting thoughts and cool off.

When the Claremont Health Club's young assistant manager heard of the incident, he asked that I report to his office. Feeling guilty for acting out at my age, I defended my actions by explaining that I had called and e-mailed the management multiple times about the club's lack of understanding for the needs of older members. Compounded by my distress about 9/11, I burst out unexpectedly in a tirade over the challenges of aging—living with glaucoma, arthritis, and knee surgeries. I also admitted that my outrage was misplaced.

As a consequence of defacing the wall, I was suspended from the club for two weeks for vandalism—a sentence that would have been more severe had I not been a founding member and a respected community elder. Yet my outburst did spur the club to finally make changes to accommodate senior and disabled members. When some of the younger women members learned of my action, they applauded me for taking on the Claremont's stodgy culture. Numerous women came up to me and said: "We heard what you did. Good for you!"

Following the incident, the club became more responsive to my requests. When I again pointed out the lack of exercise classes for seniors, they promptly offered a tai chi class that I had been asking for and a special non-aerobic "core" class to help build strength and alignment. Eagerly I joined both. Without fail I come away from tai chi and core feeling invigorated, taller, and full of energy.

Race Walking

Once I stopped running, I found that I was gaining weight and missing my "runner's high." One day some neighbors passed in front of my house, pumping their arms and wiggling their hips in a funny-looking, fast-paced walk. I learned they were "race walking" and I was instantly intrigued.

I signed up for a race walking class at outdoor equipment store REI, where I learned the basics, including how to move forward quickly while keeping my feet in contact with the ground at all times. I started race walking around Lake Merritt in Oakland and joined a group that met Saturday mornings at Marin Junior College.

The course instructor, Jack Bray, encouraged me to enter the race walking division at the National Senior Games in Napa, California. He helped me train and then showed up to watch and encourage me as I won my first race! I took first place because I was the only person in my age group in the race. I was pleased to win, but even more pleased to have found a way to continue exercising aerobically. Welcoming the challenge of competitive racing, I entered more senior race walking events and kept winning, even when there were other competitors in my age group.

Though I continued to walk and exercise, the recognition of my mortality became keener as I lived through my eighties and friends were diagnosed with life-threatening diseases such as cancer and Parkinson's.

The Death of Close Friends

As my ninetieth birthday approached, I was reflecting on friends who were no longer here to celebrate with me. In a sorrowful mood I watched the video taken at my eighty-fifth birthday party. That had been such a joyful day, surrounded by family and friends, many of whom I had known for more than half my life. I felt a surge of love and affection for those men in bright ties and women in their colorful party dresses who were here with me just five years ago but were now gone forever. My friends had all looked so happy and alive, and we had shared so much. I wished them to be with me forever. I didn't want to watch them in a video—I wanted them here, now, in the flesh, so I could hug and kiss and tell each one how much our many years of friendship meant to me.

Justine, who had been my roommate in the navy and with whom I had lived at the Casbah during World War II—my most intimate woman friend—died in 2007. I had loved her from the moment we met at age twenty-three, and that love only deepened over our sixty-five-year friendship.

As a communications officer stationed at the Twelfth Naval District Headquarters in San Francisco, Justine's job had been to decode confidential messages that came in over the radio from all the ships in the Pacific. Her work was highly sensitive and she was not allowed to discuss it with anyone. Every day she relayed messages of terror and disaster. "Ship torpedoed. 1,000 men lost. Ship sunk"—such messages barraged Justine daily for months on end. It was more than her psyche could handle, and she had a mental breakdown. She was admitted to the Mare Island Naval Hospital, where she received treatment for several weeks until she obtained a medical discharge.

Afterward, when Justine began Jungian analysis, I noticed a transformation that helped her move past this most traumatic time in her life. Analysis also influenced her return to graduate school in social welfare at the University of California, Berkeley; later she became a professor in UC's social welfare department and a much-sought-after Jungian therapist in her own right. She became a specialist in sand tray therapy, focusing on children.

In her thirties, Justine met the love of her life, Larry Fixel. She had a passion for art, was an artist herself, and had always wanted to marry an artist; Larry was a poet. Their marriage of fifty years was an incredible blending of compatible beliefs and values. Justine became the breadwinner while Larry followed the creative life, writing and taking care of their home in San Francisco. He'd shop and have dinner ready for her when she came home tired from work.

With Larry's encouragement, Justine set up a studio in

their basement where she began painting and sculpting again, as she had in earlier years. Over the years I grew to appreciate Larry's friendship, his creative approaches to living, and his questioning spirit, which came alive in his politically critical poetry. I was thrilled that Justine had such a compatible, loving marriage. Theirs was a stimulating life in San Francisco, with a large group of artist and activist friends.

When Justine and Larry privately acknowledged they were nearing the end of their lives, they questioned whether they could continue to fulfill meaningful and responsible roles in society. During these years they told me how important it was for them to remain engaged intellectual elders, and to have young people in their lives who visited and learned from their wisdom.

Over the years, Justine was a frequent visitor at our house across the bay. She had loved Rudy since he and I were courting and the three of us had lived together. She was also close to my children as they were growing up. Having made a conscious decision not to bring children into what she saw as a terrible world, she threw her energy and love into mine, all three of whom absolutely adored her.

During the years leading up to my divorce, Justine was my closest confidante; she drove over regularly from San Francisco to spend the night. Knowing I had to come to my own decision about Rudy, Justine did not advise, just listened as I poured out my frustrations. I felt totally loved and supported by her, never judged, which is an unusual trait in a friendship. She loved Rudy, too and never took sides. I'm sure it was very hard for her to see us break up, and she was especially worried about the children.

When I first began seeing Don, Justine subtly let me know that she thought I was using the relationship to avoid the inner psychological work I needed to do. She felt I should take the time to grow and discover who I was; that jumping from one relationship to another was a mistake. She encouraged me to explore myself through analysis, which thankfully I did. When Don and I finally came together, years later, she became very fond of him and felt we were good together. Likewise, Don thought the world of Justine.

Justine and I were totally in sync in our political beliefs but complete opposites when it came to lifestyle. She didn't like to do anything physical, whereas I was a whirlwind of activity. She smoked for many years and in her seventies and eighties got easily winded and found it difficult to walk. She couldn't understand why I enjoyed hiking and running. She made fun of friends who bounded out of bed at six in the morning to go for a run. If I suggested a short stroll in Golden Gate Park, she'd counter with, "Let's sit on a bench and talk." Deep conversation—connecting on a profound level—was what she valued above all else.

Justine was skeptical about my travels and passion for outdoor adventure, considering it frivolous, or a type of tourism that did not help the local people. "Do you really have to travel that far to climb a mountain?" she'd ask. "Why would anyone want to endure the exertion of hiking up a mountain to spend the night in the discomfort of a sleeping bag in a tent?" She would shake her head at my daily exercise regime.

I worried that her sedentary lifestyle was bad for her health. I thought she needed exercise and once signed her up for an all-day tai chi workshop at Grace Cathedral. An hour into it, I saw her standing and watching, shaking her head. During a break she told me to never, ever try to get her to go to one of those physical classes again.

Once, in an attempt to interest her in a healthier lifestyle, I offered to take her to Rancho la Puerta Spa, just over the border in Baja California, Mexico. "How much does it cost?" she asked. "It's $2,500 a week but totally worth it," I told her. With her nose in the air, Justine said: "Give me the money. I'll give it to the homeless." There was no circumventing her liberal beliefs; she had no tolerance for what she called a bunch of bourgeois women getting massages and eating alfalfa sprouts. I couldn't help noticing, however, that she bought nice bourgeois clothes and had a large collection of sculpture and paintings, mostly by friends, in her home.

In her late seventies Justine got breast cancer and underwent a mastectomy. It was a tough period; she was angry, yet she wanted to live and tolerated chemotherapy and tamoxifen for the rest of her life. She had to tell her patients that she had cancer, and she herself did a lot of Jungian therapy around it. Larry was, of course, very supportive. Justine lived another 15 years until the cancer metastasized, and at that point she decided not to take chemotherapy any longer.

As a painter, Justine found it agonizing when she lost her sight to macular degeneration. Toward the end of her life, I took her to Carmel and we walked arm in arm on the path above the beach. This was a favorite spot for her; she knew just where she was. I became her eyes as I described the high, tumultuous waves. "I'm hearing the waves and smelling them, and through you I can even see them!" she exclaimed.

After her beloved Larry died, Justine closed their home and moved to the Broadmoor Residential Hotel in San Francisco, where a group of sophisticated older people lived. A caregiver came to help her on a daily basis. When Justine was in severe pain or distress, the caregiver stayed overnight. Toward the end, she was cared for by hospice at the Broadmoor.

When her death was close, Rudy, his wife, Janet, Don, and I visited Justine to say goodbye. I was with her the night before she died. We declared our love for each other and said that, had we had a choice of sisters, we would have chosen each other. I didn't cry in front of her; only when I left her room did the sobbing start—in pain because I'd never see her again, and in gratitude for having had her friendship in my adult life.

I loved Justine for her humor and her wonder about all things in life. She had a gleeful, childlike quality that made her charming, and despite her anger at the terrible politics of the Reagan and Bush eras, she ultimately believed in goodness. I loved her for her intuition and insights into my family as well as me. I loved how she loved my children, and the way she could tell what was happening with me just by looking at me, and how after she lost her sight, all she needed was my voice to know what was going on.

The following year, Mel Gladstone, whom I had met at a

freshman dance at UC Berkeley seventy years earlier and who remained one of my dearest friends throughout my life, died at the age of eighty-nine. Our friendship spanned college, World War II, marriages, children, divorces, single life, remarriages, and career changes. The slim, good-looking young man with dark, curly hair and a disarming smile had barely aged over the years, except that his dark hair became more salt than pepper. He still talked so fast that I often had to ask him to repeat himself, so I could understand his Massachusetts accent.

Always a go-getter, Mel had myriad passions, ranging from Shakespeare and Gilbert and Sullivan to baseball and golf. While most of our contemporaries seemed to lose vitality, Mel became more passionate and vigorous with age, looking and moving like a much younger man. He would enter a room bursting with energy, welcome me with a hearty hug, and tell me how "smashing" I looked. In Mel's company I always felt I was the center of his attention. While many of my other friends disapproved of my decision to divorce with three children still in their formative years, Mel remained a confidant even though he was also a close friend of Rudy's. Mel understood my lost sense of security as I faced family life without a husband.

In our fifties, when we both found ourselves single, Mel and I relished going out on the town together. During those years we lunched regularly at fantastic places, taking turns choosing the spot and treating each other. He loved women and appreciated how they dressed, giving me a reason to get dolled up in my slinky black dress when we went out on the town. Together we explored every inch of North Beach, San Francisco's exciting Bohemian neighborhood. We loved going to nightclubs and restaurants, starting the evening with martinis before tooling off to dinner at Ernie's, Amelio's, or some other "in" spot. We would end the evening with spiked cappuccinos at Tosca Cafe, a popular bar that bustled late into the night with artists, beatniks, dancers, and writers. Talk flowed easily and loudly at the tightly packed bar, and jazz blared from the jukebox.

Mel and I remained friends even after we were no longer single, sharing the bad times as well as the good. After my first knee surgery, he sat next to me at Alta Bates hospital, reading the paper aloud, keeping me company and my mind off the pain. The time Don rushed me to the hospital when he thought I was having a stroke, Mel was there to lend support. I reciprocated that support whenever I had the chance and was at his side through his daughter Michelle's long, losing battle with lymphoma. We had believed our children would outlive us, and we cried together for the uncertainty and fragility of life.

In our late sixties, when I complained to Mel about Don watching a lot of TV, he advised that I just "leave him alone." Soon he invited Don to join his golf group, a perfect example of how Mel would extend himself to help friends. Mel and Don enjoyed playing golf weekly for the next 15 years.

After his heart valve replacement, Mel became well versed in living with illness. Continuing to live life to the fullest, he provided a positive role model for friends our age. In fact, he was invited to teach, and helped prepare the syllabus for, a course at Kaiser Permanente on living successfully with chronic conditions. A believer in the benefits of exercise, Mel faithfully walked 10,000 steps a day, tracking his steps with a pedometer. He bought me one as well and showed me how to use it after my knee surgeries.

After Mel died, I asked myself, "Can I ever again find a friend who loved me as Mel did?" When I cried, he cried. We could be together and just be ourselves. I miss his spontaneity, honesty, and loving acceptance. Nothing could ever substitute for his supportive friendship, or the way we reflected and complemented each other.

Another cherished friend I deeply miss is Gordon Bermak, who saw me as an individual when I was searching for an identity beyond mother and wife. He was trained as a Freudian analyst, but he treated me as a friend and not as a patient. I first became friends with his wife, Dolores, while putting on an art auction for the Liberal Democrat, an organization we both belonged to that supported progressive causes. I was fascinated by Dolores's wit and chic style—for example, she once entered a room dressed all in beige, with tight-fitting wool pants, a cashmere sweater, designer turquoise jewelry, and an alligator purse and heels.

After Rudy and I divorced, when other married couples we knew had dropped me, Dolores and Gordon continued to welcome me into their lives. During our early friendship, I hosted a shower for Alicia, their first adopted daughter, and was happy to see them adopt Jason a few years later. They invited me to dinners, outings, and even on family vacations with Jason and Alicia—whom I have remained friends with to this day—including a trip to a rented cabin on Vancouver Island, where we enjoyed wonderful hiking, cooking, and exploring. Gordon and I shared a passion for exercise and would challenge our physical limits. On these vacations we dared each other to push ourselves to new heights.

Often Gordon would swim the entire length of Pinecrest Lake, returning invigorated and glowing, while I headed for the highest summit. Then we compared notes. When we skied, our companions kept to the reasonable slopes while Gordon headed for the most difficult. He called our feats "counter-phobic," believing that we took on such challenges to prove ourselves and overcome subconscious fears.

Gordon was an animated talker, whether discussing people's behavior or spinning a tale. Although he often made fun of himself, he took life, friendships, and his role as husband and father seriously. He drove an old MG sports car with the top down, rain or shine, a cap set rakishly on his head and bundled up in rain gear or a ski jacket in bad weather. Gordon was eccentric, too. For many years he drove to work with his beloved parrot riding on his shoulder. During sessions with his clients the parrot often talked, which Gordon said was a great conversation starter.

Our friendship was able to grow because Don and Gordon also liked each other and admired each other's talents. The fact that these two men in my life admired and loved each other, as Dolores and I also did, enabled and enriched a lasting dynamic between the four of us. Don was a straightforward thinker and talker who could build anything with his hands. Gordon worked with his mind and told dramatic and humorous stories that kept us on the edge of our seats. The two men savored competing on the ski slopes and over the years developed deep affection for each other.

As a meditative contrast to his psychiatric practice, Gordon loved working on the two acres of land surrounding his and Dolores's Grizzly Peak home. The trees and bushes he had planted decades before had grown into a lush forest, and he enjoyed trimming his trees and chopping firewood. He spent weekends clearing the land and laying bricks in beautiful patterns for the patio.

When I visited them, he invariably asked, "What's happening in your life, Cec?"—expecting me to tell him honestly. If I replied, "Everything is fine," he would snap back: "Oh come on! What's really going on?" This was his opening for meaningful talk. From his leather chair in their living room with views of the San Francisco Bay sparkling in the distance, he would lean forward and listen intently to what I had to say, and we would fall into deep conversation that lasted far into the night.

We had watched each other's children grow from an early age to adulthood and shared thoughts about them and our deep love for them, as well as our worries and concerns. When I had problems with my children, Gordon offered his perspective: "Tell them you love them. That's the most important thing. That's what they need to hear." Over the years I have come to recognize how important these words of advice were.

During the 1991 fire in the hills of Berkeley and Oakland that destroyed 3,400 homes, the fire department warned the

Bermaks to evacuate, but Gordon refused to leave. For hours he stood courageously atop his house and sprayed water on his and his neighbor's roofs. Theirs were the only two homes in the area still standing after the fire. When Gordon would retell his story of fighting the fire, it wasn't to brag but rather to demonstrate how strength, determination, and will can be used to overcome adversity. He faced his lymphoma and prostate cancer with the same inner strength and fortitude. Gordon had developed low-grade, chronic lymphoma that left his immune system weakened, so when he developed prostate cancer, it became very aggressive.

Gordon discovered he had cancer about five years before his death. In earlier years, when one of his clients canceled, Gordon would go for a run in the hills. As his cancer progressed, he would call me when there was a cancellation and ask me to join him for a walk, since his office was only a few blocks from my house. He was walking more slowly by then and was thinner and more stooped. Yet his passion for his practice did not diminish. Gordon was a devout believer in analysis and its regenerative powers, and as long as he was helping his patients, he felt his life was worth living. His patients gave him a reason to keep going. Even when his cancer became advanced, Gordon would not miss a day of work. He worked until the week before he died.

As death grew closer, Gordon continued working on his land and fighting to live as long as possible. We talked at length about his battle with cancer and continuing to live with illness. I told him I was facing my own mortality. So many of my friends who had been so healthy and vital were now ill or dying. I missed them and was also afraid that I might be next. "I'm glad you're facing your shadow now," he said. With Gordon's death, three of my closest friends were gone.

I can still hear the voices of these beloved old friends, and I see them in my dreams. They have inspired me to live fully in good times and bad, and their loyalty and love has given me courage.

Reconfirming a Meaningful Future

Witnessing the deaths of my three closest friends in three years shook me to my core, and I found myself slipping too often into doubt and negativity as I yearned for them. Some of the friends who had died were younger than me—Gordon by ten years. I missed the voices at the other end of the phone, the reassuring hugs and their physical presence. That depth of being known by another person, the sense of continuity that comes from decades of friendship, leaves an immeasurable hole when it is gone. I was inconsolable.

Don couldn't bear to see me that way and lovingly became the positive force in our relationship, catching me before I could sink too deeply into depression. Mornings he brought me tea in bed while we read the paper together. We would talk, and talk some more. He listened to my pain and new vulnerability as we made love through the deep sharing of our thoughts and words.

As I struggled with loss and change, it became clear that it was time to make a deliberate choice to continue to live a meaningful life. What would the older women whom I had spent so much time and energy studying do? It was time to put into practice the lessons I had learned about aging vitally from my thesis research. Continuing to experience life as meaningful was the most important characteristic I had found in my study of vital older women, and I reviewed how each of these women had created a life with meaning.

I was inspired to ask, why do I want to persevere? What passions keep me going? I knew I wanted to leave the world a better place and, with little time left, my sense of urgency was increasing. For years I'd been active in causes that meant a great deal to me. Now helping the planet seemed more important than ever. To me, my own health and survival are inseparable from the health and survival of the environment and our planet's ecosystems. How can I leave the beauty of our community, world, and natural environment when I know it is in serious danger? It was time to increase my activism and philanthropy in environmental causes.

Some of my happiest moments in life have been hiking mountain trails, carrying a backpack filled with only the basics and a good book. Away from urban commotion and pared down to essentials, I feel an expansiveness and, at the same time, an extraordinary sense of connection to the earth beneath my feet. Drinking in high alpine views always reminds me that I am a small part of a much bigger universe, and that I am a steward of the earth. Though I can no longer backpack, in my mind's eye I can vividly see, smell, and feel my favorite wilderness areas, peaks, trails, lakes, and streams.

During the summers I spent working in Yosemite National Park while in college, I saw for myself some of the heartbreaking damage that humans had done to that beautiful place, and that awareness spurred my lifelong environmental activism through such organizations as the Sierra Club, the Arkay Foundation, Great Old Broads for Wilderness, Earth Elders, and the Yosemite Conservancy.

One of my earliest forays into activism had been with the Sierra Club's Save the Redwoods campaign in the 1960s. I canvassed door to door, wrote letters, raised funds, and visited congressional representatives in Washington, D.C. The campaign resulted in a bill—passed by Congress in 1968— that established Redwood National Park. My involvement in this campaign gave me such a sense of accomplishment and pride. Years later, when Don and I drove through Mendocino County in northern California, we gasped with pleasure as we passed groves of magnificent old redwoods that, in a small way, I felt I had helped save.

I found a way to express my passion for the health of our planet and our society through my work as the senior member of the board of directors of Arkay, a nonprofit foundation dedicated to progressive issues. I brought—and continue to bring—to Arkay my dedication to addressing the negative impacts of climate change, globalization, and money in politics. Through its environmental grants, Arkay has provided funds for work on global environmental issues such as promoting alternative energy, sustainability, and educating people about the ramifications of over-consumption.

A photo accompanying my profile in Legacy,
Portraits of 50 Bay Area Environmental Elders,
published by Sierra Club Books

Bringing the Sierra Club's Beyond Coal Campaign to the
attention of Arkay's board was one of my most rewarding

experiences. The more I learned about the devastating effects of coal mining and coal burning on both the environment and public health, the more urgently I felt that this information should be conveyed to community leaders, the media, and policymakers. I was compelled to advocate for Arkay funding to support Beyond Coal when I found out that mountaintop removal coal mining pollutes water, killing fish and wildlife, and increasing cancer rates for people who live nearby.

The campaign achieved substantial successes in 2009 with the closure of 150 mines. Arkay's funding helped educate the public that there is no such thing as clean coal. My efforts and engagements with Beyond Coal showed me how useful I can continue to be, and how my input is appreciated by people involved in activist campaigns.

I am also extremely proud of the other efforts that Arkay grants have supported. For example, we contributed seed money for the Edible Schoolyard, a Berkeley school program started by the innovative food advocate Alice Waters that teaches children healthy eating habits and provides hands-on learning about food. This program was an early model for nutritional education in schools, and it has since inspired school nutrition and lunch programs across the country.

Another Arkay grant was awarded to migrant workers in the Salinas Valley to enable them to become independent organic farmers. Through this program, farm workers were trained in organic farming methods, provided with farm tools and equipment, and offered support to become independent farmers achieving their own financial security.

In recent years one focus of Arkay has been combating the overwhelming and corrupting influence of money in the American political process—a barrier to achieving our goals relating to the environment, economic justice, education, and human rights. With our limited resources, we are grappling with how to counteract the overwhelming influence of money and address its negative impacts on the environment. We are working on strengthening the capacity of environmental organizations to make the linkages between money in politics and the degradation of our environment. We hope to amplify grassroots voices and inspire people to take action.

As meaningful to me as the programs Arkay supports are the friendships with board members whom I admire and hold dear. We meet three or four times a year. Prior to our meetings we study the many complex proposals sent in by grantees on a variety of critical issues facing our society. I love the intellectual stimulation and exposure to alternative ideas generated by this process. How good it feels to work with these intelligent younger colleagues to change the world.

Recently I became incensed about the mining of the Canadian tar sands, oil-rich soils that lie beneath a huge area of pristine forest in Alberta, Canada. Some of the world's richest energy corporations see the tar sands as a virtual gold mine from which they can extract billions of barrels of oil. Tar sand mining is much more destructive than conventional oil drilling. When I heard about a plan to build the Keystone XL pipeline to bring oil from Alberta's tar sands to the Gulf of Mexico, I joined a major effort to block it that was being organized by environmental groups, Bill McKibben, and many others.

One of the most devastating effects of extracting oil from the tar sands would be the destruction of North America's boreal forest, the largest remaining intact ecosystem in the world, not to mention the danger of pipeline breakages and spills. James Hansen, a leading U.S. climatologist, has said that mining the tar sands would mean "game over" for climate change. According to a Pew Charitable Trust report, the forest "provides an estimated $700 billion value annually as a buffer against climate change and food and water shortages—storing more than 400 trillion pounds of carbon in lakes and river delta sediment, peatlands and wetlands—more than any other terrestrial source in the world."

It was encouraging when our coordinated efforts paid off six months after we began rallying around the Keystone XL issue, a delay and reevaluation of the project was announced. The Keystone XL issue has alerted concerned individuals and organizations to the danger of these oil pipelines.

Our campaign against tar sands and big oil is based on the lessons learned from the successful fight against big tobacco. By clarifying the debate as one of public health versus oil profits and by exposing the wrongdoing of big oil companies, we can build outrage and channel it to affect policy. We propose to limit the market for dirty fuels and shift the environmental and health burdens from the public to companies responsible for the pollution. We worked to build alliances with grassroots organizations, environmental justice communities, landowners, and health, faith, and military groups to block the Keystone XL pipeline.

As an alternative to tar sand mining, we are promoting clean transportation and improved fuel economy standards to reduce oil consumption. We hope to accelerate the adoption of oil-efficient and electric engines for "green" vehicle fleets, focusing first on large corporate and university fleets. Our campaign will put grassroots pressure on fleet operators that are Beyond Oil laggards to reduce their levels of oil consumption.

Another focus that I brought to Arkay is the human rights issues that are closely related to environmental concerns, such as the direct action of indigenous peoples throughout the world to keep from losing their lands to multinational corporations. I had lived with the indigenous people in Orissa, India, and came away with a deep understanding of and appreciation for their humor, spirit, and music. I found them to be severely marginalized economically and socially, fighting a tenuous battle to protect their forest lifestyle from encroachment by the adjoining Indian villages.

With this background, I felt compelled to alert the Arkay board to the need to send indigenous delegates to the Copenhagen Climate Change Conference in 2009 and the meetings in 2010 for the United Nations Climate Change Conference in Cancún, Mexico. I am constantly on the lookout for how to translate my concern about these problems into effective action. I often wonder, did I do enough?

The 2005 White House Conference on Aging

With the first baby boomers turning sixty in 2006, the timing of the 2005 White House Conference on Aging in Washington, D.C. couldn't have been more relevant. Its focus was "The Booming Dynamics of Aging." I felt privileged to be selected again for this conference, ten years after my first appointment as a delegate from California. More than 2,000 seniors from every walk of life and from all over the country met in our nation's capital to develop recommendations on such issues as privatizing Social Security and Medicare, housing and transportation for seniors, promoting healthy aging, and aging in place. Once again our recommendations were submitted to Congress and the White House. The first time I participated in the conference, Bill Clinton was president and many of our suggestions were implemented; this time, under President George W. Bush, few were.

Upon my return from Washington, D.C., I worked to implement the conference resolutions in Berkeley. I met with Mayor Tom Bates and insisted he ensure that some of the millions of dollars of federal funds granted to the State of California for housing and transportation were targeted for low-cost senior housing in our community.

In Berkeley, older persons with disabilities or those who can no longer drive often become separated from their friends and community. Because California lacks adequate subsidized senior transportation, elders find it increasingly difficult to continue to live in their homes and lead satisfying and engaged lives. While Berkeley's senior population is growing and citizens are living longer, the city has only two small low-cost senior housing units. Many low-income seniors have been forced to enter Medicaid nursing homes or end up on the streets, homeless. Funds for housing were available, but the city needed a specific request for them. Following my meeting with Mayor Bates, Berkeley did request federal grant funds for senior transportation and housing, and part of this money was used to construct additional senior housing in the community.

The Call of Faraway Places

In addition to activism, exercise, and friends, travel has remained a high point of my life. At an age when most people are happy to retire their suitcases to storage, I found my desire to travel remains as strong now as it was in my youth. An adventurer at heart throughout my life, I continue to be lured by the call of faraway places. Stepping beyond my comfort zone, I thrive on coming face to face with what is unknown. Mark Twain was right when he said, "Travel is fatal to prejudice, bigotry, and narrow-mindedness." Travel has immeasurably expanded my heart, mind, and psyche.

To me, the most rewarding aspect of travel is making personal connections. Wherever I might go, I'm fortunate to be able to make friends. Trusting people and believing in them overcomes language barriers. I gesture with my hands and express myself through body movements and eye contact. Something as simple as a smile while leaning toward a person is a powerful tool for breaking the ice, and strangers usually smile back.

When I first traveled to India in 1970, it was in the spirit of discovery and a personal quest. Impulsive, spontaneous, and fearless, I didn't care where I stayed—a tiny room, someone's hut—or what the amenities might be—a hole in the ground for a toilet, a bucket of cold water poured over my head for a shower. It was the adventure and the chance of a lifetime, and I embraced it.

In my eighties, travel was no longer as easy as tossing a backpack over my shoulders. I still had the desire to travel in my heart, but now I needed to check in first with my head, think through the logistics, plan and make numerous telephone calls, written inquiries, and arrangements in advance. I was now concerned with Don's and my health, making sure that the food we ate was safe, that we had all the medications we needed, and that the walking was within our abilities. It was often difficult to convince Don to go with me. For the last twenty years, after every trip Don would say, "It's the last one." But he soon remembers the trip's highlights and begins bragging about it to his friends.

Don and I returned to India and Rajasthan for a month in 2003. Before we left, I contacted Faith Singh, an Indian textile and clothing designer whom I had met more than thirty years before, to let her know that I wanted to see her. I still held a clear image of the first time we met. She was working in her atelier with a small baby on her hip. The bright blues and deep maroon reds of the fabric called out to me, and the primitive block-printed designs were beautiful. I marveled at her creative designs and enthusiastic energy. I remember that she introduced me to her husband and told me about her background in England and a little about her spiritual life following a guru. I came away admiring her and feeling that she was on a unique life journey.

I had seen Faith only three or four times in the last three decades but had followed her career with great pride. That winter of 2003, when I saw her again, a mature woman now, we connected as if no time had passed at all.

In the intervening years she had built her small design firm, Anokhi, into a bustling enterprise with six locations in India. She organized the village women who specialized in appliqué, and who worked in their homes on embroidery, patchwork, beadwork, weaving, and hand-blocking, into cooperatives so they could have an outlet for their crafts. In organizing these cooperatives, Faith was able to provide work for the women and raise their standard of living as her own business expanded. Her success gave value to this kind of village craft.

Another most rewarding trip was one I took with my two daughters to the hill towns and coastal trails of Tuscany, Italy, in 2006. Since both my daughters live far away from Berkeley, I rarely see them except on my birthday or on holidays. The chance to travel together was something to savor. I worriedly thought this might be my last walking trip with them. I was eighty-six, my knees were wearing out, and I was wearing knee braces. I knew my walking would be limited, but I thought the trip to Tuscany would suit the three of us just fine.

Our small group met in Florence. I found Tuscany a paradise for walking—gentle slopes over ancient rock paths winding through orchards, vineyards, and open countryside, all the way from magical Siena through wine country and walled hill towns to the Tuscan coast on the Tyrrhenian Sea. Since some of our travel companions were U.S. representatives for the famous Barolo wines, we were served the best Italian wines at dinners. One of the best parts of the trip was that, rather than taking separate rooms, we three slept together in the same room, taking turns sharing double beds.

Lyn, BJ, and I would rise early in the morning and enjoy pecorino cheese, Italian bread, and strong coffee, then head out with the small group for the day's walk. On the long walks my daughters would run back to rest with me, since I walked more slowly and carefully, and offer me water and goodies from their backpacks. The three of us chatted happily as we enjoyed the lush, vine-covered slopes of Tuscany and the beauty of the stone-walled hill towns.

After an alfresco lunch put on by the tour company, I'd take the "sag wagon" back to the hotel while Lyn and BJ walked another five or six miles. This was our daily routine for two weeks, and it was a time together with my daughters that I treasure.

In 2010, for my ninetieth birthday, Don and I traveled to India—my fourteenth trip to that incredible country. People often ask me why I keep going back, with all the squalor and poverty. I don't even try to explain any more. India is a country and civilization that you have to experience to appreciate.

I sometimes wonder whether I might have been an Indian in another life. It may have something to do with how keenly alive my senses are when I'm in India—the constant noise of people chattering and music blaring from street vendors or cars; the fragrances of spicy food cooked in small batches by vendors or filling people's homes; the brilliant colors of women's saris, the splendor of the exotic architecture, and the special light from the sun that one experiences only in India. When I'm there, I feel vivacious, stimulated, and truly a part of things.

When I walked into the tribal village of the Bondas in Orissa, India, I found the villagers eager to chat and to practice English. Some graciously invited me into their homes, showing me their musical instruments and crafts. The humbleness of their lives and the depth of their trust never failed to moved me.

Onward with Meaning

The challenges and changes of aging cannot be erased by denying they exist, and false bravery is a poor tool for coping with the symptoms of aging. But they are to be faced with guts, determination, and perseverance, if one is to continue to embrace life and find meaning. I believe in saying yes to life, and to me that means remaining open to new experiences no matter how old I am. This is what keeps me feeling young and joyful. It feeds my feelings of excitement and wonder.

Top: Mel, my close friend from college
Bottom: My friend Gordon with whom I shared
many happy talks

Celebrating my 92nd birthday with Don in Hawaii

Ninety-Two and Dancing

A test of our spiritual strength began one morning in 2008, when Don had a stroke while working in the garden. I was upstairs in our bedroom, unaware of what had happened. Don suddenly stumbled into the room and sank to his knees. I was aghast at his ashen face. His lips were trembling and he was trying to speak, but no words came out. His eyes were vacant. Realizing that he must be having a stroke, I frantically dialed 911, and a short time later the paramedics from the fire station just two blocks away rushed Don to the emergency room at Alta Bates.

With knots in my stomach, frightened and desperate, I prayed for him to pull through. In the emergency room, Don was unable to reply coherently to the doctors' questions. He grasped my hand as if by holding on to me, he could hold on to his life. Terrified, I didn't know if he was going to live. How empty life would be without him.

Within about an hour, Don was able to speak a little and

asked me why he was in the hospital. He couldn't recall what had happened. In the moments that we were left alone together in the emergency room, we kept repeating, "I love you." "You're going to pull through this; you're going to be OK," I told him, believing that by repeating these positive thoughts they would come true.

Don remained in the hospital for four days. During the first two, his spirits were up because he felt glad to be alive, but later his memory loss and inability to find the right words became evident to him, and he became disoriented and depressed. A therapist friend suggested that rather than countering his lows with my usual "up" talk, I say, "No wonder you feel low and depressed," and ask him to tell me more about how it feels to have a stroke.

This was useful advice. Don began to express his feelings of despair. "What is there to live for?" he asked. I pointed out all the reasons to live: his newly returned vision, his sons and granddaughters, and the projects he might undertake in the future, such as restoring another old car. "The only reason I have to live is for you," he said despondently. I told him that living for me wasn't enough of a reason, and it felt like a burden; he needed to find other reasons and meaning within himself, beyond his love for me. "I believe with all my heart that you will recover," I said.

Don's stroke was shocking in its suddenness and alarming ability to instantly alter our lives. When he started speech therapy, he could not remember how to write a check and had lost much of his vocabulary. The therapist taught him how to describe the words or places he had trouble recalling. His tenacity throughout the long haul of physical, occupational, and speech therapy revealed a surprising and admirable inner strength. The therapy took more than six months, during which time he was unable to drive and I became his driver. Not until the neurologist cleared him could he again get behind the wheel of his beloved car.

Fortunately, over the last three years Don has made an amazing recovery. He is almost back to his old self, except for impaired short-term memory. He forgets who visited us last week or where we went a few weeks ago but does remember when I remind him. It is difficult to keep track of so many things for both of us. I make sure that his appointments are in his calendar as well as mine and remind him to look at it daily, and to take his medications and reorder them.

With a nurturing spirit, Don shops for groceries and is pleased to do other useful errands. He maintains and repairs things around the house, taking pride in his handiwork. Most recently he sanded and stained our wooden patio chairs. He reads prolifically, walking to our Claremont Library to check out books, and he remains fit by walking to the gym, where he lifts weights and exercises three times a week.

Occasionally he plays golf, with younger partners now, since his three close golf buddies have died. Some people view Don as very sober and wonder how he gets his kicks. To this he says: "I don't get kicks! What I like is to sit in my comfortable white leather easy chair, look out the window at the trees and the pretty girls who walk past, and read my books.

Life with the Man I Love

When I imagine life without Don, I am overwhelmed with loss and sorrow. For more than thirty years we have shared a deeply romantic and sexual relationship. He is my best friend and confidant. We can talk about anything, and our different perspectives add a greater dimension to our relationship. I also value that he's so responsible. After my charismatic but completely irresponsible father, I needed a man I could count on. With our years together, we've also learned to embrace each other's mishegoss with humor and compassion.

I'm emotional; I express my feelings freely and am not afraid to argue. Although Don and I share the same values, we at times disagree about day-to-day matters. He is a big procrastinator. When he puts things off, I often counter with, "How could you do that!?" For example, if we have heavy items we've purchased in the car, and I ask if he would please bring them in, he walks into the house and replies, "I'll do it later." Weeks may go by before we find we are missing items that are still in the car.

Don is uncomfortable with disagreements and feels criticized if I suggest an alternative way of interpreting his behavior or language. I've found, however, that if I talk from my heart, he can really hear me, which helps him open up and creates room for a meaningful discussion.

Don doesn't recall ever seeing his mother and father hold hands, kiss, or show affection toward each other. With this background, early in our relationship he was reluctant to show emotion and affection except in private. When I threw my arms around him and spontaneously kissed him on the street, he found it embarrassing. Now he likes it!

Although it bothers me that my skin sags and my body isn't tight any more, Don doesn't mind, and despite his physical changes, I'm as attracted to him as the day we met. Our excitement and attraction continues as we blend the visual and sexual memories of who we were when we first met with who we are now.

Don remembers how I looked and acted when we were in our thirties, and I feel the sexual excitement of our earlier years as if it were yesterday. The combination of young and old is part of our reality, and it is always with us. Until Don received his pacemaker, I worried that he might have a heart attack during lovemaking, but our cardiologist assured us that if he could walk up the hill to the Claremont, he could make love! Sex may not be as frequent as when we were younger, but it's just as exciting. We set aside time to make love, finding that creating the right moment and ambience helps.

For me, cooking is also a way of showing love. I make the shopping lists for fresh produce, meat, poultry, and fish, and Don shops at the Berkeley Bowl, Trader Joe's, or Costco for the staples. We could not have such a delicious home-cooked cuisine unless Don helped -- both cooking and shopping would be too tiring for me. We savor having younger and older friends over to share conversation over food.

In addition to the meditative and creative aspects of preparing food and cooking, I cherish the huge collection of recipes that I keep in a little wooden box, gathered over the years from my mother, grandmother, and many good friends who also love to cook. Some of these recipes are in my mother's beautiful old-fashioned script.

Our freshly cooked and delicious meals pay close attention to our nutrition. Food and sex fall into similar categories for me: I get hungry for both, and I feel most satisfied after both.

Writing and Mentoring

In 2011, I took a six-week course in memoir-writing through Berkeley's OLLI −− the Osher Lifelong Learning Institute for UC Berkeley alumni −− that has evolved into a collaborative support group for memoir writers. Malcolm Margolin, founder and executive director of Heyday Books, hosted the group in his conference room at Heyday for a month, and after that we continued meeting weekly at the North Berkeley Senior Center, critiquing and supporting each other's writing. The group has met for over a year now.

Most of the members are in their fifties and sixties; I am the only one who is old enough to be one of their parents. The women all consider me a role model and tell me that they hope they have as much energy and wits about them when they turn ninety. One of the women, Meg, picks me up, and we've become friends, as I have with Deborah and Sally and others in the group, going to lectures and plays or welcoming them to convene at my house when the senior center is closed. The best part is their perceptiveness and astonishing writing skills—if I am uncertain about my writing, they always encourage me or suggest positive directions.

I'm also privileged to be able to mentor women who regularly contact me about vital aging. Recently a handwritten letter arrived from a professor at the University of Maryland who found my work inspiring for her dissertation, "Old Yankee Women: Life Histories and Cultural Significance," which she completed at age seventy-four. More and more inquiries now come from my website and the Internet. Some women are inspired to return to school or to change careers after reading one of my publications or hearing me speak. Receiving grateful letters from women I've inspired is deeply satisfying and makes all my years of study worthwhile. When women ask me about changing careers at midlife, I tell them: "Go for it. Follow your passion. Go back to school or try a new activity. Find a fertile environment, where you can grow and develop." When women I encounter at conferences, on my travels, and at my health club ask me about aging, I respond: "Don't be afraid of aging! There are lots of rewards."

Coping with the Challenges of Aging

I am losing my sight. Years ago, the ophthalmologist informed me that because of my glaucoma, if I live long enough I will eventually be blind. My decrease in vision has been gradual. Two years ago I noticed that I needed more natural light and stronger light bulbs in order to see. Field-of-vision tests have indicated that I am losing all sight in my left eye and peripheral vision in my right. Direct, bright sunlight hurts my eyes. I cannot see at all in glare without sunglasses. Finding the best color tint for the lenses to help cut down glare has been challenging, as my eyes have been changing rapidly. We installed an additional overhead lighting system in the kitchen so that I can see well enough to cut vegetables and cook. At the computer, I find that I need to enlarge the text for it to be visible.

I had to stop driving at night a year before I was told by my ophthalmologist that I should not be driving at all. What a devastating blow to my day-to-day autonomy! Unfortunately, neither can I see well enough now to do the fine sewing that helped me relax and gave me much pleasure for many years. One of the most frustrating consequences of my loss in vision is that now when I drop something on the floor, I can't find it for the life of me, especially if it's small, like a tack, pill, or pen cap. I don't see the stains on my clothes, and so I must ask Don (who doesn't see so well, either!) to assist me, or wait for Carmen, our cleaning lady who comes every Thursday.

I've also noticed that I am losing my ability to distinguish colors—and I love colors! If my bright-red purse is missing in my bright-red office, I have trouble finding it. I once had perfect color sense, similar to perfect pitch. Weeks after glancing at a color, I could still identify it. A few weeks ago, when I was out shopping, I had to ask a salesperson if a sweater was pink or orange. All these losses make me feel less equipped and confident. These days, as I lose my vision, Don and I have reversed roles: he is now learning to be my caregiver.

I have learned that I can live my life and function well

despite loss of vision because of the help and inspiration of the University of California Low Vision Support Group. The people in our group have macular degeneration, glaucoma, or some other disease of the eyes. We meet twice monthly, and the group provides me with exemplary psychological and practical support. Knowing that I am not the only one out there coping with vision loss is a tremendous help. We share with each other the many challenges of vision loss, such as no longer being able to drive.

The low-vision group has helped me find information about public transportation options and other support groups, such as the Lions Blind Center in Oakland and the Lighthouse Center for the Blind in San Francisco. I am especially excited about the outdoor adventure programs that I learned about through the group, such as the Bay Area Outreach and Recreation Program (BORP) and Environmental Traveling Companions, which guide outdoor activities for people with disabilities, including double kayaking, tandem bicycling, whitewater rafting, and alpine meadow skiing and hiking. Our group is now planning a four-mile roundtrip hike on the Tennessee Valley trail in Marin County, ending at the beach where we will picnic and play games. Groups outings such as this one demonstrate to us that we can hike on flat trails on our own.

Jerome, one of our members, gave me a useful suggestion recently, to wrap white tape around the mountaineering walking stick I use for balance so that when I'm out in public it will be clear that my vision is impaired. Jerome and some of the others in our group who are completely blind have offered to help me learn to use an iPad or iPhone that has Siri, a voice-operated personal assistant. Paul, our supportive low vision counselor, drove me to the Apple store to check the possibility of using one of these devices. Recently, I told the group that my laser surgery for glaucoma pressure hadn't been successful, and that my doctor was recommending surgery to reduce pressure in the eye. They advised me not to go ahead with that surgery until I received a second opinion from Dr. Andrew Iwach in San Francisco, a world-renowned glaucoma ophthalmologist. He advised me that surgery is too risky at my age.

One of the reasons I am so concerned about my eyesight is that I love reading good books. Over the years books have been a source of tremendous pleasure, stimulation, and relaxation. At times I can't wait to get into bed, just to read, though over the last few years we've had to install more and brighter lights by my bed so I could continue to see. Just as I have a zest for traveling and exploring other worlds, I love the new imaginative landscapes—the historical times and different perspectives—that books transport me to. I am one of the lucky ones in our group, because I can still read books; other members listen to books from the Talking Book Library or use their iPads to listen to audiobooks. My ophthalmologist recently approved a talking book player from the Library of Congress for my future use.

I joined a local fiction reading group in 1980, and a nonfiction reading group in 2002 that meets at our nearby Claremont Public Library. I welcome these groups because they have introduced me to hundreds of books, in genres I wouldn't have imagined exploring. Reading is another form of exercise for me—mental stimulation and visualization. Talking about each book with others in the groups, I hear enlightening and opposing viewpoints. When Don and I are side by side in bed, reading, I often reach over and squeeze his hand, because sharing this intimacy feels like making love.

Late in 2011, without warning, I could no longer climb the stairs to my second-floor bedroom. Strolling down the street, I would become completely out of breath. These were activities that took no effort just the week before. Checking with the cardiologist, I discovered that I have congestive heart failure, for which there is no cure; it is a condition of aging that I must live with. Yet another blow to my active life of walking, dancing, and the outdoors, a lifestyle that has been so energizing and healing for me.

For ten years I have lived with atrial fibrillation controlled by medications. Five years ago, on the morning after Thanksgiving, while talking over breakfast with Don's daughter-in-law and son, I suddenly stopped speaking in the middle of a sentence. I came to a few seconds later not knowing what had happened. If Don's daughter-in-law, Ann, a nurse, hadn't been there to verify that the incident was indeed a TIA (transient ischemic attack), I would not have realized what happened to me. Immediately we checked that my speech, smile, body parts, and thinking ability were all undamaged. This was a warning, and Ann insisted that I visit a doctor soon.

Instead, I blanked out the TIA episode and the recommended doctor's appointment. In retrospect I can see that I didn't want to face the reality of what might be ahead. I knew my father had died of a weak heart. I went on living with a vengeance—writing, exercising, cooking, making love, staying active in environmental issues and aging groups, and happy to greet each day. But three years ago, as I was about to serve dinner to Don, Lyn, and my friend Georgette, who was visiting from France, I fell down hard and passed out on the kitchen floor. I was rushed by the fire department and paramedics to the emergency room at Alta Bates hospital, where it was determined that my heart wasn't pumping properly and I might need a pacemaker.

Before they would do the surgery for a pacemaker, I was required to wear a Holter monitor to record my EKG events. During that week, the monitor recorded numerous incidents, which convinced the electrocardiologist that a pacemaker was required. After it was inserted on my left side under the skin, I again returned to my active life. However, I noticed that I was moving slower, and sadly I could no longer tolerate higher altitudes, so hiking in Yosemite's Tuolumne Meadows was no longer possible. Some time after the pacemaker was implanted, I experienced severe palpitations that stopped me in my tracks and woke me in the middle of the night. I then underwent another surgical procedure, catheter ablation, which made the palpitations less disturbing.

Each of these challenges, whether knee replacements, vision loss, or various heart issues, meant additional limitations to my functioning, narrowing down my active life.

For the past decade Don and I have helped each other through these challenges and more—surgeries, hospitalizations, and all kinds of setbacks that ultimately have given us the strength to go on and the confidence that we can overcome challenging times ahead.

How different our life is now from five to ten years ago, when Don would go off to play golf with his buddies and come home tired but rejuvenated, and often in the mood to make love in the afternoon. At that time I was still driving my car, presented talks on aging all over the United States, was actively engaged in the environmental movement, and was in top physical condition, since I was exercising almost every day.

How fortuitous it is to be with a man as even-tempered, uncomplicated, and devoted as Don. He is my rock, calm and easygoing amid my highs and lows. Some nights when my thoughts wake me, Don rubs my back and eases me into sleep. How fortunate he and I are to have a soul mate who fills the other half —as Jung would say, the animus and anima, representing wholeness and completion—creating a rich and whole partnership.

Without inner strength and resourcefulness, it would have been impossible to make it through the setbacks of these past years. We have less energy and are both exhausted at the end of the day. I feel disappointed that we miss so many stimulating events we're invited to because we don't have the energy. Our doctors claim that a decline in energy is natural at our age, but giving in to the limitations imposed by aging is hard for me to accept. Because I continue to have the ambition to move mentally and physically each day, I engage in activities such as exercising, writing, traveling, advocacy, and socializing with family and friends. But I sometimes push myself beyond what my body can take.

In preparing my living trust, I recently visited with my lawyer and accountant. This was an opportune time for Don and me to talk about whether he wants to continue living at our Hillegass Avenue home if I die before him. "Where else would I go?" he asked. Ours was a poignant conversation, ending with a lingering embrace and a declaration of our love and devotion.

On a quest to improve our energy and health, Don and I traveled with Lyn and BJ to the Comprehensive Medical Center in Kirkland, Washington—the preeminent integrative medical center in the United States, where people from all over the world seek treatment. The center offers counseling on holistic health, naturopathic medicine, and nontoxic treatment options and specializes in restoring the body's innate self-healing abilities.

For our first visit we were asked to bring samples of all our medications, vitamins, and supplements, to document our food menus for three typical days, and to bring small samples of foods we consume regularly. I brought a bag of Twining's Lady Grey and Earl Grey teas, a homemade bran muffin, sliced cheese, and an apple. The doctor and her assistants examined all of this. We were given thorough physical exams, blood tests, urine tests, and brain-imaging scans that were meant to give a picture of our whole health.

Following the center's protocols and treatments has been an exciting opportunity to learn alternative methods for health as we age. They recommended oral supplements to support brain and neurological health, bone density health (I have osteoporosis), bladder and kidney health (I have had numerous bladder infections), and heart health. I was told to avoid the two teas and sliced cheese I brought and four of my vitamin supplements—taurine, vitamin C, carnitine, and lecithin—for two months. These were later reintroduced one at a time without negative effects.

Visiting the Comprehensive Medical Center helped us achieve a more holistic conception of health. In my adult life, I have chosen a lifestyle that enhances my health and well-being. To this day I continue to prepare nutritious organic meals at home and enjoy the sociability of inviting friends for dinner and conversation. I meditate and attend a core exercise course regularly and participate in my reading and writing groups. I pay attention to current politics and read history and literature, so that I am better informed about my choices as a citizen, a traveler, a consumer of foods and products, and so on. I make laughter and love an integral part of my health and happiness.

I'm determined to help make the quality of the rest of my life the best possible. I listen to and trust my inner wisdom and recognize what enhances my well-being. Though it is not physically easy any longer, and I must exert my will, I choose to walk to my exercise classes up the hill because when I return home I feel better, and it is easier to go up and down our stairs.

Living Independently at Hillegass

It's impossible not to think of our realities as we age. How can Don and I continue to live in our two-story home on our own? What would it be like if Don were to die before me? How would I go on living in this big house? If I die before Don, how will he manage? It is Don's and my goal to continue living at Hillegass as long as possible. Since life has become more challenging in recent years, we recognize that we might need more support in the future.

With these thoughts uppermost in our minds, toward the end of 2010, we invited some close friends and family to our home to brainstorm about how we could remain living at Hillegass into our old, old age. We received support and creative ideas from the fourteen people who responded to our invitation. Our younger friends recognized that they too might find themselves in similar situations in the future, and that as they helped us create a support system that would enable us to stay in our beloved home, they could learn how they might later create a similar network for themselves. Our friends left feeling good, knowing how they can help us.

In recent years we have felt a loss of social interaction and connection—many of our contemporaries are now gone, three of our closest friends were in hospice and have since died, and Don's sons and my daughters live in other states—so at our support meeting, we came up with the idea of inviting friends to be our guests at events such as the San Francisco Symphony, the opera, and lectures, if they would kindly drive us. We also told our friends and neighbors that we would appreciate joining them when they attended a movie or other events of interest. Some friends now graciously offer to let us know when they go grocery shopping, and others regularly invite us over for casual dinners.

Our friends created a telephone contact list for us and suggested that we call neighbors and friends in case of emergency, or if we needed help. Don and I assured the group that we can afford to pay for assistance; the support we crave and need is mostly psychological, social, and emotional.

Since that meeting, friends called regularly to ask if we need help with errands, shopping, or driving. One friend has helped me with computer questions, while David, an optometrist, researched and made special orange lenses for my reading glasses to minimize the effects of glare due to my glaucoma. We appreciate our friends' kind and generous help and reciprocate by inviting them to lunch or a home-cooked dinner. Their caring and support not only enhance our lives but make it easier to remain comfortable in our home. Not only do our friends help us, but they thoughtfully follow up, asking if I find the shoes we bought together comfortable, if the computer is now working, or if I need another ride across the bridge to San Francisco. Our friendships have become more intimate and deeper as a result of this support group.

In 2011, Don and I joined Ashby Village, a comprehensive

service network offered to older people in Berkeley so they can continue to live independently at home. For an affordable fee, Ashby Village offers services such as transportation to medical appointments by volunteers, shopping assistance, referrals to home medical health care workers, financial services, and referrals to volunteers who can help with odd technical jobs such as with computers or lighting. We feel that if one of us dies, the Village can provide additional support for the other. We haven't used their services often, but when we had a computer problem, they sent a knowledgeable volunteer who fixed it. The social aspect of Ashby Village was not why we joined, although we have enjoyed attending two of their functions (they have many), where we met interesting members.

Home: A Symbol of Self

When Rudy and I first moved into the house on Hillegass Avenue, we were young marrieds with no furniture except the beds. The children had rollicking fun riding their tricycles about. Relatives and friends gave us a used kitchen table, chairs, and an old sofa. After living in the house a few years, we added a larger kitchen with windows facing the garden and a new deck, and installed maple hardwood floors across the entire downstairs for dancing and exercise. For many years, I spent early mornings working out in the family room, looking out into the garden, doing yoga, stretching, and lifting weights. When I was pregnant with Rob or Lyn, I hosted prenatal exercise classes, asking each woman to bring her own mat.

I think the birds

Standing inside the front hall, one can look through the wide windows out to Hillegass Avenue, and in the other direction see all the way back to the verdant garden and trees. Sunshine pours in through the sliding glass doors and kitchen windows. We welcomed this open space for dining, cooking, entertaining, and dancing. Over the years we hosted many celebratory parties here for our children, for birthdays, anniversaries, family gatherings, and weddings.

Each of our children chose their bedroom. BJ wanted a blue room facing the garden; Rob chose a red carpet, bunk beds for his friends, and cork walls for playing loud music; Lyn preferred bare floors with a view of the hills. As we could afford it, we gradually furnished the rooms to their taste. The children loved the house and garden. For a number of years a croquet set on our back lawn was the center of attraction. As the children grew older, they invited friends for sleepovers. I recall cooking enormous amounts of food for Rob's ravenous teenage friends and for family parties.

Don has grown to love our Hillegass home as much as I do. Over the years he has used his skills to make some needed changes. He knocked out a wall and remodeled BJ's former room to make a larger room for his study. As our book collection grew, he built additional shelves in the hallways and landings.

The house feels secure and protective, while at the same time its aesthetics and bright colors offer us both stimulation and tranquility. My home is a symbol of my personal identity. With its brilliant primary colors, expanse of windows, and artifacts from travels, the house is a metaphor for who I am and have become. I have lived here for over fifty-five years; it is filled with fond memories of children, laughter, travels, dancing, twenty years of building a family base with Rudy and nearly thirty years of loving companionship with Don. My home is my anchor: it represents stability, safety, and a place for continuous nurturing. I have told my children that I intend to die here.

I recently painted our bedroom a beautiful marigold color. When I enter the bedroom I find light and sun in my life. My marigold-colored bedroom is my sanctuary. As I look out the window at the variegated greens of the eucalyptus pulverulenta tree, reading on our comfortable chaise lounge on the deck, absorbing the fragrances of the garden and trees, I feel in nature and am invariably rejuvenated by the peace and tranquility of our garden. It would be hard to find this kind of natural, old-growth landscape in a garden elsewhere. I cannot imagine that any retirement home could provide it. While many senior communities have beautiful gardens, they are meticulously manicured and do not have our garden's overgrown, spontaneous feel.

Recently I have been overwhelmed by the tumult of world events. I wake up in the middle of the night thinking about the troubling issues facing our planet: rapid loss of biodiversity, global warming, and nuclear radiation. I am concerned about the loss of civil liberties for workers and the expanding inequalities that have led to uprisings such as the Arab Spring and Occupy-type events around the world. In contrast to the dramatic and rapid changes in our world and in my own health, my Hillegass home is a place of permanence and safety. When I feel vulnerable, the presence of my sturdy, tranquil home supports and lifts my spirits.

Going Forward

I tire more easily these days and attempt to counteract these feeling by looking at the sunny side of things, yet this has become more difficult in my nineties. I seem to have lost some of my innate optimism and often feel low in spirits. I can't help wondering if it's because I'm feeling more vulnerable as I grow older, or whether it's valid to feel insecure about the state of the world today. Did my positive outlook come from my youth, when I believed in the future and had the energy and commitment to make the world a better place?

I have faced, and lived through, many challenges in life. The years of the Great Depression were hard for my mother and me, but there was always the hope that our lives would be better again. World War II was devastating. I enlisted in the navy because I wanted to help my country; I believed in democracy and opposed fascism. But my country also did terrible things: the bombings of Hiroshima and Nagasaki were criminal acts. When the war was finally over, we moved on. What alternative was there? I believe in persevering. After the trauma of divorce, I grew, learned, and traveled.

When younger, I would have flown to Occupy Wall Street in New York, or to Madison, Wisconsin, to voice my protest alongside the public workers there. I firmly believe in the energy of collective action and the power of the people. But since the onset of my congestive heart failure last year, it has been hard for me to muster the energy—though I have the enthusiasm —to write letters of protest or attend demonstrations.

At ninety-two, my time is limited. What can I do in this short period that is left? How do I balance my passion to change the world with taking care of myself? Perhaps they aren't mutually exclusive. Part of energizing myself is remaining engaged in life and surrounding myself with positive people.

Instead of delving into death and dying, I would like to talk about living fully to the end.

Looking forward to an abundant future, I sense that now is the time to go inward. I feel I need more inner process and quiet time to examine. As I breathe deeply in Vipassana meditation, I let the outside world recede by sensing each part of my body. Releasing and dissolving tensions, I encourage those "Ah ha!" moments of awareness, presence, and clarity. Throughout life I've been active and have neglected to give myself quiet time alone, except during vacations or when injuries have required rest. Now I am striving for balance between remaining active and finding inner tranquility.

If I feel out of balance or not conscious, I bring forth a spiritual element of oneness with something larger than myself. I visualize the wilderness. Extraneous concerns fall away. Life is put in perspective. I know there is a natural world that transcends the self. When living is painful and hard to get through, I am reminded that there is a spiritual harbor out there, a vast wilderness that I can visualize and feel even though I can't always get to it. Wallace Stegner believed that not only is the wilderness good for us when we are young for the sanity it can bring into our lives, but also good for us as an idea when we are old because it is there for us to contemplate and visualize.

As long as I feel balanced within, I view the outer world with a positive perspective, able to envision the many possibilities that life holds and allow my innate optimism to flow outward. Regular tai chi is not only a deeply spiritual practice but also gives me flexibility, balance, and energy. Breathing and meditating as I sense each part of my body, inside and out, carrying the energy to each point, reconnects my mind, body, and spirit. Knowing that I have within me the possibility of achieving inner harmony makes me feel rejuvenated. This, my most recent revelation, evokes a big smile.

I recognize the importance of intimate times with close friends and my children, grandchildren, and great-grandchild. I don't want to wait until I am no longer articulate or on my deathbed to tell people how much I love them. I invite friends to stay overnight, so that we really have time to talk, instead of having short conversations over dinner. I tell my son and daughters how much I love them, and how fortunate I feel that we are family.

Four years ago, at the Berkeley Public Library Foundation's annual fundraising party, Don and I won a bid on a silent auction for round-trip airfare and a week's stay at a private home in Nairobi, Kenya. That was the year Don had his stroke, and we had to cancel our trip. At the same fundraiser the next year, we again bid for a trip—a week on a small island off the coast of Denmark—and won again! Sadly, that year I was challenged with heart issues, was put on medication, and ended up in the hospital. We had to cancel once again.

As I approached ninety-two last December, I wanted to share intimate time with my family by celebrating my birthday with them. Unsure if I would ever be able to do another major trip with my children and grandchildren, I decided that year to bid on a location closer to home that would be more manageable—a week on Oahu, Hawaii, which we again won. I chose the week of December 4 to 11 because I had received an invitation from the U.S. Navy to be honored as a veteran of World War II at the seventieth anniversary of Pearl Harbor. I invited all my children and grandchildren to come with us. New to our clan and special to us was my grandson Jon Robin's new wife, Mary, and six-month-old baby, Alana.

Each of us had our own condominium looking out on the water, all in the same building. We met at the white sandy beach daily. BJ had brought a duffel bag filled with special foods from home for each of us. BJ organized the menus. We cooked together and shared meals; together we decided what should be for dinner, and the kids did the shopping. It was a happy family joint venture. BJ and Lyn and my grandkids learned something new about me, as well, at the anniversary of the tragedy at Pearl Harbor, when I stood up to be acknowledged as one of the few surviving women officers of World War II.

My children and grandchildren were surprised to learn that over 2,000 people died in the December 7, 1941, attacks. Eight battleships were sunk and hundreds of planes were lost on the ground. Many of those on reconnaissance mistakenly believed the Japanese aircraft were American, so there was no advance warning, and no evacuation or bunkering before the strike. Nearly 1,200 died on the USS *Arizona* alone. The ships and the planes on the ground weren't manned for a counter-attack; the planes had no fuel. The unprepared military personnel and civilians looked up in defenseless terror. At the ceremony, I was touched to see a few of the survivors from the *Arizona* stand up haltingly or wave their hands from their wheelchairs, to wild applause.

Lyn and I took off by ourselves one day to a deserted beach. We had a glorious time together lying in the sun, sharing a picnic, and reading. We didn't need to talk; each felt the other's loving presence. Later Lyn and I explored the nearby town and a Samoan grocery store. It was a completely different Hawaii from that of our Marriott condo, and the local people we talked with invited us back. Another day, BJ, Don, and I visited a lush state forest reserve, enjoying its many waterfalls and flowers. My twenty-five-year-old granddaughter, Eliana, on vacation from her Ph.D. program in clinical psychology at the University of Denver, and I were able to spend the kind of time with each other that we both delight in, talking about our lives while working out at the condo's gym. The trip also gave me the opportunity to know and appreciate the special qualities and talents of Mary, my new granddaughter-in-law, who is a talented seamstress and made a few of the outstanding outfits that she sported, as well as to enjoy my new great-granddaughter, Alana, who was just beginning to crawl.

If I'm Around—Keinahora

I feel grateful to be alive at ninety-two. How fortunate I am to have lived so long and to still be traveling, meeting new friends, attending concerts, going to museums, continuing to be vitally engaged in cultural, social, and political activities. Not every woman my age has the privileges I have.

Sometimes I ask myself: How long can this go on? How can I get it all in? I can't last forever. How much time is left? Then I remind myself that nobody ever knows the answers, and all I have is the day I'm living right now. How do I want to spend this day, and then the next?

Recently I was talking with my friend Henry Elson about arranging a reunion with our old and dear friend Hack Fain, a professor emeritus in Madison, Wisconsin, who visits the Bay Area during the cold Wisconsin winter months. Henry Elson has been a friend of ours since Liberal Democrats days. In the following e-mail, I told Henry how I feel about planning for the future in these later years.

April 10, 2012
Dear Henry,

I hear that Hack and Linda are off to Madison again. Let's get together when they return. I might have inserted, "If I am around," but this statement irks Don and bothers my kids, yet I can't help thinking it when I plan an event in the future. How lucky can I get, living on so long? Any thoughts on this age-old transcendental question, Henry?

Warm regards,

Cec

April 13, 2012
Dear Cec,

I can understand your feeling about planning for the future at advanced age. I often feel the same. I can't speak for you, but in my case it is sort of a "warding off" of a fear of being "jinxed" by predicting a good result in regard to a future happening. In this case, by planning "too far ahead" you suggest that you'll live that long, and at our age we're afraid of being punished for something like hubris, and not wanting to get the gods angry, we make the qualification to which you referred. It's like keeping your fingers crossed or throwing salt over your shoulder under certain circumstances.

There's a Jewish expression that applies here. When one says something positive, like, "I'm feeling better after being sick," often the following is added: "keinahora," which means something like warding off the "evil eye" that the devil may give you for boasting about your health. So to protect yourself in the situation you mentioned, you would say, "Let's get together with Fains next winter, keinahora," thus hoping to avoid the evil eye for being presumptuous in suggesting that you'll live that long. Those are my thoughts about the transcendental question you posed.

Say hello to Don. Pat sends regards, as do I,
Henry

Today I have the time, wisdom, and energy to live fully. I hope tomorrow allows me that pleasure, keinahora.

With BJ at a conference in Boulder, Colorado

Sharing a happy moment with Rob in the garden at Hillegass

Enjoying time with Lyn in our garden

My grandson Jon with his wife, Mary, and my
great-granddaughter, Alana

Cousin Diane, me, and my granddaughter, Eliana,
posing in San Francisco

About the Author

Few people in this world practice what they preach, but in the field of aging, Cecelia Hurwich is at least one extraordinary exception. Proving that "we can deliberately create the conditions we need to maintain our health and well-being," she exercises regularly, maintains an active work schedule, guards her nutrition, enjoys friends of all ages, and stays spiritually healthy.

Dr. Hurwich is a psychologist, researcher, writer, feminist, environmental activist, and worldwide speaker on the subject of vitality in aging. She loves life and believes in living every minute of it to the hilt. She teaches all over the world, inspiring others to pursue healthy aging, physical activity, and the healing powers of nature. A graduate of the University of California, Berkeley, she served as a lieutenant in the navy during World War II. She has three children, two grandchildren, and one great-granddaughter.

Dr. Hurwich lives in Berkeley, California, with her loving partner, Don Ross. In her free time she enjoys climbing mountains, hiking, dancing, reading, and listening to live jazz and classical music.

About the Cover

Colors make my life! My favorites are oranges, which give me a feeling of peace, and reds, which I find pleasurably exciting. I knew that I wanted to incorporate both in the cover for this memoir. My original working title for the book, *Vitality in Aging*, was not interesting, so I sent out an email to colleagues and friends for help, and received over a hundred suggestions. The one I chose was *92 and Dancing*, suggested by my close friend Ailish Schutz. As soon as I heard it, an image popped into my head that I knew would make a perfect cover for the book: a silhouette of myself dancing.

When it came time to turn this vision into reality, two special friends, Alicia Roldan and Leah VonEhrenkrook, both photographers, offered to photograph me as I danced. What fun I had prancing in my back garden in a swirling dress as these two talented women took my picture! The biggest design issue was how to combine the dancing silhouette, the bright colors, and some visual references to my adventurous life to achieve a compelling and airy cover. Carol Salvin, my designer, came up with the brilliant idea of using multiple silhouettes with some subtle allusions to my sojourns in India and South America. Happily, the dancing silhouettes pulled together all the key elements. From there on the challenge was to select exciting color combinations to achieve this vibrant and eye-catching cover.

Publications by Dr. Cecelia Hurwich

"Self-Care, Your Responsibility." *American Society on Aging Journal,* USA, March 1998.

"Vital Women in their 70s, 80s & 90s." World Congress of Gerontology, August 1997.

"Older Women and Personal Growth." *The Gerontologist,* USA, November 1995.

"Self-Care: My Responsibility." *Generations,* October 1993.

"Still Vital After All These Years: Older Women and Personal Growth." *Ageing International,* September 1993.

"Late Life Potential." Congress of the International Association of Gerontology, August 1993.

"Vital Women in their 70s & 80s." World Congress of Sociology, July 1993.

"Health of the Elderly." Proceedings of the IFA Global Conference on Aging, August 1992.

A Jewish Woman in the Military During World War II: Cecelia Hurwich, Judah L. Magnus Memorial Museum: Western Jewish History Center, 1991.

"Vital Women in Their 70s, 80s and 90s: Ten-year longitudinal Study," UMI Dissertation Services, 1990. This widely acclaimed research provides greater understanding of the aging process.

Dr. Hurwich has conducted workshops, lectures, symposia, and conferences at numerous colleges, universities, and organizations in the United States and abroad.